Lecture Notes in Computer Science 9221

Commenced Publication in 1973
Founding and Former Series Editors:
Gerhard Goos, Juris Hartmanis, and Jan van Leeuwen

More information about this series at http://www.springer.com/series/7409

Alessandro De Gloria (Ed.)

Games and Learning Alliance

Third International Conference, GALA 2014
Bucharest, Romania, July 2–4, 2014
Revised Selected Papers

 Springer

Editor
Alessandro De Gloria
Electronic Engineering
University of Genova
Genova
Italy

ISSN 0302-9743   ISSN 1611-3349 (electronic)
Lecture Notes in Computer Science
ISBN 978-3-319-22959-1   ISBN 978-3-319-22960-7 (eBook)
DOI 10.1007/978-3-319-22960-7

Library of Congress Control Number: 2015948154

LNCS Sublibrary: SL3 – Information Systems and Applications, incl. Internet/Web, and HCI

Springer International Publishing AG Switzerland is part of Springer Science+Business Media
(www.springer.com)

Preface

The third edition of the GALA Conference was held on July 2–4, 2014 in Bucharest, Romania. The conference was organized by the Serious Games Society and the Games and Learning Alliance, the European Network of Excellence on Serious Games (SGs).

The conference provided the opportunity for gathering and nurturing a community of experts on SGs, a community which is growing year by year and involves academics, industrial developers, teachers, and corporate decision makers, to promote knowledge sharing, technology transfer, and business development. This year, we also welcomed the participation of indie developers, which we believe represented a great opportunity and potential for improving and extending the technologies and applications of SGs.

As in previous years, the research presented covered a variety of aspects and knowledge fields. These have been grouped into four sessions: pedagogy, technology, design, and applications. The pedagogy session hosted studies about deployment of SGs at different school levels and on different topics. This constituted a significant advancement with respect to previous years, as it demonstrated that SGs have started to be used and deployed in authentic educational settings. One paper specifically investigates the role of the teacher in this new context.

The design and implementation session covered various aspects ranging from mobile games to multiplayer games, from formats to gamification of co-design processes and models for scaffolding game-based learning experiences.

The technology session included some very interesting papers about applying the Service Oriented Architecture paradigm to the field of SGs and multimodal emotion recognition in SGs.

Finally, the new games session presented some very interesting educational games, for instance in the field of physics, for training working memory, and for using social networks. Attention was paid in particular to special users, such as children with depression. Some papers presented interesting information on SG mechanics, which are at the core of SG design. Among them, we cite particularly virtual tutors and minigames.

This book collects the studies presented during the conference, addressing the above mentioned topics, with authors from a variety of countries and bringing knowledge from several different fields. Not only does this highlight the growing interest in SG applications in various domains, but also the multidisciplinary collaboration that is typically involved in SG design and deployment.

It is important to highlight that the papers presented at the Gala 2014 conference closely reflect this year's trend in research on serious games. In particular, we underline topics such as SG design research, rapid development frameworks, learning analytics, analysis of deployment in educational settings, brain-computer interaction, and applications in the health domain. Collaboration is targeted as well, and games are also cited as an appropriate tool within learning networks, the emerging paradigm through which more-experienced people help less-experienced people learn new skills and form new networks and communities. Mobile games and supporting technologies are also focused upon.

Like for the 2013 edition, the selected best papers of GALA 2014 will be published in a dedicated special issue of the International Journal of Serious Games, which represents a great opportunity for the scientific/technological community and for the industrial world as well to publish original research works on SGs and to be informed about the latest developments in the field. This year, the GALA 2012 best papers were published in an Entertainment Computing special issue.

July 2015   Alessandro De Gloria

Organization

GALA 2014 was an event organized by Carol I National Defence University and the University of Genoa, and sponsored by the Games and Learning Alliance (GaLA) European Network of Excellence and by the Serious Games Society. The organizational structure was as follows:

General Chair

Alessandro De Gloria   University of Genoa, Italy

General Co-chair

Ion Roceanu   Carol I National Defence University, Romania

Workshop and Tutorial Chair

David Wortley   UK

Program Committee

Aida Azadegan	The University of West Scotland, UK
Albert Angehrn	INSEAD, France
Alessandro Berni	NATO, Italy
Ana Paiva	INESC-ID, Portugal
Andreas Oikonomou	University of Derby, UK
Anthony Brooks	Aalborg University, Denmark
Audrius Jurgelionis	Fraunhofer, Germany
Baltasar Fernandez-Manjon	Complutense University Madrid, Spain
Bianca Falcidieno	CNR IMATI, Italy
Brian Goldiez	University of Central Florida, USA
Carmen Padron	ATOS, Spain
Carolina Islas Sedano	University of Eastern Finland, Finland
Christos Gatzidis	Bournemouth University, UK
Damien Djaouti	IRIT, France
Daniel Burgos	UNIR, Spain
David Wortley	UK
Dirk Ifenthaler	Open Universities Australia, Australia
Donald Brinkman	Microsoft, USA
Erik Duval	Catholic University Leuven, Belgium
Erik van der Spek	Technical University of Eindhoven, The Netherlands
Fabrizia Mantovani	Università di Milano-Bicocca, Italy
Francesco Bellotti	University of Genoa, Italy

Rob Nadolsky	Open University, Netherlands
Rosa Maria Bottino	National Research Institute, Italy
Rui Prada	Inesc-Id, Portugal
Sandy Louchart	Heriot-Watt University, UK
Sara de Freitas	Coventry University, UK
Simon Egenfeldt-Nielsen	Serious Games Interactive, Denmark)
Staffan Bjork	Chalmers Unibersity, Sweden
Stephen Lane	University of Pennsylvania, USA
Steve Ellis	NASA, USA
Sung Hyun Cho	Hongik University, South Korea
Tanya Krzywinska	Brunel University, UK
Theo Lim	Heriot-Watt University, UK
Travis Ross	Indiana University, USA
William Fisher	Quicksilver, USA
Wim Westera	Open University of the Netherlands, Netherlands
Yiorgos Chrysanthou	University of Cyprus, Cyprus

Local Arrangements Committee

| Daniel Beligan | Carol I National Defence University, Romania |
| Elisa Lavagnino | University of Genoa, Italy |

Publications Chair

| Riccardo Berta | University of Genoa, Italy |

Communication Chair

| Francesco Bellotti | University of Genoa, Italy |

Administrative Chair

| Elisa Lavagnino | University of Genoa, Italy |
| Antonie Wiedemann | University of Genoa, Italy |

Contents

Beyond Serious Games: The Next Generation of Cultural Artifacts

Federico Fasce[✉]

URUSTAR, Genova, Italy
federico@urustar.net

Abstract. Beyond quizzes, cold simulations, and educational content placed inside non-meaningful games, serious games are evolving and becoming a more mature class of artefacts.

1 Introduction

Serious games are experiencing a new generation of artefacts, what in this paper is called "the second wave", which is the symptom of an evolution and the result of a general improved understanding about how games themselves work. In order to analyse these changes and deconstruct them, this paper starts with a consideration about the definitions of what a game is.

2 About Definitions

Almost every game scholar has they own definition of what a game is. Every single one is fine, but they often fail in describing as a game something that the public and the critic regards as such. Being the game a social object often negotiated by the players, a definition of games should act like a loose guide rather than a prescriptive definition of what a game is and what it is not. Therefore this paper suggest the following definition:

A game is a system capable to generate emotions through agency in a ritual space.

The word system comes directly from Katie Salen and Eric Zimmerman's definition[1]. The idea of "system" is central because it implies the game designer has defined mechanics from which the content of a game can emerge. It is capable to generate emotions which are the main reason we play. These emotions are generated or evoked by the interaction with the system, the *agency*.

---

[1] "A game is a system in which players engage in an artificial conflict, defined by rules, that result in a quantifiable outcome." – Katie Salen, Eric Zimmerman, *Rules of Play: Game Design Fundamentals* (The MIT Press, 2004)

© Springer International Publishing Switzerland 2015
A. De Gloria (Ed.): GALA 2014, LNCS 9221, pp. 1–4, 2015.
DOI: 10.1007/978-3-319-22960-7_1

The idea that emotions come indirectly from the player exploring the system comes from Jesse Schell [8] and from Will Wright's definition of a game as *possibility space*[2] the player explores and give sense to. All of this happens in a ritual space. This idea is the very same of Huizinga's *magic circle*[3], and it's the negotiated space (physical or imaginary) where the rules of the game apply: if the players doesn't acknowledge the ritual space, no game can really exist for them. Now, game is a structured activity, for it needs a system, a negotiation and a ritual space. It can produce play (Zimmerman, 2003), though.

3   The Problem with "Serious" Games

Even if the term *serious game* has been used since 1975[4] and at least since 2002 [7] has been referred to digital games, it could lead to misinterpretations of what a game is. Bernard De Koven [3] has stated that playful is the path to happiness. Play is something that enables positive emotions. A structured game has also a great power as a learning machine. Raph Koster [5] analyses how games, by enabling and improving the dopamine processes in our brain, are the perfect way to learn. While playfulness can evoke positive emotions, games are great learning systems. That's not a dichotomy, of course, but two aspects of a whole artefact. And that's why the term "serious" game fall short: when considered as an artefact, a game – being a learning machine – is inherently serious.

3.1   Where Serious Games Fall Short

What we have learned to call "serious games" sometimes take the form of quizzes you need to solve in order to make a story progress. These have questionable educational value, because often rely on sciolism rather than trying actually teach something

---

[2] "So it's time to reconsider games, to recognize what's different about them and how they benefit - not denigrate - culture. Consider, for instance, their "possibility space": games usually start at a well-defined state (the setup in chess, for instance) and end when a specific state is reached (the king is checkmated). Players navigate this possibility space by their choices and actions; every player's path is unique." – Will Wright, "Dream Machine", published on *Wired*, 14/04/2006 – http://archive.wired.com/wired/archive/14.04/wright.html

[3] "All play moves and has its being within a play-ground marked off beforehand either materially or ideally, deliberately or as a matter of course. Just as there is no formal difference between play and ritual, so the 'consecrated spot' cannot be formally distinguished from the play-ground. The arena, the card-table, the magic circle, the temple, the stage, the screen, the tennis court, the court of justice, etc, are all in form and function play-grounds, i.e. forbidden spots, isolated, hedged round, hallowed, within which special rules obtain. All are temporary worlds within the ordinary world, dedicated to the performance of an act apart." – Johan Huizinga, Homo Ludens: A Study of the Play-Element in Culture (The Beacon Press, 1955

[4] "We are concerned with serious games in the sense that these games have an explicit and carefully thought-out educational purpose and are not intended to be played primarily for amusement." – Clark C. Abt, *Serious Games* (University Press of America, 2002 – first ed. 1975)

throughout the game itself. In other examples, the educational content is breaking the rhythm of the game which is designed without any educational purposes in mind. This has been called by Ian Bogost [2] the "Mary Poppins effect", because like in the popular movie it's like adding a spoonful of sugar to help the medicine go down. But they lack of continuity and that's not how games work as learning machines.

Then there are simulations: they often lack any real playfulness, resulting in something non-emotional we cannot relate to. These kind of simulations are a great example of how not play-centred systems miss something. When people play good simulation games (e.g., flight simulators) it is not in place of the real life experience. They are looking for sensations and emotions. One good example of introducing the real power of games in a simulation environment is *Relive*[5]: built to teach people how to correctly perform a CPR manoeuvre, its sci-fi setting and storyline, along with credible characters and a very strong game direction, moves away from the simulation and proposes an emotional and enjoyable game. Relive is just one example of the new wave of serious games. These games, rather than proposing themselves as educational, choose to play in the same field of traditional video games, albeit largely in the independent niche. They focus on their playful content, but they're still able to send powerful messages and teach complex systems in a very interesting way.

4 The New Generation

The game which best represent this new wave is *Papers, Please*[6] winner of two 2014 Games for Change Awards (Most Innovative & Best Gameplay Awards[7]) as well as of the Seumas McNally Grand Prize and the Excellence in Design at the 2014 Independent Games Festival[8]. In the game, the player takes the role of the border agent in a fictional totalitarian country. Day after day, they must decide if the arriving people can be let in or not, while the documents to be controlled grow in number and complexity as the government implement stricter immigration rules. Though the fictional setting, *Papers, Please* shows the players how immigration systems work, how government choose to control people entering a country and even how work conditions and wages can deeply influence the humanity of people. *Papers, Please* present a nuanced commentary about immigration, politics and also democracy, while retaining its nature of game.

5 Conclusions

Papers, Please looks like a tipping point. It's a commercial product, sold on platforms like Steam and due to be released on PSVita; its success sits on top of a lot of games using the power of game mechanics to teach, make people think and comment about every kind of topic. The second wave of serious games is mainly born out of the

---

[5] StudioEvil, *Relive*, in development (http://relivegame.com)

[6] Lucas Pope, Papers, Please, 2013 (http://papersplea.se)

[7] (http://gamesforchange.org/festival/gameplay/papers-please–2/)

[8] (http://www.igf.com/02finalists.html)

independent game community, as the result of a democratisation of game development, due to the diffusion of simple game-making tools and the liberalisation of digital distribution platforms [1]. The use of game development as an expressive form made by people who are not necessarily game developers could lead to a better understanding of how games work and to novel approaches to serious games. At the Games for Change Festival 2014, developer Paolo Pedercini[9] pointed out the necessity of a turning point for serious games, rather than focusing on making educational games: what will happen if we enable more people expressing themselves through games?

The next step of games for impact doesn't lie in some technological advancement but rather, in helping people to engage with the practice of game design.[10]

Therefore, the second wave of serious games are games which don't consider themselves "serious" but instead implement a coherent system design to enhance messages without forgetting the basic rules of games, like the emotional link with the player, because the term is not to be considered as opposite of fun. In "fun" lies the learning machine and every message we want to deliver through it should be designed accordingly.

References

1. Anthropy, A.: Rise of the Videogame Zinesters: How Freaks, Normals, Amateurs, Artists, Dreamers, Drop-outs, Queers, Housewives, and People Like You Are Taking Back an Art Form. Seven Stories Press, New York (2012)
2. Bogost, I.: Persuasive Games: The Expressive Power of Videogames. The MIT Press, Cambridge (2010)
3. De Koven, B., A Playful Path. Lulu (2014)
4. Huizinga, J.: Homo Ludens: A Study of the Play-Element in Culture. The Beacon Press, Boston (1955)
5. Koster, R.: A Theory of Fun for Game Design. Paraglyph Press, Scottsdale (2010)
6. Salen, K., Zimmerman, E.: Rules of Play: Game Design Fundamentals. The MIT Press, Cambridge (2004)
7. Sawyer, B., Rejeski, D.: Serious Games: Improving Public Policy Through Game-based Learning and Simulation. Woodrow Wilson International Center for Scholars, Washington, DC (2002)
8. Schell, J.: The Art of Game Design: A Book of Lenses. CRC Press, Boca Raton (2008)
9. Wright W., "Dream Machine", published on Wired, 14/04/2006

---

[9] Paolo Pedercini, "Making Games in a Fucked Up World", presentation held at the Games for Change Festival 2014 (http://www.molleindustria.org/blog/making-games-in-a-fucked-up-world-games-for-change–2014/)

[10] ibid.

Investigating the Deployment of Serious Games in Secondary Education: A Pilot Study Inspired by Design-Based Research

Jeffrey Earp[1(✉)], Chiara Eva Catalano[2], and Michela Mortara[2]

[1] Istituto per le Tecnologie Didattiche, CNR Via de Marini 6, 16149 Genoa, Italy
jeffrey.earp@itd.cnr.it
[2] Istituto di Matematica Applicata e Tecnologie Informatiche,
CNR Via de Marini 6, 16149 Genoa, Italy
{chiara,michela}@ge.imati.cnr.it

Abstract. This paper describes a pilot deployment in lower secondary school of a serious game dedicated to the learning of history. The primary aim of the initiative was to investigate the integration of Serious Games-based learning environments in the school study of humanities subjects. The pilot was carried out as part of investigations that researchers in the Games and Learning Alliance (GALA) Network of Excellence are conducting into the adoption and deployment of Serious Games (SG) in formal learning contexts. In this regard, the paper outlines the sequence of deployed pilot activities, which was shaped with the intention of responding to the needs of all the participants involved – researchers, educators and learners. This approach is inspired by the principles of design-based research, as illustrated in the strategies adopted both for piloting activities and data gathering. The paper reports the outcome of these and considers some implications of the adopted approach both for SG deployment in formal education and for implementation of experimental SG pilots of this kind.

Keywords: Serious games · Game-Based learning · Experimental pilot · Design-Based research

1 Introduction

The widespread integration of serious gaming is looked on by many as a promising path towards more effective learning in formal education contexts, and as a means for instilling and consolidating technology-enhanced innovation, especially within school contexts. In this light, increasing attention is being focused on the drivers and obstacles to such integration, especially with regard to curriculum [1] and to pedagogy and praxis [2]. Moreover, a clear need has emerged for evidence-based research to support policy-level efforts towards integration [3]. These aspects are currently the subject of investigation by researchers in the Game and Learning Alliance (GALA)

© Springer International Publishing Switzerland 2015
A. De Gloria (Ed.): GALA 2014, LNCS 9221, pp. 5–15, 2015.
DOI: 10.1007/978-3-319-22960-7_2

Network of Excellence[1], who are exploring ways to foster wider and more effective use of Serious Games (SG) in formal learning contexts.

The research activities reported in this paper were carried out as part of that effort. They concern the pilot deployment of a SG dedicated to the study of history by students in primary and lower secondary school. As well as investigating the educational efficacy of the SG as the core component within a technology-enhanced learning environment, the pilot examined key issues in the deployment of serious games in school education such as integration in the organisational and educational praxis followed in schools, the design and orchestration of game based learning activities, and the teacher's pivotal role in leveraging the educational potential that SGs offer.

The following section begins by describing the key elements involved in the experience, namely the SG and the experimental context for the deployment. It then focuses on the sequence of activities undertaken, explaining the rationale underpinning the design of the sequence and, more generally, of the pilot SG implementation as a whole. This is illustrated through description of the activities, their implementation and outcomes. Finally, some considerations are provided about the implications of the adopted approach, both for SG deployment in formal education and for the implementation of experimental SG pilots of this kind.

2   Pilot Design and Preparation

2.1   The Adopted Serious Game

The game adopted for this pilot is "The Plague", the first title in a series of three SG called "Playing History" produced and published by Serious Games Interactive[2]. The Plague is a narrative-based game that gives youngsters between the ages of eight and thirteen the opportunity to experience and learn about a key event in European history, namely the plague epidemic that struck Europe in the Middle Ages. The game is set in Florence in 1348 during the Black Death. The player takes the role of a young boy whose family is threatened by the disease and who must discover a way to protect them from the rapidly worsening epidemic. The central game mission is to gather key information that could help the family avoid the advancing ravages of the plague. This is done by interacting with Non-Player Characters (NPC) and following the clues they give to complete a sequence of tasks. In this manner, the player unlocks vital information for deciding what course of action to take in the game to avoid the family's contagion. The game also features a parallel treasure hunt for historically inappropriate artefacts "hidden" throughout the environment (a PC, antibiotics, etc.). Each of these embeds information or powers that are useful for progress in gameplay. The player can also earn extra points and status by playing embedded mini-games, some of which are also learning opportunities.

The game primarily targets the acquisition of knowledge about the Black Death and awareness of its impact on medieval society. This mainly occurs through the

---

[1]   http://www.galanoe.eu/.
[2]   http://playinghistory.eu/front.

unfolding of the central narrative/mission, but also via the artefact hunt and mini-games. Immersion in and exploration of the gameplay setting also contributes to the learning experience by conveying a sense of medieval life generally: the behaviour and beliefs of ordinary people, the role of faith and religion, the nature of medical and scientific knowledge and practice, types of economic activity, etc. Of course, the representation is suitably stylised for youngsters, dealing as it does with a dark and gruesome period in human history.

To facilitate use in a school setting, the digital game comes with a supplementary educational package that includes student and teacher guides, summative evaluation tests, and activity sheets for further studies.

2.2 Deployment Setting

The pilot was carried out in 2013 at an international school in Italy where the lower-secondary grades follow the International Baccalaureate Middle Years Programme and the official teaching language is English. This choice ensured that the participating students possessed the English language skills demanded to play the game. The socio-economic background of the students is generally higher than average.

Thirty-five students aged 12-13 from two Year Seven classes took part in the pilot; preparation for final exams prevented more extensive participation. Both classes were taught by the same history teacher, who had no previous experience with game-based learning. The year before the pilot was run, most of the students had briefly studied the Great Plague of London (1665–1666) as part of their history course with the same teacher. For this reason, the chosen SG was considered to fit closely with curriculum objectives, even if the students were at the upper limit of the game's target age range.

2.3 Design of the Pilot Activity Sequence

A central aim of this research initiative was to investigate issues surrounding the deployment of serious games in formal education. So, as well as ascertaining the nature and degree of generated learning, interest also centred on the design, implementation and effectiveness of the classroom activity sequence intended as a pilot educational intervention.

Given this focus, particular importance was placed on recognition of, and respect for, the intertwined-but-distinct needs of all the pilot participants - researchers, educators and learners. Accordingly, an explicit effort was made to design and implement a sequence of pilot activities that reconciled the researcher's data gathering requirements with the teacher's (and students') need - and right - to a fruitful and engaging educational experience supporting the attainment of expected learning outcomes.

This consideration is one of guiding principles of Design-Based Research (DBR), an approach adopted in educational research that acknowledges the intrinsic complexities and ethical responsibilities involved when pilots are run in real school environments [4]. Furthermore, DBR recognises that piloting educational innovations for research purposes means "engineering" a "working" instance of the self-same innovation within experimental settings that have been shaped, explicitly or implicitly, to a greater or lesser extent, to fit the specific research agenda [5]. DBR proponents in the game-based learning field [6] concur that "the enacted intervention is a dependent, not an independent, variable" [7] and indeed, in a sense, "…the intervention (itself) is the outcome." [4]. This, and the many other variables at play in real educational environments, place limitations and strains on quasi-experimental research methods, particularly with respect to assessment of learning gains through pre- and post-testing - the prevailing strategy adopted in educational (and game based learning) research [8–10]. While DBR does not eschew quantitative methods altogether, as is the case in the pilot study reported here, it stresses the need for careful attention in experimental design and, especially, recognition of the agendas that the design embeds.

Bearing this in mind, the activity sequence in this pilot was designed and implemented through researcher-teacher collaboration with the express intent of reconciling the respective agendas as far as possible. For example, limited student access (a common constraint in school-based pilots) restricted the scope for administering questionnaires, interviews etc. So activities were designed to be meaningful and engaging for students, educationally fruitful and pedagogically sound for the teacher, and of a kind yielding useful data for the researcher (overhaul of the server-end SG management application posed some doubt about the ultimate availability of analytics data from the pilot). Accordingly, the following pilot phases were designed.

Preparation. To begin, a structured interview was conducted with the teacher using a question matrix specifically designed for use with practitioners approaching game based learning for the first time [11]. The intention was to elicit the teacher's expectations, plans and ideas about the intervention, to raise awareness of critical aspects involved in implementing and orchestrating GBL activities, to establish the basis for teacher/ researcher understanding, and to benchmark attitudes for evaluation purposes. A follow-up structured interview was conducted in which the question matrix responses given at the outset were reviewed and reappraised in the light of the experience (see below).

Subsequently, a unit of learning was developed with the aid of an online pedagogical planning tool developed at ITD-CNR and customised for supporting the design of game-based learning interventions [12].

Classroom Activities. Both classes took part in three 120-150 min sessions held over a period of three weeks. The sequence was fashioned to fit the standard briefing/gameplay/debriefing structure but, as outlined above, was conceived especially to meet both research and educational objectives.

- Session 1: introduction; pre-test of domain knowledge; co-construction of a mind map about the plague; group-based paper & pen designs of a digital game on the plague; introduction to the SG.
- Session 2: gameplay with SG in computer lab (2 players per PC) monitored by research team (three student pairs per researcher).
- Session 3 – post-test; review and updating of session 1 mind map; integration of "favourite" SG aspects in groups' game designs; class-based listing of desired modifications to the SG for a new 2.0 version of the game.

Teacher Briefing & Debriefing. The pre-pilot questionnaire revealed that the teacher largely foresaw the experience as an opportunity to innovate and diversify her teaching practice, aligning this with demands for digitally oriented school preparation, and to enhance student engagement by stimulating their imagination. From the pedagogical viewpoint, she foresaw a chance for task-based learning that leverages the educational affordances of multimodality. She considered the chosen game to be a good match with the teaching curriculum but nonetheless expressed concerns about how the experience would be accepted by students and parents alike; her own inexperience with GBL was also an issue.

After the pilot the teacher confirmed most of these initial thoughts. She expressed satisfaction with learning outcomes (especially consolidation of domain knowledge), the level of student acceptance/engagement, and their willingness and capacity to collaborate, something she had not foreseen. She would have preferred the SG to be more graphic, challenging and content-rich. She evaluated the design of the activity sequence positively, particularly the "supplementary" briefing/debriefing activities (listed above), and appreciated the benefits of the design effort. This was especially true given the technological and classroom management challenges she saw such sequences as posing, something that was facilitated in this case by teacher-research co-presence. In retrospect, she would have included an out-of-class phase and she thought mind-mapping would be more fruitful if a group-based phase were added to the plenary work (see Sect. 3).

3   Pilot Implementation & Outcomes

3.1   Benchmarking Knowledge & Assessing Learning Outcomes

Two different strategies were adopted for benchmarking students' entry-level domain knowledge and assessing their knowledge acquisition: standard pre-and post-testing and an experimental mind-mapping activity. Both are reported here, with a twofold aim: firstly to give a general picture of learning outcomes resulting from the pilot; secondly, to examine whether and how the deployed activity sequence might meet educational needs and, at the same time, generate useful research data.

Pre- and Post-testing. This activity was carried out using an adapted version of the 21-question multiple-choice quiz contained in the game's resource pack for educators. Thirty-one out of the 35 participating students completed both tests. Their results are briefly outlined below to give a general idea of learning outcomes; a more detailed statistical analysis is to be reported elsewhere.

Figure 1 above shows individual students' pre-test (dark-coloured bars) and post-test results (light-coloured bars), arranged according to the latter. For reference, the academic pass mark of 50 % (10.5 out of 21) is indicated by the dotted line. In the pre-test, the mean score (dashed line) is 13.6 out of 21 (64.8 %), with 28 out of the 31 students (90 %) achieving a pass (dark-coloured bars above dotted line). By comparison, the mean score in the post-test (dot-dashed line) rose to 15.9 out of 21 (75.7 %), and all but one of the 31 learners (97 %) achieved a pass (light-coloured bars above dotted line). Looking at students' progress individually, we see that 28 (90 % of the total) improved on their pre-test score, eight (26 %) doing so by a margin of 25 % or more. Conversely, three (9.7 %) actually regressed, by margins of 11.1 %, 12.5 % and 35.7 % respectively. Despite this, the outcome can be deemed positive, generally speaking, especially as pre-test results indicate domain knowledge was already relatively solid.

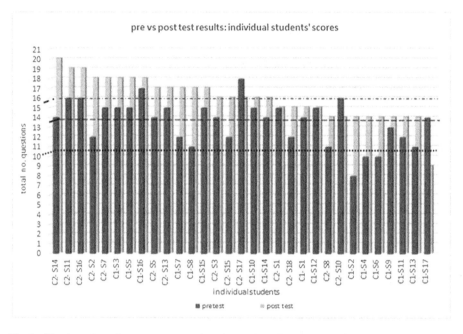

Fig. 1. Total number of correct answers given by each student in pre- and post-tests (Color figure online)

Figure 2 above compares the total number of correct answers generated for each question in the pre- and post-tests, with results arranged according to post-test outcome (light-coloured bars). Looking across the test, we see a cluster of four questions (Q19, Q04, Q18, Q11) that generated distinctly more errors than the remainder, especially in the pre-test. Comparison of total pre- and post-test scores (dark vs light bars) reveals a mean increase in correct answers (learning gains) per question of 3.5 (11.3 %). Four questions generated particularly strong gains: two of the above-mentioned initially "difficult" questions – Q19 (73.3 %) and Q04 (50 %) – together with Q20 (51.7 %) and Q05 (31.8 %). These four questions all deal with information that is mission-critical in the game. By contrast, one question - Q06 - actually generated a net *decrease* in students' correct answers in pre- vs post-testing (-10.3 %). In this case, the related information only emerged incidentally to gameplay (mentioned in passing in a branching dialogue with a NPC). So some players may well have missed it or paid it little heed. What's more, all those who got Q06 wrong (16.1 %) did so by choosing an option (high food prices caused by a ban on peasants entering towns) that, in the context of gameplay, is ostensibly plausible; the player has to sneak past guards to pass the town gate. So the game narrative may have confused some players on this aspect, especially those who were less attentive to the domain content presented in the series of branching dialogues.

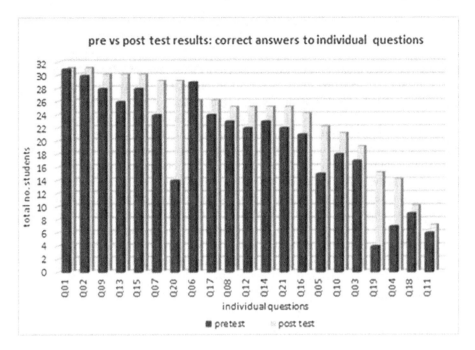

Fig. 2. Total of correct answers to individual questions in pre- and post-tests (Color figure online)

3.2 Joint Mind Mapping

As mentioned in Sect. 2, the application of quasi-experimental research methods in real learning contexts in subject to various limitations, especially in gauging learning outcomes. With these and context-specific educational needs in mind, an experimental strategy based on mind mapping was devised and implemented. The aim was to gather useful data on learners' domain knowledge within an activity that makes an education-ally meaningful contribution to the pilot activity sequence (and to the learning process), rather than simply interrupting it or, at worse, undermining it.

Pre-existing knowledge was captured in whole-class, on-the-fly construction of a digital mind map that established "what we already know" vs. "what we need to find out" in a tangible, jointly-owned construct [13–15]. After gameplay, the map was re-presented for the class to clarify, correct and expand through integration of their new knowledge. The final map thus represented a (mediated) measure and embodiment of their collective learning; it is also a testament to – and fruit of – their collective progress. In this manner, the assessment process (and the overall pilot) acquire greater intrinsic meaning for students and teachers. Usually, pre and post-test results, along with other data, are the exclusive preserve of the researchers, indicating that members of the learning community are treated purely as experimental "subjects", even outside the strict confines of Randomised Controlled Trials [16].

Pre-game mapping generated a substantial body of generally accurate and detailed information that was almost perfectly balanced across the two classes (54 and 56 concepts respectively), in part due to the uniformity of time allocated (20 min). Surprisingly, only a few of the 110 items appear to have been drawn directly from the contents of the pre-test, even though the concept map activity was run immediately after the test.

The classes' contribution to the postgame mapping was starkly different. The first class made 21 changes to their original map, 17 integrations of information gleaned from the game, two manifestly gained from external sources (indicating some self-guided study), and two regarding unconfirmed information "suspended" in the original map. By contrast, the second class made only six changes: three game-based integrations, two from external sources, and one item expressing a reflection spurred by both the original map and the game. This considerably weaker response was not a reflection of lesser ability or lower engagement in pilot activities; indeed monitoring and data analysis suggested this class was actually stronger in both cases. Rather, the cause almost certainly lies with contextual factors: their debriefing session was held on the second last (and extremely hot) day of the school year, when enthusiasm and attention levels were at a very low ebb. It is reasonable to suppose that more felicitous timetabling would have produced a stronger response for this class.

3.3   Reflections on the Two Approaches

The mapping activity generated a largely positive response from students, who participated actively and enthusiastically. The quantity and accuracy of information gleaned from gameplay, especially by one class, were a good indication of knowledge acquisition and appeared to confirm the test results reported in Sect. 3.1.

That said, some caveats apply to the results obtained from both strategies. The pupils had already studied the topic somewhat the previous year, so a focused intervention of any kind was bound to reactivate "submerged" knowledge to some extent. In addition, the demands posed by school timetabling placed limits on the scheduling of the class sessions in the pilot sequence and so timing of the respective activities was far from optimal, as mentioned.

During joint mind mapping, efforts were made to elicit responses from as many students as possible and teacher/researcher intervention was deliberately kept to a minimum. However, it should be recognised that the outcomes reflect a collective effort, are shaped to some extent by class dynamics, and inevitably involve some degree of meditation. By the same token, active, student-centred information encoding in mind mapping presents advantages over decoding of a narrow set of options in multiple-choice tests. This is certainly the case from the educational viewpoint, both for formative/diagnostic assessment prior to gameplay and summative post-game evaluation. From the research angle, mind mapping is certainly subject to contextual factors but avoids the clouding of results often caused when students apply guesswork and/or deduction strategies in answering multiple choice tests.

Mind mapping was singled out in teacher debriefing as having been particularly successful. It was agreed that its effectiveness would be increased if mapping were first carried out in small groups, whose maps would subsequently be merged through plenary negotiation. It was also agreed that running both mapping and pre- and post-testing generates a fairly high cognitive load and could pose a problem of cross-contamination, although there was very little sign of this happening in the pilot.

3.4 Brainstorming a Plague Game Design

The activity sequence foresaw a further activity in which the students worked in teams with paper and pen to brainstorm an imaginary digital game on the plague. This activity was implemented in two phases: game design in the briefing session, before gaining any notion at all of the SG; modification of the original designs in the debriefing session after having played the game. Phase One was a chance to re-engage the class after the pre-testing, to gain some insights into their attitudes to - and experience with - digital games, and to gauge expectations about the SG. Phase Two provided a meaningful, student-centred basis for expressing positive reactions to the SG. Negative feedback was gathered in a supplementary step, described later in the paper.

In the briefing session, self-formed teams comprising 3-5 students had about 20 min to imagine and devise a digital game on the plague. To help them, they had a worksheet with five headings that they were to expound on with descriptive text, brief points or illustrations, as they preferred. These headings were:

- setting (real or fantastic, in any time)
- plot (rough storyline)
- characters (invented or borrowed)
- gameplay (object of the game, rules, mechanics, interaction, etc.)
- "must-haves" (at least three elements considered indispensable to the game)

At the conclusion of that first phase, a representative from each team presented their game design to the whole class.

In phase two after SG gameplay, the students were asked to consider incorporating a maximum of three aspects gleaned from the SG that they wanted to include in their own game design; no minimum threshold was set. The assumption was that, given the students would likely invest a sense of identity and ownership in their designs; they would only choose elements from the SG that they genuinely valued. From a research perspective, this had the advantage of not having to prompt the students about what aspects in the SG to evaluate. Additionally, the students had to negotiate and rank the relative merits of their feedback suggestions on their own terms and mindful of the consequences, rather than being tempted simply to gratify the adults with positive numerical scores.

Outcome of Game Design. All ten teams in the classes collaborated closely on their game design and practically all the students were motivated and engaged. Group discussion was intense: most individuals vigorously advocated their ideas, and proposals were strongly contended before acceptance, rejection or compromise. The students clearly invested value in their team products, as demonstrated by general eagerness to share ideas with the adults and, in some cases, with other teams. This was also evident in the attentiveness and mutual encouragement shown when the various designs were presented to the whole class at the conclusion of phase one.

Overall, the first-round designs reflected enthusiasm, thoughtfulness and creativity. Familiarity with digital games was evident, especially among the boys. Some interesting parallels with the SG emerged, including one design for a plague-themed serious game and two designs sharing exactly the same setting as that in the SG.

Phase two also proved to be engaging. Group participation was strong and discussions were earnest: all the groups managed to identify three features without any trouble and only one of the thirty proposals was insignificant. Analysis of the responses revealed that 57 % regarded more entertainment-oriented features, such as amusing characters and fun mini-games, while the other 43 % were more closely aligned to game mechanics and disciplinary content. This fairly even split is interesting given the young age of the user group, and also in view of the oft-expressed need to reconcile and balance game and educational factors goal in SG design.

Negative feedback was gathered by asking the classes to provide concrete suggestions for a revised version of the SG and for new titles in the same series. The rationale was that framing criticism as inherently constructive and valuable would limit stigma and encourage the students to speak freely. This was organised as a plenary class discussion, with spontaneous proposals being briefly discussed and then put to a (non-compulsory) show-of-hands vote. Although subject to peer pressure, the voting step was considered useful for both engagement and motivation. The ideas attracting strongest consensus indicate that, overall, the students would have liked a more dynamic, engaging game experience with a richer content base. This is understandable given that the students are at the very top of the SG's target age range.

4   Conclusions

This paper has examined a pilot deployment of a serious game in formal education that was intended to pursue both research and educational objectives. The author has proposed an approach to serious game piloting that draws inspiration from the principles of Design-Based Research. These were adopted in the pilot design in an attempt to address some fundamental issues arising from enactment of experimental activities in formal education contexts. Among these are the inevitable bias resulting from implicit embodiment of the researcher's agenda in pilot design and deployment, limitations in applying quasi-experimental research methods to game-based learning pilots enacted in "real-world" contexts, reliance on pre- and post-test results alone to substantiate learning outcomes, and making due allowance for the need of teachers and students to pursue educational objectives while engaging in research undertakings.

Results from the pilot implementation, although limited in scale, are encouraging. Enactment of the activity sequence designed to meet various piloting needs yielded generally positive results. These indicate that further investigation is warranted. In particular, more extensive field testing of the strategies and activities outlined in this contribution would help to substantiate their validity and applicability on a wider scale.

Acknowledgement. The work reported in this paper has been performed as part of research activities conducted within the Game and Learning Alliance (GALA) Network of Excellence, co-funded by the EU under the Seventh Framework Programme.

References

1. de Freitas, S., Ott, M., Popescu, M.M., Stanescu, I. (eds.): New Pedagogical Approaches in Game Enhanced Learning: Curriculum Integration. IGI Global, Hershey (2013)
2. Arnab, S., Berta, R., de Freitas, S., Earp, J., Popescu, M., Romero, M., Stanescu, I., Usart, M.: Serious games in formal education: discussing some critical aspects. In: Gouscos, D., Meimaris, M. (eds.) Proceedings of 5th European Conference on Game-Based Learning, pp. 486–493. Academic Publ. Ltd, Reading (2011)
3. Caponetto, I., Earp, J., Ott, M.: Aspects of the integration of games into educational processes. Int. J. Knowl. Soc. Res. **4**(3), 11–21 (2013)
4. Design-Based Research Collective: Design-based research: an emerging paradigm for educational inquiry. Educ. Researcher **32**(1), 5–8 (2003)
5. Cobb, P., Confrey, J., diSessa, A., Lehrer, R., Schauble, L.: Design experiments in educational research. Educ. Researcher **32**(1), 9–13 (2003)
6. Barab, S., Squire, K.: Design-based research: putting a stake in the ground. J. learn. Sci. **13**(1), 1–14 (2004)
7. Hoadley, C.: Methodological Alignment in Design-Based Research. Educ. Psychol. **39**(4), 203–212 (2004). doi:10.1207/s15326985ep3904_2. ISSN 0046–1520
8. Field, A., Hole, G.: How to design and report experiments. Sage Publications, London (2003)
9. Baalsrud Hauge, J., Boyle, E., Mayer, I., Nadolski, R., Riedel, J.C.K.H., Moreno-Ger, P., Bellotti, F., Lim, T., Ritchie, J.M.: Study design and data gathering guide for serious games' evaluation. In: Connolly, T.M., Hainey, T., Boyle, E., Baxter, G., Moreno-Ger, P. (eds.) Psychology, Pedagogy, and Assessment in Serious Games, pp. 394–419. IGI Global, Hershey (2014). doi:10.4018/978-1-4666-4773-2.ch018
10. Bellotti, F., Kapralos, B., Lee, K., Moreno-Ger, P., Berta, R.: Assessment in and of serious games: an overview. Hindawi Adv. Hum. Comput. Interact. **2013**, 11 (2013). doi: 10.1155/2013/136864
11. Ney M., Emin V., Earp J. Paving the Way to Game Based Learning: A Question Matrix for Teacher Reflection. In: Proceedings of 4th International Conference on Games and Virtual Worlds for Serious Applications (VS-GAMES 2012), Genoa, Italy. Elsevier Procedia (2012)
12. Earp, J., Ott, M., Pozzi, F.: Facilitating educators' knowledge sharing with dedicated information systems. Comput. Hum. Behav. **29**(2), 445–455 (2013)
13. Jonassen, D.H., Reeves, T.C., Hong, N., Harvey, D., Peters, K.: Concept mapping as cognitive learning and assessment tools. J. Interact. Learn. Res. **8**, 289–308 (1997)
14. Heinze-Fry, J.A., Novak, J.: Concept mapping brings long-term movement toward meaningful learning. Sci. Educ. **74**(4), 461–472 (1990). doi:10.1002/sce.3730740406
15. McClure, J.R., Sonak, B., Suen, H.K.: Concept map assessment of classroom learning: Reliability, validity, and logistical practicality. J. Res. Sci. Teach. **36**(4), 475–492 (1999)
16. Woolfson, L.M.: Educational Psychology: the Impact of Psychological Research on Education. Prentice Hall, Pearson Education, London (2011)

To Facilitate or Not? Understanding the Role of the Teacher in Using a Serious Game

Jannicke Baalsrud Hauge[1(✉)], Theodore Lim[2], James Ritchie[2],
Matthias Kalverkamp[1], Francesco Bellotti[3], and Claudia Ribeiro[4]

[1] Bremer Institut für Produktion und Logistik,
Hochschulring 20, 28359 Bremen, Germany
{baa,kvp}@biba.uni-bremen.de
[2] Institute of Mechanical, Process and Energy Engineering,
School of Engineering and Physical Sciences, Herriot-Watt University,
Edinburgh EH14 5SJ, UK
{T.Lim,j.m.ritchie}@hw.ac.uk
[3] DITEN – University of Genoa, Via Opera Pia 11/a, 16145 Genoa, Italy
franz@elios.unige.it
[4] INESC-ID, Instituto Superior Técnico,
Universidade Técnica de Lisboa, Lisbon, Portugal
claudia.sofia.ribeiro@inesc-id.pt

Abstract. The challenge of delivering personalized learning experiences in a large class, and through groups or teams, is an undertaking fraught with difficulties. Yet it is a necessary experience for engineering education since engineering in the real world are team-based events that build from individual knowledge. This paper reports on the learning of supply chain management (SCM), a fundamental component in engineering manufacturing operations and logistics planning. The study investigates the use of SHORTFALL a team-based game in conjunction with various degrees of facilitation, supported with taught material. Early results from two separate and independent studies indicate that the usefulness of using SHORTFALL in classes regarding the students' experience and learning outcomes depends on the prior knowledge of the students as well as on the use of an expert facilitator.

1 Introduction

1.1 Game-Based Learning in Higher Education

For students, the supply chain (SC) and its management are still mostly addressed primarily at a theoretical level. When they graduate from a SC-related discipline of a business school, most students will need to make decisions in variable environments, lacking the previous experience of anticipating their strategic impact on the other SC stakeholders in practical terms. Game-based learning (GBL) [2–4] - in particular through Serious Games (SGs), including ad-hoc games designed for joining fun and instruction [5–7] – have shown to be advantageous in delivering an otherwise difficult subject [8, 9] fostering more direct student participation of the students [10–12].

© Springer International Publishing Switzerland 2015
A. De Gloria (Ed.): GALA 2014, LNCS 9221, pp. 16–30, 2015.
DOI: 10.1007/978-3-319-22960-7_3

Such games also motivate children, contextualize teaching and/or offer opportunities to exercise and verify knowledge and skills.

Educational simulations enhanced with gaming features do enable learners to cope with real problems and authentic situations that are close to reality [5, 13, 14]. For the subject on SCM it only requires that the bounded rationality of economic actors [15] and the nonlinearities, time delays and feedback structures can be visualised without sacrificial performance [16].

Although Semini [17] pointed out that games are more suitable than simulations to teach decision making in SCs the deployment rate of SGs for SCM remains low. To a large extent because the facilitation is challenging as most games are not course specific requiring an experienced lecturer [18]. This article intends to contribute in reducing the barrier of integration of existing games in the classes by reporting our experience in using SGs within the education of engineers at different universities, namely: Herriot Watt (HWU, UK) and Bremen (UNIHB, Germany), while considering the role of the teacher and facilitators for the game.

1.2 Integration of Serious Games and Curriculum Adaption

The adoption of new learning/teaching tools always raises several questions regarding traditional techniques of classroom instruction. Some of those questions are related to how it will affect the way learners carry out educational tasks and how teachers might/must facilitate learning [19]. Another important question that results from the integration of serious games in formal education is how it will affect the role of the trainee and the role of the teacher. As argued by Iverson [20], serious games offer a paradigm shift in training as it changes the role of the trainee from passive to active and the role of the trainer changes from just delivering material to being a facilitator. The role of the teacher becomes central as the facilitator balances the educational game experiences to other practices. For the teacher to become a facilitator means, in design terms that he or she must be involved in the game experience itself, either participating in the game or as a close observer.

In order to guarantee an effective use of serious games for educational purposes, these questions need to be addressed, not simply from the nature of games but also how the game and its characteristics can be adopted and leveraged to enhance learning within the structural, organizational and cultural constraints of institutional education [21]. In this regard, the integration of serious games requires teachers to take into account a variety of different elements (timing, contents, assessment, etc.), in order to guarantee that (a) that the information being taught is indeed generalizable outside the context of the game and (b) that deeper, metacognitive gains are attained as a result of socially constructed game play [22–24]. Even though most games used for teaching purposes within engineering and business schools are in-house developments, there are some propositions about which games can be used for SCM education [25, 26].

The most well-known SCM Game is the beer distribution game [27]. A variant has been redesigned as an Internet based SC challenge Simulation game (ISCS) [34]. Role-play mechanics is the mainstay of SCM gameplay dynamics whichever the variant. ISCS also includes a Management Information System (MIS) built in to support decision making allowing it to test SCM strategies in the game. ISCS has been used at post-graduate level in the University of Greenwich since its launch in 2005. The Lean Leap Logistics Game [32] is another variation of the beer game more appropriate for application to a manufacturing process. It considers set up times, process reliability and capacity issues across multiple stages and constraints.

In terms of engineering the objectives are to provide students a detailed understanding of how to identify the pinch points for modern manufacturing SCs. In particular for e-manufacturing, where production planning and logistics are key learning topics, such games provide a more realistic alternative to classical teaching methods.

One main challenge for the integration of a serious game in a new environment is their adoptability. The next section therefore describes a game that can be used for supply chain management, followed by how it was integrated in three different curricula at two different universities.

2 Shortfall Game

SHORTFALL [36] is a strategy game with implicit role-play mechanics. The game is played in teams of three players per computer. Each player manages their individual entity (company) that makes up a whole supply chain (Fig. 1). The aim is to maximize profits across the whole supply chain, i.e. across all stakeholders, by achieving a benign manufacturing enterprise. To achieve this objective, the players have to take decisions and select options, as seen in Fig. 2. Communication within the team is the key to success as each team competes with others.

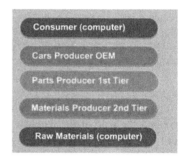

Fig. 1. SHORTFALL material, parts and cars managed tiers.

The game is a repetitive loop of 10 rounds interspersed with real-world events (e.g. strikes). First, the player is informed about the status of the chain (which is expressed in five target dimensions: profit, green compliance, number of sold products, etc.) and about the external conditions (prices of material, parts and products). Although not explicit, a turn-base mechanic regulates each player role to set some numerical values (e.g. the quantity of material to be purchased, products to be sold or stored). Events may occur impacting the next period.

In each round, the players make investment decisions. With three options available and with each option having a different environmental impact, the player should apply any knowledge accrued in this field to select the optimum solution for green and sustainable production. To aid decision-making and to meet certain criteria, the team can access information related to costs and revenue, including waste (Fig. 2).

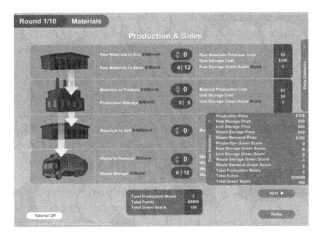

Fig. 2. SHORTFALL GUI - overview costs- materials

The difficulty level increases with the rounds since events become ever more difficult to deal with, forcing the player to reflect and think of more complex counter-actions to avoid losses and to fulfil the objective. The scoring (Fig. 3) for the game is based on five factors: Total profit; Green score; Total waste removed; Waste disposal expenses; Total number of cars sold.

Fig. 3. Web-based SHORTFALL score board.

3   Educational Setting

The integration of SHORTFALL varies both within an institution as well as from one institution to another. However, it can be clearly stated that traditional teaching methods are mostly used, and SGs remain as a niche tool either as a supplement to normal classes or as a GBL course for a specific module. The usage depends very much on the topic and the flexibility of the curriculum. In this article two different approaches are presented. In the first setting, SHORTFALL is used as an extension that parallels conventional teaching whilst being played regularly throughout the course. In the second setting it is used as a part of a GBL course, in which the students shall apply methods and knowledge acquired in earlier semesters at the university.

3.1   Heriot Watt University Engineering Manufacturing Course

The context of SHORTFALL used in this investigation pertains to supplementing taught material on engineering manufacturing at Heriot-Watt University in the UK for final year mechanical engineering students. The course comprises theoretical understanding of manufacturing and technologies that influence its workflow. Within this course lies e-manufacturing. The aim was to provide students an alternative approach to classical teaching about the principles of manufacturing enterprises and the technologies employed therein. From the academic perspective, it was about how SHORTFALL could be used as an abstraction layer to broaden their knowledge and implementation strategy of manufacturing concepts and as a platform for engineering related information sharing. On completion of this course students are expected to demonstrate how various principles of manufacturing methods can be applied and its role in the modern engineering processes. To further establish the game's effect an exam question was designed to ascertain the learning outcomes.

The students formed teams of three and play three game sessions, with each session lasting 2 h over a 12-week period. No corroboration between teams is allowed. UK students were largely un-facilitated other that the tutor explaining where to locate the game, which game scenario to be played and responding to simply "how-to" queries with regards to the game's interface. A reflective class was held after each game session.

In 2013 there were 17 groups of three while in 2014 a total of 9 groups of 3 were available in UK. After each session played, a team spends two weeks reflecting on how they performed, their strategy and how the taught material compares to real world scenarios, and how it aligns with the game. A reflection class was held after each game week for students to discuss the game in context with the taught material. Course lectures are scheduled such that incremental knowledge accrued would increase the relevance of game play. This was further supplemented with industrial visits where students have the opportunity to question industrialists on matters such as tradeoffs among economic and environmental policies that influence technology implemented or even which current strategies are used in industry to address environmental issues.

After the 12-week case-study, each team gave a short presentation on how they conducted their game sessions; each team member was graded on their understanding of manufacturing methods and the use of technologies therein. A System Usability Scale (SUS) report [37], which is a well-established a tool used in usability engineering, was modified to establish the class perception on using SHORTFALL.

3.2 University of Bremen Course 1: Decision Making

At the University of Bremen SHORTFALL was used as an introduction to a game based course on decision making in distributed production and supply chain for 3rd Semester Master students studying production, industrial or systems engineering. The course aims to strengthen the capability of strategic thinking as well as to support the process of constructing new knowledge. On completion students are expected to be able to demonstrate how various methods for strategic decision making can be applied to support collaboration, reduce network risks and thus increase the resilience of the supply chain or production network. Furthermore, it is expected that they also experience how different technologies affect the production in different ways and how their decisions have an impact on the overall success as well as on the efficiency of the network.

The academic use of SHORTFALL was to investigate if the game could either replace or act as an extension to the games already in used. SHORTFALL was played by 18 Master students from the second year on Oct. 21, 2013. It was played directly after a short introduction to the game, to the learning objective, a very brief introduction to the different production and supply chain strategies relevant for the SHORTFALL game (meant as a repetition). No detailed introduction to sustainable production was given. The students were divided in 6 groups sharing one PC with an allocated 4.5 h for completing the whole game, which was far more than the lecturer would expect that the students needed. Initially it was planned to have a short debriefing after rounds 5 and 10, and not give additional information and help during game play, so that we could check if it might be possible to use the game unfacilitated, but due to the observation of the lecturer during game play, there were debriefing session after round 3, 7 and 10 and she also had to provide help during game play. The game play was facilitated by the teacher and much time was dedicated to the reflection and discussion phase after round 3, 7, and 10. In order to establish the game's effects, and to be able to compare the results with the exisiting results from Heriot-Watt, the student used the same questionnaire and had to deal with the same questions as the students at Heriot-Watt. A questionnaire with the 10 questions listed in Sect. 4 was completed directly after the game play, and also added a reflection and documentation part to the lab protocols.

3.3   University of Bremen Course 2: Reengineering of Manufacturing Processes

This game based course deals with reengineering of manufacturing processes. It is aimed at applying methods on quality management, reengineering, project and change management within the context of production and manufacturing. During the course students apply different creative techniques and methods to solve different problems. The course has a blended learning concept, with a short introduction to the theory before the experiential learning experience takes place. The majority of students in this course are first semester industrial and production engineering Master students. These students have not yet selected a main topic within their master studies and have their undergraduate degree from different universities, however many of them come from industrial and production engineering at the university of Bremen.

In this course SHORTFALL was played by 19 master students in 1st Semester 2013. It served as an intersectional part between a game re-engineering (a physical game where the students have to produce mini elevating truck) and the management section dealing more with process quality and project management topics. The idea was to see if SHORTFALL would help the student in reflecting on what they learned and transfer this knowledge and the methodological approaches learned during the first part of the course in different settings. Before playing, a short introduction to the course was given including an overview of different production and supply chain strategies relevant to SHORTFALL was provided by the teacher who was also responsible for carrying out the reflection and discussion phases in between the game rounds. She was also available during game play for explaining the different manufacturing strategies and technological solutions during game play. The same questionnaires and lead question during game play was used.

4   Methodology

SHORTFALL was administered in a digital format where students access the game online. To ascertain the strengths and weaknesses of SHORTFALL as a supplement to classical teaching and purely as a game-based learning, the approach was to:

- Capture or collect usability data, such as scores, task completion time, error records, and subjective ratings;
- Analyse and interpret usability data to identify fitness of purpose;
- Critique and suggest solutions or improvements to mitigate problems.

The protocol (Fig. 4) for HWU and UNIHB differs in that HWU UK provided minimal facilitation while UNIHB conducted the game with full facilitation. In terms of game rounds, three were conducted by HWU over a 9 week period while UNIHB played a single game for 4 h for the first course in the first class, and the second course in the middle of the course. At HWU, students were incrementally taught material in parallel with each game round, followed by 2 weeks of reflection and analysis. That is, lectures were provided at the beginning of the week followed by gameplay at the end of the week. Thus by the third round all taught material would have been covered and it is anticipated that the accrued knowledge would be exercised by the students.

HWU	Wk1 (Game 1)		Wk2 (Reflection)		Wk3 (Summation)			Wk9 (Game 3)	
	SHORTFALL	Reflection	Lecture	Reflection	Lecture	Analytic report		Lecture	Final report

UNI HB	Wk1 (Game Shortfall)		Wk2-7 (Game Seconds)		Wk8-10 (Game Beware)		Wk11	
	SHORTFALL	Reflection	Theory Game1- Reflection		Theory Game2- Reflection		Presentation Reflection Report	

UNIHB2	Wk1-3 (reeng. Game)		Wk4 (Game Shortfall)		Wk5-7 (mgt. games)	
	Theory Game1- Reflection-Presentation		SHORTFALL ......Reflection		Theory Game4-6-Reflection and presentation	

Fig. 4. Protocol for conducting SHORTFALL at HWU and UNIHB.

Reflection activities were facilitated at both HWU (other than the summation weeks) and UNIHB. To support reflection and gameplay the students were given the following similar tasks:

- Work with your team to achieve the highest score by managing the most profitable and environmentally benign supply chain
- Use information accrued in lectures to help you make major decisions in the game
- Reflect on the gameplay and log your understanding of how a new technology or a manufacturing paradigm influences production
- Reflect on how the elements in the game enable you to identify and link the knowledge and information accrued in lectures

- Establish your learning from each stage
- To identify shortcomings of using the game

To establish the games' quotient as supplementary SC material a post-game questionnaire as used by Gennett [38] was applied. Given that SHORTFALL is utilised here as a technical subject, i.e. on SCM and production strategies, the questions of interest to both HWU and UNIHB are Q1- 4, Q8 and Q10:

- Q1: Shortfall increased my knowledge of the automotive supply chain.
- Q2: Shortfall increased my knowledge of supply chain management.
- Q3: Shortfall increased my knowledge of manufacturing practices.
- Q4: Shortfall increased my knowledge of environmentally benign manufacturing practices.
- Q8: Playing Shortfall again would further increase my knowledge of environmentally benign automotive manufacturing.
- Q10: I would enjoy playing Shortfall in tandem with class lectures about environmentally benign manufacturing and/or supply chain management.

While slight differences in the protocol were required to match the institutional requirements, the questions as well as the tasks were similar at both universities. This was necessary to enable comparison of results.

5   Results

The results herein are in part to ascertain the long-term use of SHORTFALL either as supplementary teaching material or as a bespoke means to teach SCM and production strategies. For UNIHB, there are two fundamental reasons for using SHORTFALL; the first concerns decision making while the second is directed at managing re-engineering. Not too dissimilar, HWU uses the game as a means to associate how technologies influence the production strategies in a supply chain. This is closer aligned with UNIHB's use of the game for decision making meaning as it pertains to formulating SCM strategies.

It should be noted that the demograph of students and the teaching methods vary. However, the analysis for both institutions is associated to how a specific serious engineering game, such as SHORTFALL, can be adapted to a specific course. The post questionnaires [38] provide more detailed answers than a simple yes/no or neither/nor. However, to quickly view the trend a 3-point Likert-type sale was adopted. These are summarised in Tables 1 and 2 which represent the HWU results of 2013 and 2014. Note the number of students on the course is shown in the column 'total'. This similar format was used at UNIHB (See Tables 3 and 4 on 2014 results).

The relevant questions of interest to HWU are related to strategic use of production technologies in a SCM are mainly Q3 and Q4. Most of the technological components and strategic decision making are related to Q3. Q4 focuses on implementing a benign SCM. The results indicate a positive experience of SHORTFALL in both years with regards to knowledge of manufacturing practices. With reference to creating a benign manufacturing enterprise there is minimal increase in the capacity (7 %) of using the

Table 1. 2013 HWU use of SHORTFALL

Question no	Description	yes	no	neither/nor	total	yes (%)	no (%)	neither/nor (%)
1	Shortfall increased my knowledge of the automotive supply chain.	39	4	8	51	76%	8%	16%
2	Shortfall increased my knowledge of supply chain management.	36	11	4	51	71%	22%	8%
3	Shortfall increased my knowledge of manufacturing practices.	30	12	9	51	59%	24%	18%
4	Shortfall increased my knowledge of environmentally benign manufacturing practices.	27	10	14	51	53%	20%	27%
8	Playing Shortfall again would further increase my knowledge of environmentally benign automotive manufacturing.	34	7	10	51	67%	14%	20%
10	I would enjoy playing Shortfall in tandem with class lectures about environmentally benign manufacturing and/or supply chain management.	35	8	8	51	69%	16%	16%

Table 2. 2014 HWU use of SHORTFALL

Question no	Description	yes	no	neither/nor	total	yes (%)	no (%)	neither/nor (%)
1	Shortfall increased my knowledge of the automotive supply chain.	19	0	1	20	95%	0%	5%
2	Shortfall increased my knowledge of supply chain management.	20	0	0	20	100%	0%	0%
3	Shortfall increased my knowledge of manufacturing practices.	17	1	2	20	85%	5%	10%
4	Shortfall increased my knowledge of environmentally benign manufacturing practices.	12	3	5	20	60%	15%	25%
8	Playing Shortfall again would further increase my knowledge of environmentally benign automotive manufacturing.	13	2	5	20	65%	10%	25%
10	I would enjoy playing Shortfall in tandem with class lectures about environmentally benign manufacturing and/or supply chain management.	16	3	1	20	80%	15%	5%

game. It is worth noting that HWU students are taught the fundamentals of engineering manufacturing from first year onwards. Thus, students are expected to build upon knowledge gained, hence the reasoning for minimal facilitation. Facilitation here refers to directing students to the website, how to operate the interface, and where to find information to enable them to construct a strategy. The lectures that parallel the game and the reflection classes allow students to have a deeper understanding of SCM and discuss how best to approach SCM bottle necks. The rationale is that students take a leading role in the pursuit of their own knowledge endeavours and the applied decision information mining during the gameplay.

Considering that 2014 has less than half of 2013 cohort, the trend remains that SHORTFALL is useful as a compliment to the taught material. What is interesting is that there is a more distinct perception of the game from the point of the students; there is a clear 'yes' and 'no' vote of confidence to the game.

For UNIHB courses on decision making in supply chain (Table 3) the most relevant questions are 1, 2, and 4. Judging from the results, half of the students did not feel that

Table 3. 2014 UNIHB use of SHORTFALL. Summative results of the post-questionnaire for the decision making course.

Question no.	Description	yes	no	neither/nor	total	yes (%)	no (%)	neither/nor (%)
1	Shortfall increased my knowledge of the automotive supply chain.	7	9	2	18	39%	50%	11%
2	Shortfall increased my knowledge of supply chain management.	12	5	1	18	67%	28%	6%
3	Shortfall increased my knowledge of manufacturing practices.	9	6	3	18	50%	33%	17%
4	Shortfall increased my knowledge of environmentally benign manufacturing practices.	12	3	3	18	67%	17%	17%
8	Playing Shortfall again would further increase my knowledge of environmentally benign automotive manufacturing.	9	7	2	18	50%	39%	11%
10	I would enjoy playing Shortfall in tandem with class lectures about environmentally benign manufacturing and/or supply chain management.	18	0	0	18	100%	0%	0%

Table 4. 2014 UNIHB2 use of SHORTFALL. Summative results of the post-questionnaire for the manufacturing and reengineering course.

Question no.	description	yes	no	neither/nor	total	yes (%)	no (%)	neither/nor (%)
1	Shortfall increased my knowledge of the automotive supply chain.	6	8	5	19	32%	42%	26%
2	Shortfall increased my knowledge of supply chain management.	13	5	1	19	68%	26%	5%
3	Shortfall increased my knowledge of manufacturing practices.	8	6	5	19	42%	32%	26%
4	Shortfall increased my knowledge of environmentally benign manufacturing practices.	11	6	2	19	58%	32%	11%
8	Playing Shortfall again would further increase my knowledge of environmentally benign automotive manufacturing.	4	13	2	19	21%	68%	11%
10	I would enjoy playing Shortfall in tandem with class lectures about environmentally benign manufacturing and/or supply chain management.	8	6	5	19	42%	32%	26%

the game increased the knowledge on automotive supply chain. This has to be seen in the relation to the high involvement of the automotive industries in the education of the engineers offering several internship, company visits etc. during study. Q2 and Q4 (66.7 %) indicate the opinion that shortfall did increase their knowledge of SCM and environmental benign of manufacturing. This is an important finding since SHORT-FALL was only intended as a short repetition of the theoretical foundation prior to using downstream games for strategic decision making in supply chains. The post-questionnaire, with its more detailed answers as well as the feedback in the debriefing sessions, however did reveal that most students thought the availability of a facilitator and the use of debriefing sessions increased their understanding on how to assess the impact a decision may have on the result and the next steps required.

In addition students lacking the expected level of knowledge reported that it was very important for their learning outcome to have a teacher explain the theory while playing.

For the course on manufacturing and re-engineering an UNIHB the most relevant questions are as for HWU, Q3 and Q4. Interestingly, even though the largest group of students indicated that they increased their knowledge of manufacturing practices, this question reveals a high number of students not knowing, such that the overall results is less positive. These results have to be verified with the next year's cohort, in order to see if an adaption of the theoretical foundation is necessary or not. 42 % of the students would like to play SHORTFALL in combination with a class lecturer focussing on environmental or supply chain aspects; while 32 % do not support this statement and 26 % are uncertain.

6   Discussion

For the University of Bremen, the use of SHORTFALL in course 1 showed positive answers regarding Q1-4, Q8 and Q10, with low percentages uncertain (neither/nor). The results from course 2 indicates the same; however, the results are not as clear (lesser percentages) while the share of uncertain (neither/nor) answers increased. In both cases the teacher was the same, but the course domain and the knowledge of the students were different.

Questions 8 and 10 however displayed contrasting differences. While course 1 (UNIHB) supports the statement, that playing shortfall again would increase their knowledge of environmentally benign automotive manufacturing, course 2 ((UNIHB2) contradicts this statement. Further, regarding Q10, course 1 fully supports that statement, while course 2 supports this with only 42 % of the students and a high percentage of 26 % uncertain (neither/nor). At HWU, where the game is played 3 times during the semester and with theoretical classes in parallel the first cohort shows similar results as the decision making course, and slightly better than the manufacturing course at UNIHB. For the cohort 2014, the results at HWU were much more positive than Bremen's. Since this was the second year it was played, it can be assumed that an adaption based on the experience of using SHORTFALL in 2013 has had a very positive influence. It needs however more long term use to see if this is also depending much on the group or only of a better integration in the curricula.

A main question that should be addressed is the role of the facilitator and teacher. In the case of HWU, the teacher gives the theoretical classes prior, with some facilitation during the first game play, but with no facilitation in the last. However, the facilitator is aware of what happens in the game, and use time on reflection with the students after game play. It is the same teacher that carried out the classes both in 2013 and 2014.

In the case of the UNIHB Course 1, the game was originally planned to be unfacilitated as a repetition. However, during gameplay it became obvious that this did not work, as the students where guessing instead of making sound choices based on prior knowledge of the subject. Thus, the approach of using the game unfacilitated had to be changed into playing the game with facilitator and reflecting phases were introduced after round 3, 7, and 10. The main reason for the change seems to be a result of a mismatch of needed as well as expected prior knowledge (based on taught topics in the

BSc degree and first year of master) and actually available knowledge. The change in the use of facilitator had according to the feedback from the students and the observation from the teacher/facilitator, a positive impact on the game play, and the usefulness of SHORTFALL as a repetition of pervious gained knowledge, but this required for some group much facilitating during game play. For some groups, with a higher level of relevant knowledge, less facilitation was required. Almost all students reported that the several debriefings and reflection phases (outside the gameplay) supported the analysing and assement of the gameplay.

UNIHB Course 2 was facilitated from the beginning since it was expected that some of the students would have too little knowledge on manufacturing practices due to a large number of students coming from industrial engineering, and also due to the experience collected in the first course. However, again contrary to the teacher at HWU who have had these students regularly over the past years, the teacher in Bremen did not know the students, their learning style and their knowledge before. This can be directly seen in the results, that indicates that there is a need for more information on the topics either beforehand or inbuilt in the game play, and that if SHORTFALL should be used in future courses a better integration in the course is necessary. The results show in all experiments that the students find that the game improves their skills on SCM. In addition, the analysis of the HWU case where the game was played three times with additional theoretical classes, show that the more they are into the topic, the less facilitation was needed. Also the impression of the teacher at UNI HB underpins this, but in order to confirm the results, the experiment has to be repeated with a more proper experimental set-up. However, in one of the cases at UNI HB, the intention of using SHORTFALL was to use it for repetition of prior knowledge, unfacilitated this was only achieved for the groups having a high level of prior knowledge, and not for the all groups. Thus, it can be indicated that for this purpose, facilitation is necessary.

7   Conclusions and Future Work

Both the HWU and UNIHB results indicate that a teacher/facilitator with some experience using SHORTFALL is important and that the regular use of the game by continuous adaption with corresponding taught topics impacts on the students learning outcomes. None of the courses were expedited through use of RCT since this was, and will not be possible even in the future. However, by comparing the results both across the institutions and with the results of previous years, it will be possible to understand better how SHORTFALL can be integrated in the curricula, the challenges and barriers and also how to overcome these. So far only two universities took part in the experiments, but it is the intention to enlarge this group in order to identify patterns and to provide more general guidelines for integration of SG in the manufacturing education. Such long term measures will also improve the understanding of how different game mechanics influence the gameplay and the learning outcome [39]. It will also help to understand for which learning types, different types of adaption are necessary and to understand how to optimise the setting.

Acknowledgments. This work has been co-funded by the EU under the FP7, in the Games and Learning Alliance (GALA) Network of Excellence, Grant Agreement nr. 258169.

References

1. Starkey, K., Tempest, S.: The future of the business school: knowledge challenges and opportunities. Hum. Relat. **58**(1), 61–82 (2005)
2. Prensky, M.: Digital game-based learning. ACM Comput. Entertain. **1**(1), 21 (2003)
3. Gee, J.P.: What video games have to teach us about learning and literacy. Palgrave Macmillan, New York (2003)
4. Ebner, M., Holzinger, A.: Successful implementation of user-centered game based learning in higher education: an example from civil engineering. Comput. Educ. **49**(3), 873–890 (2007)
5. Bellotti, F., Berta, R., De Gloria, A.: designing effective serious games: opportunities and challenges for research, special issue: creative learning with serious games. Int. J. Emerg. Technol. Learn. (IJET) **5**, 22–35 (2010)
6. Greitzer, F.L., Kuchar, O.A., Huston, K.: Cognitive science implications for enhancing training effectiveness in a serious gaming context. ACM J. Educ. Res. Comput. **7**(3–2), 10 (2007). doi:10.1145/1281320.1281322
7. De Gloria, A., Bellotti, F., Berta, R.: Building a Comprehensive R&D Community on Serious Games, 4th International Conference on Games and Virtual Worlds for Serious Applications, VS-Games 2012, Genova (2012)
8. Kerns, S.E., Miller, R.K., Kerns, D.V.: Designing from a blank slate: the development of the initial Olin college curriculum, in Educating the Engineer of 2020: Adapting Engineering Education to the new century (2005). http://www.nap.edu/catalog/11338.html. Accessed 20 December 2012
9. Cheville, A., Bunting, C.: Engineering students for 21st century: student development through the curriculum. J. Adv. Eng. Educ. **3**(4), 1–37 (2011). http://advances.asee.org/wp-content/uploads/vol02/issue04/papers/aee-vol02-issue04-p10.pdf. Accessed 30 April 2014
10. O'Sullivan, B., Rolstadås, A., Filos, E.: Global education in manufacturing strategy. Intellect. Manuf. **22**, 663–674 (2011)
11. Chryssolouris, G., Mavrikios, D.: Education for Next Generation Manufacturing, Paper presented at IMS Vision Forum 2006 (2007). ftp://cordis.europa.eu/_/gc_to_ims-visionforum2006-paper.pdf
12. Baalsrud Hauge, J., Hoeborn, G., Bredtmann, J.: Challenges of serious games for improving students' management skills on decision making, handbook of research on serious games as educational, business and research tools: development and design. In: Cruz-Cunha, M., Varajao, J. (eds.) IGI Global, pp. 947–964 (2012)
13. Narayanasamy, V., Wong, K.W., Fung, C.C., Rai, S.: Distinguishing games and simulation games from simulators. Comput. Entertain. **4**(2), 1–18 (2006)
14. Kriz, W.: How to facilitate the debrief of simulations/games for effective learning. In: Psychologische Bericht (2001)
15. Simon, H.A.: Models of bounded rationality: Empirically Grounded Economic Reason. MIT Press, Cambridge (1997)
16. Sterman, J.D.: Modeling managerial behavior: misperceptions of feedback in a dynamic decision making experiment. Manag. Sci. **35**(3), 321–339 (1989)

17. Semini, M. Fauske, H. Strandhagen, J.O.: Simulation methods and educational games: application areas for learning asd strategic decision-making in manufacturing operations. In: Conference Proceedings, Multidisciplinary Research on Simulation Methods and Educational games in Industrial Management, SINTEF, S3771, Trondheim Norway (2006)
18. Baalsrud Hauge, J., Bellotti, F., Nadolski, R., Kickmeier-Rust, M.D., Berta, R., Carvalho, M.: Deploying serious games for management in higher education: lessons learned and good practices. In: Escudeiro, P., de Carvalho, C.V. (eds.) Proceedings of 7th European Conference on Games based Learning, pp. 225–234, 2–3 October 2013, Porto (2013). ISBN: 978-1-909507-66-1
19. de Freitas, S., Kiili, K., Ney, M., Ott, M., Popescu, M., Romero, M., Stanescu, I.: Gel: exploring game enhanced learning. Procedia Comput. Sci. **15**, 289–292 (2012)
20. Micael, D., Chen, S.: Serious Games: games that educate, train and inform. Thomson Course Technology (2006)
21. Hanghøj, T., Engel, B.C.: Teacher roles and positionings in relation to educational games. In: Meyer, B. (ed.) ECGBL 2010, pp. 115–122. Academic Conferences and Publishing International Limited, Reading (2010)
22. Young, F., Slota, S., Cutter, B., Jalette, G., Mullin, G., Lai, B., Simeoni, Z., Tran, M., Yukhymenko, M.: Our princess is in another castle: a review of trends in serious gaming for education. Rev. Educ. Res. **82**(1), 61–89 (2012)
23. Jonassen, D.H.: Certainty, determinism, and predictability in theories of instructional design: lessons from science. Educ. Techn. **37**(1), 27–34 (1997)
24. Bellotti, F., Kapralos, B., Lee, K., Moreno-Ger, P., Berta, R.: Assessment in and of serious games: an overview. Adv. Hum. Comput. Interact. **2013**, 11 (2013). doi:10.1155/2013/136864. Article ID: 136864
25. Campbell, A., Gontzel, J., Savelsbergh, M.: Experiences with the use of supply chain software in education. Prod. Oper. Manag. **9**(1), 66–80 (1999)
26. Lewis, M.A., Maylor, H.R.: Game playing and operations management education. Int. J. Prod. Econ. **105**(2007), 134–149 (2007)
27. Forrester, J.W.: Industrial Dynamics. a major breakthrough for decision makers. Harvard Bus. Rev. **36**(4), 37–66 (1958)
28. Nienhaus, J., Ziegenbein, A., Schoensleben, P.: How human behaviour amplifies the bullwhip effect. a study based on the beer distribution game online. Prod. Plann. Control **17**(6), 547–557 (2006)
29. eBeer. The electronic Beer game. http://www.responsive.net/ebeer.html
30. Wu, D.Y., Katok, E.: Learning, communication, and the bullwhip effect. J. Oper. Manag. **24**(6), 839–850 (2006)
31. Macdonald, J.R., Frommer, I.D., Karaesmen, I.Z.: Decision making in the beer game and supply chain performance. Oper. Manag. Res. **6**(3–4), 119–126 (2013)
32. Holweg, M., Bicheno, J.: Supply chain simulation – a tool for education, enhancement and endeavour. Int. J. Prod. Econ. **78**, 163–175 (2002)
33. Bodner, D.A., Wade, J.P., Watson, W.R., Kamberov, G.I.: Designing an experiential learning environment for logistics and systems engineering. Procedia Comput. Sci. **16**, 1082–1091 (2013)
34. Zhou, L., Xie, Y., Wild, N., Hunt, C.: Learning and practising supply chain management strategies from a business simulation game: a comprehensive supply chain simulation. In: 2008 Proceedings of IEEE Simulation Conference on WSC 2008, pp. 2534–2542 (2008)
35. Louchart, S., Lim, T., Al Sulaiman, H.: Why are video-games relevant test beds for studying interactivity for engineers? In: Proceedings of International Simulation and Gaming Association Conference paper O-25, vol. 4, Singapore (2009)

36. Corriere, J.D.: Shortfall: An Educational Game on Environmental Issues in Supply Chain Management. M.S. thesis. Mechanical and Industrial Engineering. Northeastern University, Boston (2003)
37. Brooke, J.: SUS: a quick and dirty usability scale. In: Jordan, P.W., Thomas, B., Weerdmeester, B.A., McClelland, I.L. (eds.) Usability Evaluation in Industry, pp. 189–194. Taylor and Francis, Brighton (1996)
38. Gennett, Z.: Shortfall Online: The Development of an Educational Computer Game for Teaching Sustainable Engineering to Millennial Generation Students. MS thesis, Department Mechanical and Industrial Engineering. Northeastern University, Boston (2010)
39. Arnab, S., Lim, T., Carvalho, M.B., Bellotti, F., de Freitas, S., Louchart, S., Suttie, N., Berta, R., De Gloria, A.: Mapping learning and game mechanics for serious games analysis. Br. J. Educ. Technol. (2013). doi:10.1111/bjet.12113. (2014)

Identifying Pedagogical Uses of Serious Games for Learning English as a Second Language

Azeneth Patiño and Margarida Romero[✉]

Université Laval, 2320 rue des Bibliothèques,
Québec, QC G1V 0A6, Canada
{irma-azeneth.patino-zuniga.1,
margarida.romero}@ulaval.ca

Abstract. Nowadays, English is a global language taught as a second language in most of non-English speaking countries. Over recent decades, Computer Assisted Language Learning (CALL) has evolved into solutions that allow a higher learner engagement in authentic active-based learning activities. In this context, the educational digital games, also known as Serious Games (SG), allow learning English as a Second Language (ESL) in a playful and engaging environment. In this study, we develop a literature review on the current uses of SG in the context of CALL, in general, and ESL, specifically, in order to create a taxonomy of pedagogical uses of SG for ESL. The taxonomy could be of utility for teachers aiming to integrate SG in their ESL courses.

1 English as a Second Language (ESL)

English is a global language with a great influence on the economic, cultural, academic and scientific fields. The influence of English in these fields implies that learning English is a competitive advantage for people and organizations working internationally in those areas [1]. According to Hüppauf [2], the globalization process and the English hegemony as a foreign language are inseparable. In this global context, educational systems in non-English-speaking countries have included learning English as a Foreign Language (EFL) or as a Second Language (ESL) as a curricular objective. According to Santos Gargallo [3], learning a second language is the process whereby an individual acquires a level of linguistic and communicative competence that allows him to interact with a linguistic community that uses that second language. Mitchell and Myles [4, p. 1] define second language learning as "the learning of any language to any level provided only that the learning of the 'second' language takes place sometime later than the acquisition of the first language."

2 Computer Assisted Language Learning (CALL) for ESL

The evolution of Information and Communication Technologies (ICT) and its uses for second language learning have evolved simultaneously. Computer Assisted Language Learning (CALL) has evolved considerably during the last 50 years. If the first programs allowed basic interactions to complete words or letters; nowadays, they allow

© Springer International Publishing Switzerland 2015
A. De Gloria (Ed.): GALA 2014, LNCS 9221, pp. 31–43, 2015.
DOI: 10.1007/978-3-319-22960-7_4

more complex pedagogical uses of Information and Communication Technologies based in web 2.0 such as podcasts [5], videos [6], webQuests [7] and social networks [8, 9]. This article analyzes one of the emerging solutions in CALL: the use of Serious Games (SG) in English as a Second Language (ESL) learning in order to classify the different types of SG that allow ESL learning according to the pedagogical intention, to the individual or cooperating modalities, and to the game interactivity.

3   Serious Games (SG) for ESL

According to Connolly, Stansfield and Hainey [10], the educational digital games support the teaching, learning, and evaluation processes. Serious Games combine the active pedagogy and the playful character of games with learning objectives based in knowledge or competences [11, 12]. The games can lead to the creation of immersive and authentic learning activities that place students as the main characters of foreign language interaction. The potential of games in foreign language learning has been analyzed by several authors in the last decade. Gee [13] points out the linguistic interaction opportunities in open games environments where dialogue is promoted. Godwin-Jones [14] indicates that games are one of the educational technologies with more potential for CALL, and he emphasizes the potential of multi-player games and the immersive contexts that integrate cultural aspects. Purushotma [15] analyzes the interest in the Massively Multiplayer Online Role-Playing Game (MMORPG) called *The Sims* as an environment for language learning that implies authentic contexts and he points out the integration of songs as an interesting resource for young learners. The mini-games that allow simple interactions with immediate feedback are as well of great interest for language learning [16]. Hansbøl [17] considers the online availability of ESL mini-games as a way to increase the English training hours outside the classroom in order to reinforce learning.

4   Integration of Videogames and Serious Games in ESL Learning

Even though the innovating experiences with the use of games in foreign language learning are increasing day by day, the use of games in formal education contexts is still a minority. The existence of a great diversity of videogames in English and the increasing number of SG specifically designed for English as a Foreign Language learning is not represented in the use of videogames and SG in formal learning contexts. We must consider different factors stopping the use of these educational technologies in English as Foreign Language learning. On the one hand, we can consider the ESL teachers development of digital competence. Currently, the ESL teachers' education has its limitations regarding the use of ICTs. Laborda [18] states that the main use of technology is of consultative type to obtain information and it leaves aside the productive reading-writing activities. On the other hand, there is a minority of ESL teachers that actually play videogames, and only a few of them transpose the videogames interest into the pedagogical context of formal ESL learning. This study aims to offer the general keys to know the different videogames and Serious Games typologies in ESL learning as well to relate these typologies to the Second Language Learning strategies proposed by Oxford [19].

5 Typology of Videogames and Serious Games for ESL Learning

Some of the main difficulties faced by ESL teachers are the constant evolution of technology and the lack of time and perspective to choose the most appropriate educational resources. According to Lam [20], the perceptions about the impact of educational technologies on learning determine the use of these technologies among the second language teachers. Stockwell [21] considers that one of the most important factors regarding the teachers who decide to use technologies in second language learning is to get familiarized with the different available options and make sure these technologies are adapted to the specific learning objectives. We have performed a literature review in the EBSCO Host database with the purpose of identifying the different game options available for ESL learning. The search strategy was performed using the terms "Serious Games" and "English" using the operator "AND". The Serious Games analyzed in the articles found in the database EBSCO Host have been classified into three categories that are further described in the next sections: (1) the pedagogical intention of the videogame or SG; (2) the number of players; and (3) the complexity of interactions and pedagogical approach (Table 1).

Table 1. Taxonomy of videogames and serious games.

Category	Typology	Games and SG
Pedagogical intention	SG specifically designed for ESL	*Mingoville, Motion English, It's a Deal!,* and *Tower of Babel ARG*
	Videogames used pedagogically for ESL	*Simcopter, Active Worlds, The Sims, World of Warcraft, Seaman, Operator's Side* or *Lifeline, EverQuest II*
Number of players	Individual games and SG	*Seaman, Motion English, Operator's Side* or *Lifeline, Mingoville, It's a Deal!*
	Multiplayer games and SG	*Simcopter, Metavals, Tower of Babel ARG*
	Massively Online Games and SG	*EverQuest II, World of Warcraft, Active Worlds,* and *The Sims Online*
Complexity of interaction and pedagogical approach	Auto-corrective mini-games	*Gemmings Rush, Pacman* or *Memory* in *Mingoville* platform
	Artificial Intelligence-based games and SG	*It's a Deal!, Motion English, Seaman, Operator's Side* or *Lifeline*
	Open Online Player Interaction games and SG	*Hello you, Tower of Babel ARG, Active Worlds,* and *EverQuest II*

5.1 Serious Games for ESL According to the Initial Pedagogical Intention

We must distinguish between the Serious Games specifically designed for ESL and the videogames that have been developed without any pedagogical intention, but that can be used for ESL learning. According to Shelton and Scoresby [22], the use of videogames like *Sim City* with learning objectives constitutes a pedagogical reuse of entertainment games. ESL teachers interested in using games for language learning can decide whether to integrate an existing entertaining videogame or to use a Serious Game specifically designed for language learning.

5.1.1 Serious Games Specifically Designed for ESL

We start analyzing the games specifically designed for ESL learning. A game that has been designed for learning and not just for entertainment can be considered a Serious Game. The Serious Games for ESL learning explicitly indicate the pedagogical objectives that are supported by the game. Therefore, it is easier for a teacher to choose the most appropriate Serious Game according to its pedagogical objective.

Among the scientific articles analyzing SG for ESL learning, we must point out the one written by Connolly, Stansfield and Hainley [10]. These authors observe that alternate reality games or immersion games like *Tower of Babel ARG* represent an educational environment with potential to motivate students and engage them in second language learning activities. These games provide a collaborative and stimulating environment and they provide opportunities of interaction with other students in different languages. The SG *It's a Deal!* has been designed for ESL learning with a competence-oriented approach [11]. Its purpose was to teach intercultural business communication in business settings where English is the spoken language. Therefore, it is oriented to teach language as an intercultural communicative competence. In the same record, we must mention other simulation environments like the SG *Tactical Iraqui* [23], which was not created specifically for ESL, but designed to facilitate the intercultural communication in second languages. *Tactical Iraqui* is a game-based and simulation-based training system designed to support the training of American military personnel in second languages. The system includes mission-based games that were created to improve the oral communication proficiency and provide awareness of the practical and intercultural uses of the language. One of the individual games we must mention is the online platform *Mingoville* that offers a series of organized mini-games (like *Pacman* and *Memory*) as well as other entertainment activities for children of 9–11 years old in a virtual city inhabited by flamingos. The platform contains 10 missions that take the learners through different themes like *The Family*, *Colours and Clothes*, *Numbers and Letters*, etc. Each mission contains a number of activities like *Stories* where children can listen to and create narratives; *Creative lab* where children can draw pictures or sing karaoke in English; and *Games* that are mini-games involving the construction of sentences and the recognition of words. The games in this platform allow ESL learning for elementary school students either inside or outside the classroom in an autonomous way [17]. Meyer [24] points out that the feedback provided by games like the ones in *Mingoville* represent a great opportunity to increase the feedback provided to students. The ESL Serious Game *Motion English* is a physical interactive game with a three-dimensional depth camera interface that detects children's movements. The movements performed by children move the main character of the game and allow them to attack or to avoid game characters' attacks [25]. This game combines ESL learning and physical interaction. The game's interface detects player's movements and it provides a motivating, fun, and interesting opportunity to learn English. Physical movement is a spontaneous activity that occurs during learning, and it also represents immediate feedback from the system. This quality makes learning a stimulating activity and it helps to reduce the sedentary lifestyle associated to the use of technological systems.

5.1.2   Videogames Used Pedagogically for ESL

In this section we analyze the videogames that were originally created for entertaining, but that have been used in educational contexts for ESL learning. First of all, most of the videogames available in English language can be used as pedagogical resources in ESL. In order to do so, a pedagogical integration or an adaptation of the videogame is required to avoid students ignoring the pedagogical objectives because they get deeply involved with the game.

Simcopter is a helicopter flight simulator game that uses a 3D interface to provide immersion in a virtual city. In the game, an individual player assumes the role of a pilot who must navigate and respond to various emergencies such as traffic jams or fires in order to gain points and bonuses. *The Sims* is a computer game where players control the daily routines of a virtual family through the challenges of everyday life. Players guide the characters through tasks like cooking food, finding jobs, managing personal hygiene, and managing the family finances. In *World of Warcraft,* players must adopt an avatar or a fantasy character like an elf or a dwarf within a simulated world. Players are required to complete quests (specific tasks) like solving puzzles or engaging in battles to gain monetary or status rewards. In the game, players must interact using the target language to explore the environment, to communicate with other players through text chat, and to interact with the game characters controlled by the software's artificial intelligence. *Active Worlds* is a three-dimensional simulation platform that provides instant text-chat and voice-based communication within the simulated worlds created by users. This platform includes avatars that can move within the worlds and can display non-verbal communication like gestures or emotions. According to Peterson [23], the simulation games like *Simcopter, The Sims, Active Worlds* and *World of Warcraft* can contribute to second language learning if they are combined with additional material or if they are adapted to be used with pedagogical objectives. Peterson [26] states that simulation games represent an environment that allows second language learning since players are exposed to second language input, they interact with their peers, and they can participate in goal-based communicative activities. Plus, games motivate students and allow them to communicate and interact with other players, which imply social collaborative relationships. Puroshotma [15] indicates that videogames originally designed for entertainment like *The Sims*, can be modified in order to contribute to vocabulary learning. By changing the language settings, a videogame becomes helpful to acquire vocabulary since it repeatedly exposes the student to words in an interactive manner. Also, it provides a rich context for meaning association and minimizes learner's stress and effort.

Seaman is a speech recognition game that presents players with a virtual baby fish-creature to be nurture into adulthood by having conversations with it about its life and conditions. With an approximate of ten minutes of speech interaction a day the creature can be raised from birth to adulthood in about a month. *Operator's Side* (also called *Lifeline* in U.S.A) is a speech recognition game with all the elements of a typical action/adventure game where players can direct the main character entirely through vocal instructions. These games with speech interfaces allow users to dialogue with their characters or to verbally provide them instructions and commands. Puroshotma [15] affirms that the ability of easily customizing the language settings in existing games or to combine them with speech interfaces and the newest features like the Massively Multiplayer Games are an incentive to use games in education rather than creating new games from scratch.

5.2 Serious Games for ESL According to the Number of Players

Considering the great importance of social and collaborative learning contexts in second language learning, we must consider the videogames and SG capacity to support massive, group or individual modes. This second category might be useful for teachers to identify the most appropriate games to be used in ESL courses or practice addressed to individual students or to small, medium and large groups. According to the number of players in a game, we distinguish three types of videogames and Serious Games.

5.2.1 Individual Games and Serious Games

First of all, the interface of individual videogames or SG like *Seaman, Motion English, Operator's Side* or *Lifeline* allows interaction with a single player and it provides immediate feedback provided by artificial intelligence. Even though the *Mingoville* online platform represents a virtual city like *Sim City*, most of the games on the platform are individual mini-games. There are other games and Serious Games like *It's a Deal!* that provide an environment of dialogue production and simulated collaboration [11], but they are individual games since the collaboration is regulated by the game's artificial intelligence module. In this case, we talk about a game based in socio-constructivists principles for ESL learning that offers an individualistic scenario where collaborative aspects are simulated by the game's artificial intelligence.

5.2.2 Multiplayer Games and Serious Games

SG and multiplayer videogames allow competitive and cooperative game dynamics depending on the game's rules [27]. Analyzing the use of the game *MetaVals* in ESL learning, Popescu, Romero and Usart [28] noticed the existence of cooperation among the students playing in pairs (within the same team) and competition against the other pairs (with other teams). In this particular case, collaboration was favored by the support granted to the meta-cognitive statements, the level of certainty on answers provided by each participant. Games like *Tower of Babel ARG* or *Simcopter* have been used for ESL learning in a collaborative manner. In the SG *Tower of Babel ARG* participants had to cooperate and interact with other participants in order to get information about languages and cultures and eventually build a tower. The peda-gogical adaptation of *Simcopter* described by Peterson for an English course took place in a two-stage task. The class was divided in teams. During the first stage of the task, a member of each team had to pilot the helicopter following directions provided by other members of the same team that were required to assist the pilot in finding the required destination by producing a set of accurate written directions that will be later used. In the second stage of the task, the pilot faced the challenge of getting to a destination on foot in a different city following directions provided by other participants. Collabo-ration among peers was crucial to succeed in the game and oral and written practice took place in an interactive task-based activity.

5.2.3   Massively Online Games and Serious Games

Recently, we have witnessed the emergence of massive environments in gaming and education with the success of Massively Multiplayer Online Games and the develop-ment of Massive Open Online Courses [29]. We observe the appearance of Massive Serious Games, also known as Massively Multiplayer Online Serious Games (MMOSG) [30]. The massive videogames and SG enable several players to participate and interact within a virtual world. The scientific articles included in the literature review we performed do not mention the analysis of any Massive Serious Games designed specifically for ESL learning, but the literature review permitted to identify the use of Massive videogames in ESL learning like *The Sims Online, Ever Quest II, World of Warcraft* and *Active Worlds. The Sims Online* is the MMOG version of the computer game called *The Sims*. In this online game, players exist as characters of a virtual world interacting with other players on the internet rather than playing with a pre-programmed environment. The text chat feature is available and allows players to interact and communicate among them.

5.3   Serious Games for ESL According to the Complexity of Interactions and Pedagogical Approach

According to Barendregt and Bekker [31], the game's interactivity level can influence its use outside the classroom in non-formal educational contexts. Also, the complexity of interactions in a game can be of great importance depending on the English profi-ciency level of students. For instance, Peterson [23] recommends using Massively Multiplayer Role-Playing Games in small groups of intermediate or advanced students since they require the use of multiple competences and they can result into a cognitive overload for beginners. For a successful pedagogical integration of the game, this third category might be useful for ESL teachers to select videogames and SG according to the students English proficiency level. We distinguish three types of games depending on interactivity level.

5.3.1   Auto-Corrective Mini-Games

Mini-games allow simple interactions and provide immediate feedback. These are SG designed for auto-corrective activities in ESL learning like *Gemmings Rush* or the *Pacman* or *Memory* games available in several missions of the *Mingoville* platform that form a series of simple learning activities with immediate feedback [17]. *Gemmings Rush* is a game that takes place on a space station and it challenges players to spell words under pressure. The player is presented with a grid filled with different colored-gems that contain one letter. When the player clicks on a letter all the gems in the same color light up and the rest of the grid goes dark. So, the player can focus on the letters inside the blue gems only, for instance. Then, the player must spell a word that starts with the selected letter. If the word is valid, the player wins points. In the *Pacman* spelling game of the *Mingoville* platform the learner leads the *Pacman* through a labyrinth to select and "eat" the exact letters that make up a certain word like "cat", or "parrot". According to Cornillie and colleagues [16], these games are of great interest for second language learning since they provide feedback to participants.

5.3.2   Artificial Intelligence-Based Videogames and Serious Games

In this section we consider the videogames and SG that imply more complex inter-actions mediated by artificial intelligence. Games and SG like *Motion English, Seaman, Operator's Side* (*Lifeline*) or *It's a Deal!* are considered in this category since they include a programming feature that adapts the game's interactions and the feedback provided to players according to the player's input. In the SG *It's a Deal!* interactive situations are simulated in order to promote intercultural communicative competences, the player interacts individually with a character that is controlled by the artificial intelligence module. The answers of this character depend on the player's input.

5.3.3   Videogames and Serious Games with Open Online Player Interaction Environment

The highest interactivity level is reached in videogames and SG that allow open interactions and promote English practice among users like *Tower of Babel ARG, EverQuest II,* and *Active Worlds* [23]. The game *Hello you* [31] provides a virtual city environment where children can interact in different linguistic open contexts. In *EverQuest II*, players can create a character to interact in the three-dimensional fictional world of Norrath. This user-created character can complete quests, explore the world, and kill monsters in order to gain treasures and experience. The *EverQuest II* gameplay allows users to socialize with other players. For a successful pedagogical integration of *EverQuest II*, Peterson [23] recommends an informative session on how to proceed during the game before playing, as well as linguistic supporting activities while playing in order to decrease the learners' cognitive overload and to assure a proper open interaction context. The storyline of the Serious Game *Tower of Babel ARG* is based in a future world where European languages and cultures have vanished from the earth. Students have to send information about languages and cultures to this futuristic world in order to save them. Communication from the future is sent by a secret rebel society to the players through email and through a special game portal. Members of the secret society ask players to solve a series of quests to help the world of the future remember what culture and languages are. In order to find answers to the quests, students have to work collaboratively with other students and with the game characters to find out information relating to the quest. If players find the right answer then they can add blocks to their virtual *Tower of Babel*. The tower was designed as a growing wiki where students can add their own building blocks, which could be narrative, videos, quests, blogs, emails, as well as text. The game was designed to enable student-student interaction as well as students-teachers opportunities to interact. In cases like these, the ESL teacher must be sure that the open interaction context where learning takes place actually allows learning among users. When implementing Open Online Player Interaction Environments, teachers must assure that the open interaction context includes mechanisms that allow developing awareness of the appropriate linguistic practice and uses of language, so they can have a proper feedback for learning.

6 Videogames and SG According to the Second Language Learning Strategies

Taking into account the interest of using videogames and SG in ESL learning and the taxonomy including the three main categories mentioned above (pedagogical intention, number of players and pedagogical approach), we now present a methodology-based design to facilitate an integration of videogames and SG for ESL learning according to the second language learning strategies proposed by Oxford [19]. Learning strategies are defined as "steps or actions taken by language learners to enhance any aspect of their learning." For this author, second language learning implies the use of direct (memory, cognitive, and compensatory) and indirect strategies (metacognitive, affective, and social). The direct strategies directly involve the language to be learned while the indirect strategies are called that way because they do not directly involve the language but are essential to language learning. In a learner-centered perspective, the use of Serious Games and videogames that provide an environment where the learners can easily develop and perform these learning strategies might contribute to successful and meaningful second language learning. Teachers interested in adapting or integrating commercial videogames or using Serious Games in ESL learning can consider these features to choose a more adequate game according to their students' needs.

6.1 Direct Strategies

Memory strategies are helpful to enter information into long-term memory and to retrieve it when needed for communication. Actions like grouping, associating, and placing new words into a context; using imagery, semantic mapping, or keywords; representing sounds in memory; using physical response, mechanical tricks or sensation represent memory strategies. Simulation games like *The Sims* represent a perfect immersive environment for memory strategies since they include images, sounds and animations that form rich contexts where students can easily create mental linkages and associations. Plus, action is employed using physical response or sensation in feedback provided to the student, like a shaking joystick when the game's character experiences a specific situation or the character not moving anymore while a message in English as a Second Language displays in the screen indicating why that happens.

Cognitive strategies are used for "forming and revising internal mental models and receiving and producing messages in the target language" [19, p.71]. Cognitive strategies can be actions like practicing with sounds and alphabets, repeating, receiving and sending messages, analyzing and reasoning, recognizing and using formulas and patterns, getting the idea quickly, analyzing expressions, translating, taking notes, summarizing and basically creating structure for input and output. Games like *Seaman* and *Operator's Side* or *Lifeline* can contribute to the development of these strategies since they have a speech interface that allows players to produce and receive messages. But, we must mention that most of the simulation or immersive SG and the games adapted for ESL learning purposes represent practice environments, like vocabulary and grammar practice, or even to practice speaking, reading, writing and listening.

Compensation strategies, such as guessing unknown meanings while reading and listening, or using circumlocution while speaking or writing, are needed to overcome any limitations in knowledge of the language. Some other examples of compensation strategies are using linguistic clues or other clues for guessing meanings, switching to the mother tongue, getting help, using mime or gesture when talking, avoiding communication partially or totally, selecting the topic, adjusting or approximating the message, coining words and using a circumlocution or a synonym. The environment of games like *Active Worlds* and *The Sims* can help to the development of these strategies when pedagogically adapted for ESL learning. The environment of these games allows players to guess the meaning of words thanks to the several visual clues on the game represented by characters' gestures, images, sounds, and words shown on the screen when action occurs in the game.

6.2 Indirect Strategies

Metacognitive strategies help learners to execute a certain control by planning, arranging, focusing and evaluating their own learning process. These strategies imply actions like linking new information with already known material, paying attention, delaying speech production to focus on listening, identifying the own language learning needs, organizing, setting goals and objectives, planning for a language task, seeking practice opportunities, self-monitoring, and self-evaluating. The videogames and SG allowing players to choose freely the order of missions and to go back and forward to previous missions or mini-games like *Mingoville*, represent a perfect environment for the development of metacognitive strategies since they grant the learner with a certain degree of learning control. If videogames and SG include a learning analytics log or a record of the scores obtained by the learners they will permit the student to monitor and evaluate his/her own learning.

Affective strategies enable learners to control feelings, motivations, and attitudes related to language learning. These strategies imply small actions like using relaxation, music, deep breathing or meditation and laughter; making positive statements; taking risks wisely; getting rewards when objectives are met; and even discussing the feelings with someone else in order to lower anxiety, and to self-encourage. In most of the games, players get rewards when they achieve game-related goals, players take risks in a safe environment and music is usually present to create either a relaxed or a challenging atmosphere that motivates players. Many videogames and SG, *Mingoville* and *Motion English* among them, contribute to develop affective strategies since they have musical backgrounds and players get rewards when achieving goals.

Social strategies facilitate interaction with others, often in a discourse situation. These strategies imply actions like asking questions; asking for clarification, verification, or correction; cooperating with peers, or with proficient users of the new language; empathizing with others by developing cultural understanding; and becoming aware of others' thoughts and feelings. Multiplayer videogames and SG encourage players to implement social strategies due to their open interaction nature. Therefore, games like *Ever Quest II, Active Worlds,* and *Tower of Babel ARG* that allow cooperation and communication among players contribute to the development of social strategies.

We notice that some of the categories in our typology of games and SG contribute to the development of specific second language learning strategies. Such is the case of social strategies and Multiplayer videogames and SG. Also, several strategies can be developed in a single videogame or SG, especially in more complex games. As mentioned above, certain games and SG have the potentiality of allowing students to execute learning strategies; and therefore, they might lead to a meaningful second language learning.

7 Discussion

Considering the great diversity of educational gaming dynamics and ESL Serious Games, this study presents an integration of videogames and SG in ESL learning according to Oxford's second language learning strategies [19] and the typology of the videogames and SG analyzed in the literature review. We propose a typology of videogames and SG based on the pedagogical design of the game, on the number of players and the game's complexity besides the second language learning strategies proposed by Oxford [19]. The videogame and SG typology aims to facilitate the integration of this kind of technologies in ESL learning. Nowadays, the ICT knowledge of ESL teachers is uneven. On one hand, there is only a minority of them that actually integrate videogames and SG in ESL courses in formal education contexts. On the other hand, ESL teachers require time to analyze videogames and SG prior to curriculum integration; that is the reason why having access to a typology and criteria of videogames and SG might facilitate the integration of these technologies in ESL learning by reducing the time of analysis. Not all classrooms are technologically equipped or prepared to host the activities of SG or videogame integration, but an increasing availability of games online allows the use of these technologies outside the classroom in an autonomous way. According to Hansbøl [17], this pedagogical use of educational technologies can contribute to increase the ESL practice hours. Finally, we must point out that choosing a videogame in English to be used as a learning resource in the classroom is of great interest for ESL teachers. Using videogames as an educational resource opens a wide range of possibilities for an interactive, immersive and motivating ESL learning among the digital generation.

References

1. Escudeiro, P., de Carvalho, C.V.: Game-based language learning. Int. J. Inf. Educ. Technol. **3**(6), 643–647 (2013)
2. Hüppauf, B.: Globalization: threats and opportunities. Glob. Future Ger. 3–24 (2004)
3. Gargallo, I.S.: Análisis contrastivo, análisis de errores e interlengua en el marco de la lingüística contrastiva. Síntesis, Madrid (1993)
4. Mitchell, R., Myles, F., Marsden, E.: Second Language Learning Theories. Routledge, Abingdon (2013)
5. Fox, A.: Using podcasts in the EFL classroom. TESL-EJ **11**(4), n4 (2008)
6. Jones, T., Cuthrell, K.: YouTube: educational potentials and pitfalls. Comput. Sch. **28**(1), 75–85 (2011)
7. Laborda, J.G.: Using webquests for oral communication in english as a foreign language for tourism studies. J. Educ. Technol. Soc. **12**(1), 258 (2009)
8. Hsu, L.: leveraging interactivities on social networking sites for EFL learning. Int. J. Engl. Lang. Educ. **1**(3), 244 (2013)
9. Razak, N.A., Saeed, M., Ahmad, Z.: Adopting social networking sites (SNSs) as interactive communities among english foreign language (EFL) learners in writing: opportunities and challenges. Engl. Lang. Teach. **6**(11), 187 (2013)
10. Connolly, T.M., Stansfield, M., Hainey, T.: An alternate reality game for language learning: ARGuing for multilingual motivation. Comput. Educ. **57**(1), 1389–1415 (2011)
11. Guillén-Nieto, V., Aleson-Carbonell, M.: Serious games and learning effectiveness: the case of it's a deal! Comput. Educ. **58**(1), 435–448 (2012)
12. Romero, M., Gebera, O.T.: Serious Games para el desarrollo de las competencias del siglo XXI. RED Rev. Educ. Distancia **34**, 1–22 (2012)
13. Gee, J.P.: What video games have to teach us about learning and literacy, Revised and Updated Edition edn. Macmillan, London (2007)
14. Godwin-Jones, B.: Emerging technologies: language in action: from webquests to virtual realities. Lang. Learn. Technol. **8**(3), 9–14 (2004)
15. Purushotma, R.: You're not studying, you're just. Lang. Learn. Technol. **9**(1), 80–96 (2005)
16. Cornillie, F., Grenfell, A., Windeatt, S., Desmet, P.: Challenges in specifying and evaluating a conceptual design for a task-based mini-game environment for language learning. In: Status Published (2012)
17. Hansbøl, M.: Alternatives and passages: english teaching, learning, and mingoville. In: Proceedings of European Conference Games Based Learning, pp. 499–503 (2010)
18. Laborda, J.G.: La integración de las TIC en la formación bilingüe: perspectivas en la formación del profesorado, Teoría Educación. Educ. Cult. En Soc. Inf. **12**(3), 101–117 (2011)
19. Oxford, R.L.: Styles, strategies, and aptitude: connections for language learning. Doc. Resume, 73 (1990)
20. Lam, Y.: Technophilia vs. technophobia: a preliminary look at why second-language teachers do or do not use technology in their classrooms. Can. Mod. Lang. Rev. Can. Lang. Vivantes **56**(3), 389–420 (2000)
21. Stockwell, G.: A review of technology choice for teaching language skills and areas in the CALL literature. RECALL-HULL THEN Camb. **19**(2), 105 (2007)
22. Shelton, B.E., Scoresby, J.: Aligning game activity with educational goals: following a constrained design approach to instructional computer games. Educ. Technol. Res. Dev. **59**(1), 113–138 (2011)

23. Peterson, M.: Massively multiplayer online role-playing games as arenas for second language learning. Comput. Assist. Lang. Learn. **23**(5), 429–439 (2010)
24. Meyer, B.: Game-based language learning for pre-school children: a design perspective. Electron. J. E-Learn. **11**(1), 39–48 (2013)
25. Shin, S.-I., Park, K.: A physical interactive game for learning english of children. In: Park, J. J.H., Stojmenovic, I., Choi, M., Xhafa, F. (eds.) Future Information Technology. LNEE, vol. 276, pp. 219–224. Springer, Heidelberg (2014)
26. Peterson, M.: Computerized games and simulations in computer-assisted language learning: a meta-analysis of research. Simul. Gaming **41**(1), 72–93 (2009)
27. Romero, M., Usart, M., Ott, M., Earp, J.: Learning through playing for or against each other? Promoting collaborative learning in digital game based learning. In: ECIS 2012, vol. 5, p. 15 (2012)
28. Popescu, M.M., Romero, M., Usart, M.: Serious games for serious learning using SG for business, management and defence education. Int. J. Comput. Sci. Res. Appl. **3**(1), 5–15 (2013)
29. Romero, M.: Game based learning MOOC. Promoting entrepreneurship education. Elearning Pap. Spec. Edit. MOOCs Beyond **33**, 1–5 (2013)
30. Muratet, M., Torguet, P., Jessel, J.-P.: Learning programming with an rts-based serious game. In: Petrovic, O., Brand, A. (eds.) Serious Games on the Move, pp. 181–192. Springer, Vienna (2009)
31. Barendregt, W., Bekker, T.M.: The influence of the level of free-choice learning activities on the use of an educational computer game. Comput. Educ. **56**(1), 80–90 (2011)

Intouch: Mobile Game-Based Learning for Non Routine Skills

Alfredo Imbellone[1](✉), Brunella Botte[1], and Carlo Maria Medaglia[2]

[1] Link Campus University, Via Nomentana, 335, 00162 Rome, Italy
a.imbellone@unilink.it
[2] Department of Computer, Control, and Management Engineering,
Sapienza University of Rome, Via Ariosto, 25, 00185 Rome, Italy

Abstract. The paper presents the InTouch project and discusses design principles and implementation of serious mobile games for the development of soft skills for SME professionals. 30 serious games for mobile devices were developed to be tested and evaluated during Learning labs participated by SMEs professionals operating in different business sectors from seven European countries. The games describe situational learning cases related to 10 non-routine skills, and use different types of interactions. Usability study findings together with qualitative results emerging from Learning labs are described, showing an overall positive evaluation deriving for the choice of the serious game approach and the use of mobile devices.

1 Introduction

The InTouch project realized 30 games for smartphones and tablets to teach adult workers how promptly answer to non routine situations at work. Developed games were made available to be downloaded on mobile devices and via Internet through the project website [1]. The project aimed to develop an ad hoc mobile learning kit for adult learners based on a set of games designed to be usable, to challenge players to confront them with non-routine tasks involving skills like planning, teamwork, communication, conflict management and others.

Time, space and place management, and their implications for learning processes are radically changing with the advent of mobile and connected society [2]. Mobile game-based learning is widely and rapidly spreading thanks to its characteristics of mobility and portability, flexibility and accessibility, social interactivity and informality [3, 4]. Applications range from the use of portable technologies to support curriculum learning in the classroom, and the use of personal mobile technologies for learning on the move [5]. M-learning main advantages are recognized in making learning contents available anytime and anywhere and linking learning to activities in the outside world environment. Furthermore educational games can enhance attention and motivation thanks to their contents in terms of challenge, control, curiosity and fantasy [6, 7].

Learning through mobile games is not only relevant but also applied and practiced within the context [8], realizing situated and active learning and giving rise to new forms of educational experience away from the classroom [9]. Time for learning

A. De Gloria (Ed.): GALA 2014, LNCS 9221, pp. 44–53, 2015.
DOI: 10.1007/978-3-319-22960-7_5

through mobile games can vary from small casual bursts [10] to a total immersion for hours in the so called "state of flow" [11–13] or "hard fun" [14].

Theories about design of mobile technologies for learning and collaboration games can be found in the literature [15–18]. As suggested by many authors mobile learning materials must be designed properly according to the small (and different) screen size of the devices, information overload must be prevented using multimedia strategies rather than textual: visuals contents and knowledge organizers showing main concepts and their relationships. InTouch's games are designed in order to be short, simple and to have a really straightforward interface with very simple functions.

Mobile applications, based on needs and context, can be used to increase cognitive and meta-cognitive growth, strengthening highly diversified skills [19, 20] and addressing many types of intelligences [21, 22]. Mobile game-based learning promotes reflections and strategies for learning [15] and meta-level thinking skills [16, 23]. Engagement, self-motivation, coping, role identification are often cited as the main targets of Mobile game-based learning [24].

Recent research-work in educational serious games (SG) is changing our understanding of the capabilities of learning with games. While early studies focused upon proofs of concept [25, 26], we now see a shift of emphasis of these environments away from early pilots, isolated research projects and silos in different disciplinary fields into a more cohesive field of SGs with research perspectives from cognitive psychology, pedagogy, computer science, artificial intelligence, business studies, health and human–computer interaction. Games are regarded as a perfect environment for teaching soft skills that support self-efficacy, self-directed learning and reflection upon performance, in addition to interpersonal skills that allow players to collaborate, communicate, cooperate and negotiate important skills for problem- solving and leadership [20, 27].

Soft skills development and assessment in-game requires a different approach and perspective from traditional approaches in order for it to be most effective. Towards defining a model for e-leadership in the educational game context, it is worth considering the findings from the literature review undertaken above, as well as reflecting some of the key game design parameters such as motivation [28]; increased engagement of learners through immersion and fidelity [29]; importance of game rules, competition, reward system, role play and narrative for effective game design [30, 31]; team work and long-term cooperation [32, 33] and the importance of immediate feedback for ensuring learning [20, 34].

Csikszentmihalyi's flow experience sheds light on a way to incorporate learning experiences with the known benefits of mobile learning. Flow is a holistically controlled feeling where one acts with total involvement or engagement with a particular activity, with a narrowing of focus of attention [11]. From a mobile learning perspective, it implies that, in order for learners to experience flow while engaged in a mobile learning activity, they must perceive a balance between their controls and the challenges of the activity, which should present them with playful interaction, exploratory behavior, and positive subjective experience [35]. Learners are more motivated when the instructional design generates curiosity and interest about the content and learning context. If the challenges of an activity are beyond the individual's skill level, demanding more than the individual can handle, they may disengage from further learning. On the other hand, if the challenges are lower than the individual's skill level, boredom may be the result, also leading to disengagement [12].

2 The InTouch Project Approach

In November 2010, a consortium of European partners started working on "Labour Market InTouch: new non-routine skills via mobile game-based learning" project, funded by Leonardo da Vinci Multilateral projects for Development of Innovation Program. InTouch aimed to define an innovative approach enabling new generations of workers to develop their crucial non routine skills according to the new exigencies of the labour market.

Following the "New Skills for New Jobs" strategy [36], an innovative m-learning kit for working adults was designed, focusing on crucial non-routine skills, in order to improve self-learning through educational serious games and to provide SMEs employees with the key skills needed to answer to labour market requests and to deal with the deep changes taking place in the economy.

Field research has been conducted to define the top 10 crucial transversal key competences for non-routine tasks with the identification of non routine situational cases for each competence. Non-routine skills have been defined through a questionnaire, while semi-structured interviews have been conducted to associate situational cases to each skill that had emerged from the questionnaire results.

The questionnaire collected 60 respondents and was formed by 51 items describing behaviors related to skill management. Respondents were asked to express their opinion about the degree of importance for each item on a Likert scale. At first all questions were factorized by principal components method, while applying factors axis rotation according the highest dispersion (VARIMAX rotation). When the structure of theoretically meaningful indicators was found, obtained single factors (12 skills) were additionally tested by applying alpha factor analysis method. Their inherent consistency coefficients were high enough (Cronbach's Alpha index ranging from 0,6 to 0,8). Among the 12 skill factors the 10 most popular ones (with higher scores) were finally selected and labeled as: Communication; Planning; Conflict management; Openness to change; Decision making; Teamwork; Flexibility; Strategic thinking; Initiative; Learning and improvement.

Personal in-depth interviews were then conducted with 62 employees and managers of European business service SMEs from the 7 different countries participating the project. During interviews, each respondent was asked to evaluate non routine tasks skills and to provide related cases. Each situational case was defined giving a description of the workplace situation/problem, the objective to be reached with the use of the addressed skill, and a list of solutions (at least 5) to face the described situation/problem. From an initial list of 50 situational cases (5 for each skill) revealed by interviews, a reduced list of 30 situational cases, obtained clustering and combining the previous ones, was finally stated as the starting point for developing games scenarios.

We elected to focus on games delivered via the two most personal and portable technologies: smartphones and tablets, even if a considerable amount of mobile games are delivered through specific game consoles. The choice for smartphones and tablets was due to their versatility that make them suitable for educational purposes, while game consoles were considered more indicated for pure entertainment.

To develop the m-learning kit InTouch partners decided not to simply port pc style games to mobile. It has been decided to adopt a user-friendly design. All games were designed to be easy to use with mobile devices. It has been considered the devices' small display dimensions and way of interaction (indeed not all devices have touch interface). Embedding too much details in a small screen can be nice to see but counter-productive to use. The InTouch games' scenarios are simple and a simple touch, or click, is enough to interact with the game, thus enabling one-hand playing. InTouch partners were mindful to keep usage costs as low as possible: indeed it was made possible to download the games and play them offline. The games are simple to use: no training or any special equipment is needed. Users are able to use the games anywhere and at any time, at work or at home or even on the way to/from work/home, at a convenient time.

Learning contents were mapped to game style, embedding them naturally in the game with a variety in game context and complexity: novelty, surprise, humour. Attention was paid to speed, level of difficulty, timing and range of feedback. Games were developed keeping user cognitive load down thanks to a limited use of text, and simple and intuitive interface.

The InTouch games present examples that are relevant to the learner in enjoyable and an interesting way. The Games take place in situations and contexts characteristic of day-to-day activities, namely within a small company titled "InTouch". Games scenarios were obtained adapting situational cases found with the initial field research to the "InTouch" company and its characters. Playing the games users discover the problems and possible solutions in a real life environment. The company proposed in the games is composed by several characters that were described giving their company role (Chief, PM-Design, PM-Development, PM-Assistance, Account, Account assistant, Supplier contact, Practitioner), personal information (name, surname, age, sex, star sign, hobbies), and a short bio (see Fig. 1).

The games foresaw different kinds of interaction:

Branching Stories: the user reads the story and has to take different decisions. The story develops in different ways according to the choices made by users and the final feedback is the result of the combination of the choices [37].

Interactive Maps: at the beginning of the game a typical trouble situation is described in the "InTouch" company. To solve the problem, the user can choose three members of the company to talk to, but he/she needs to pick the right people to get the useful information. Once the user has read the three clues he/she can take a decision choosing one of the three available alternatives.

Multiple Choices: at the beginning of the game there is a description of a scenario and the aim of the game. The user has to help the main character with three different decisions and has limited time per question. The difficulty increases: in the first decision point only three out of the five listed options are correct, in the second one only two and in the third one only one. The final score and the feedback depend on how many correct answers the user chooses.

Fig. 1. Screenshots of the games: the "InTouch" company team; a single character description; and an interactive map game example.

Quizzes: the game begins presenting a brief introduction of the main topic, than the player has to try to correctly answer the related questions. The player gets immediate feedback on the answer and a summary at the end of game. The key objective of gameplay is to gain points for fast and correct answers.

Simulations: during the game the user has to achieve a goal, which foresees different tasks. He has to make sure to do the right tasks in the right order and then he/she has to answer to a question focused on the selected task. The score is determined from the number of correct answers and from the order the user chose to prioritize the tasks.

3   Testing and Results

Evaluation of the games has been developed through usability studies during the formative phase and a formative evaluation during Learning labs which took place in the 7 countries participating the project.

Usabilty analysis was held to guarantee an adequate level of user friendly interface and game functions. Tests were conducted with two small groups of participants (10 people for each group) utilizing 5 game prototypes (one for each kind of game inter-action). Participants had the possibility to test each game prototype. Just after this test, the participants have been asked to fill in a game grading grid, to give a mark to numerous criteria about the game design (colours, graphics, characters, general aesthetics) and other aspects of the game (playability, duration, interest of the goal, fun degree, clarity of the instructions, type of interaction), about the training content (scenario, learning aspect, clarity of the final feedback...), and some additional questions about the level of difficulty or the will to play again with the game. The marks done by the participants went from 0 (weak) to 10 (excellent). Table 1 summarizes the averages calculated on a basis of 20 answers.

Table 1. Games grading grids average results (n=20 participants).

Type of game	Branching story	Quiz	Interactive map	Simulation	Multiple choice
Design	8.2	6.7	5.3	5.5	4.5
Playability	7.6	6.1	7.1	7.0	6.7
Duration	6.5	4.2	7.3	6.8	6.7
Interest of the goal	6.8	3.9	5.7	5.9	5.5
Fun aspect	4.8	3.8	4.7	5.5	5.5
Clarity of the instructions	8.0	6.8	8.3	8.2	7.0
Type of game	7.0	6.0	6.9	7.7	6.8
Would you like to play again?					
Yes	64 %	18 %	45 %	46 %	55 %
Game scenario	7.2	5.5	6.9	5.9	5.9
Reality of the situation	7.7	5.1	6.1	6.9	5.8
Learning/educative content	5.5	4.2	7.1	6.5	6.2
Interest of the questions	6.6	4.4	6.6	6.0	6.1
Relevance of the answers	5.9	4.8	6	6.4	5.8
Clarity of the feedbacks	6.1	5.6	6.2	7.0	6.5
Relevance of the feedbacks	5.5	4.0	5.7	6.5	5.6
Did you find this game:					
Too easy	18 %	55 %	9 %	27 %	27 %
Normal	82 %	45 %	91 %	63 %	73 %
Too difficult	0 %	0 %	0 %	10 %	0 %
Did you learn something?					
Yes	56 %	0 %	73 %	64 %	40 %

At the end of the grading grids participants were asked to write down their comments about the testing experience. Most of the test participants said they wanted the games to be not too easy. Numerous players asked for a first easy level to understand the game's objectives, and then, more difficult levels/situations. They also wanted longer games with more content. Short but thorough instructions in the beginning of the game session were also requested, together with a quick and complete feedback at the end. A larger explanation of the reasons associated to the score was generally required, understanding how the score was calculated, so to be able to improve it. Many players suggested to classify the games according to their objectives and not only according to the skills to which they are linked.

Useful indications for the further development of the games emerged from usability sessions. The most critical type of interaction was found to be the Quiz perceived as too easy and substantially not instructive, so that people was not motivated to play it again. On the contrary the best results were those obtained by Branching story, Simulation and Interactive map that were perceived as engaging, challenging and motivating. As a general issue more fun content was suggested as an improving factor to be developed for every kind of interaction.

To tryout the usefulness of InTouch m-learning kit, the project partners held dedicated events (Learning Labs) in seven countries (Italy, England, Sweden, Switzerland, Austria, Lithuania, Bulgaria). Learning Labs involved in all 54 person (28 managers and 26 employees) of SMEs operating in different business sectors (ICT, business support, education/training, etc.). There were 30 men and 24 women. Age distribution was: 20–35 years: 16 people, 36–50 years: 23 people, 51–65 years: 15 people.

The main objectives of the Learning Labs were to raise awareness and to promote the advantages of InTouch m-learning kit; to give participants an opportunity to test the InTouch m-learning kit; to collect information/feedback/suggestions from the participants on how mobile technologies can be used for teaching, learning and empowerment within SMEs.

Each learning lab was articulated in three phases:

(1) *presentation:* InTouch m-learning approach, the "Be competitive" handbook, and the 30 learning games were presented at the beginning of each Lab;
(2) *testing*: during this session participants had the opportunity to play the InTouch m-learning games;
(3) *discussion*: a final debrief aimed to collect additional information /feedback / suggestions about the use of the InTouch m-learning kit.

The evaluation was made through the observation for the whole duration of the learning labs to identify the first reactions of the participants. A structured questionnaire was proposed after the 2nd session (testing), and a group discussion with a Focus group took place after the completion of the evaluation questionnaire.

The results of the evaluation, summarized in Table 2, showed that the main advantages of the InTouch m-learning kit noted by the participants were the accessibility of training content every time and everywhere (82 % of respondents selected this as one of the advantages of the m-learning kit), the funny and amusing approach of games (64 %), and low/no cost of the training (55 %).

Even if the InTouch m-learning kit received an overall positive evaluation, the participants of the learning labs pointed out some limits of the kit: games were too basic and not enough challenging (38 % of respondents selected this as one of the disadvantages of the m-learning kit); in order to increase the learning value of the games the

Table 2. Main findings from Learning Labs (n=54 participants).

	Tot	Sex		Role		Age		
		Males	Fem.	Manager	Empl.	20-35	36-50	51-65
Accessible	82 %	80 %	83 %	86 %	77 %	94 %	83 %	67 %
Funny	64 %	67 %	63 %	57 %	73 %	94 %	57 %	47 %
Low cost	55 %	53 %	58 %	61 %	50 %	63 %	61 %	40 %
Too easy	38 %	37 %	42 %	39 %	38 %	56 %	39 %	20 %
Poor feedback	25 %	23 %	29 %	25 %	27 %	19 %	22 %	40 %
More social media	13 %	13 %	13 %	11 %	15 %	31 %	9 %	0 %

players asked for more extensive feedback (25 %); younger employees demanded to insert games into social media (13 % of the total sample, 31 % of the 20-35 years aged participants).

Taking into account all advantages and limits outlined by the participants of the Learning labs it is possible to conclude that m-learning games were perceived as a funny and innovative way of learning that is also time saving and economically attractive. It could be good as addition to other training or as a teaser to start a group face to face discussion.

Furthermore among the limits of the InTouch solution it must be mentioned that a deeper and more systematic evaluation, supported by quantitative data and analysis, should be conducted for evaluating learning experience and integration within existing educational and organizational contexts [38].

These limits of the project will be soon addressed, in fact European Commission recently approved the InTouch-ICT Transfer of Innovation project (2013–2015). The InTouch-ICT Project will transfer InTouch project results to suit the learning needs of business professional in ICT SMEs in Turkey. The transfer will be made by adapting the existing m-learning kit to the new requirement of Turkish ICT SMEs and taking advantages of the new opportunities offered by the evolution occurred during the last years in the field of mobile technologies applied to educational contexts.

References

1. InTouch project Games Homepage. http://www.intouch-european-project.eu/. Accessed on 6 August 2015
2. Traxler, J.: Distance education and mobile learning: catching up, taking stock. Dis. Edu. **31** (2), 129–138 (2010)
3. Kinshuk: Adaptive mobile learning technologies, Global Educator, Department of Information Systems Massey University, New Zeland (2003)
4. Campanella, P.: Mobile learning: new forms of education. In: 10th IEEE International Conference on Emerging eLearning Technologies and Applications. Stara Lesna, The High Tatras, Slovakia, 8–9 November (2012)
5. Sharples, M.: Mobile learning: research, practice and challenges. Dis. Edu. China. **3**(5), 5–11 (2013)

6. Prensky, M.: Digital Game-Based Learning. McGraw-Hill, New York, London (2001)
7. Kurkovsky, S.: Mobile game development: improving student engagement and motivation in introductory computing courses. Comput. Sci. Educ. **23**(2), 138–157 (2013)
8. van Eck, R.: Digital game-based learning: it's not just the digital natives who are restless. EDUCAUSE Rev. **41**(2), 16–30 (2006)
9. Klopfer, E., Squire, K.: Environmental detectives – the development of an augmented reality platform for environmental simulations. Edu. Tech. Res. Dev. **56**, 203–228 (2008)
10. Froschauer, J. et al.: ARTournament: a mobile casual game to explore art history. In: 12th IEEE International Conference on Advanced Learning Technologies (2012)
11. Csíkszentmihályi, M.: Flow: The Psychology of Optimal Experience. Harper and Row, NewYork (1990)
12. Park, J., Parsons, D., Ryu, H.: To flow and not to freeze: applying flow experience to mobile learning. IEEE Trans. Learn. Technol. **3**(1), 56–67 (2010)
13. Admiraal, W., Huizenga, J., Akkerman, S., Dam, G.T.: The concept of flow in collaborative game-based learning. Comput. Hum. Behav. **27**, 1185–1194 (2011)
14. Lazzaro, N.: Why we play games: four keys to more emotion without story. XEODesign,® Inc. (2004)
15. Sharples, M., Corlett, D., Westmancott, O.: The design and implementation of a mobile learning resource. Pers. Ubiquit. Comput. **6**, 220–234 (2002)
16. Roschelle J., Pea, R.D.: A walk on the WILD side: how wireless handhelds may change computer-supported collaborative learning. In: Stahl, G. (ed.) Proceedings of the International Conference on Computer Support for Collaborative Learning 2002, Lawrence Erlbaum Associates, Mahwah, NJ (2002)
17. Parsons, D., Ryu, H., Cranshaw, M.: A design requirements framework for mobile learning environments. J. Comput. **2**, 4 (2007)
18. de Freitas, S., Liarokapis, F.: Serious games: a new paradigm for education? In: Ma, M., Oikonomou, A., Jain, L.C. (eds.) Serious Games and Edutainment Applications. Springer, London (2011)
19. Kebritchi, M., Hirumi, A.: Examining the pedagogical foundations of modern educational games. Comput. Educ. **51**(4), 1729–1743 (2008)
20. de Freitas, S., Routledge, H.: Designing leadership and soft skills in educational games: the e-leadership and soft skills educational games design model (ELESS). Br. J. Edu. Technol. **44**(6), 951–968 (2013)
21. Gardner, H.: Intelligence reframed: Multiple intelligences for the 21st Century. Basic Books, New York (2000)
22. Becker, K.: Pedagogy in commercial video games. In: Gibson, D., Aldrich, C., Prensky, M. (eds.) Games and Simulations in Online Learning: Research and Development Frameworks. Idea Group Inc., Hershey (2006)
23. Gee, J.: What Video Games Have to Teach us About Learning and Literacy. Palgrave Macmillan, New York (2003)
24. Colella, V.: Participatory simulations: building collaborative understanding through immersive dynamic modelling. In: Koschmann, T., Hall, R., Miyake, N. (eds.) CSCL2: Carrying Forward the Conversation, Lawrence Erlbaum, Associates, Mahwah, NJ (2002)
25. van der Spek, E.D., Wouters, P., van Oostendorp, H.: Code Red: triage or cognition- based design rules enhancing decisionmaking training in a game environment. Br. J. Edu. Technol. **42**(3), 441–455 (2011)
26. Knight, J.F., Carley, S., Tregunna, B., Jarvis, S., Smithies, R., de Freitas, S., Dunwelle, I., Mackway-Jones, K.: Serious gaming technology in major incident triage training: a pragmatic controlled trial. Resuscitation J. **81**, 1175–1179 (2010)

27. Dondlinger, M.J.: Educational video game design: a review of the literature. J. Appl. Edu. Technol. **4**(1), 21–31 (2007)
28. Garris, R., Ahlers, R., Driskell, J.E.: Games, motivation, and learning: a research and practice model. Simul. Gaming **33**(4), 441–467 (2002)
29. de Freitas, S., Rebolledo-Mendez, G., Liarokapis, F., Magoulas, G., Poulovassilis, A.: Learning as immersive experiences: using the four-dimensional framework for designing and evaluating immersive learning experiences in a virtual world. Br. J. Edu. Technol. **41**(1), 69–85 (2010)
30. Järvinen, A.: Games without Frontiers. theories and methods for game studies and design, Doctoral dissertation study for Media Culture, university of Tampere, Finland (2008)
31. Ducheneaut, N., Moore, R.J.: More than just 'XP': learning social skills in massively multiplayer online games. Interact. Technol. Smart Edu. **2**(2), 89–100 (2005)
32. Gorlinsky, C., Serva, M.A.: Leveraging online gaming for teaching student leadership and teamwork. In: SIGMIS CPR 2009 Proceedings of the Special Interest Group on Management Information System's 47th Annual Conference on Computer personnel Research, pp. 73–76. ACM, New York (2009)
33. Siitonen, M.: Conflict management and leadership communication in multiplayer communities. In: Proceedings of DiGRA 2009: Breaking New Ground: Innovation in Games, Play, Practice and Theory (2009)
34. Dunwell, I., Jarvis, S., de Freitas, S.: Four-dimensional consideration of feedback in serious games. In: Maharg, P., de Freitas, S. (eds.) Digital Games and Learning. Continuum Publishing, London (2011)
35. Hoffman, D.L., Novak, T.P.: Marketing in hypermedia computer-mediated environments: conceptual foundations. J. Mark. **3**(60), 50–68 (1996)
36. mGBL European Project. http://www.mg-bl.com/. Accessed on 6 May 2014
37. Aldrich, C.: The Complete Guide to Simulations and Serious Games: How the Most Valuable Content Will Be Created in the Age Beyond Gutenberg to Google. Pfeiffer & Company, San Francisco (2009)
38. Vavoula, G., Sharples, M.: Meeting the challenges in evaluating mobile learning: a 3- level evaluation framework. Int. J. Mob. Blended Learn. **1**(2), 54–75 (2009)

Multiplayer Serious Games and User Experience: A Comparison Between Paper-Based and Digital Gaming Experience

Luca Argenton[1(✉)], Marisa Muzio[2], Esther J. Shek[1,2], and Fabrizia Mantovani[1]

[1] Centre for Studies in Communication Sciences – CESCOM,
University of Milan-Bicocca,
Building U16, via Giolli, angolo Via Thomas Mann, 20162 Milan, Italy
{luca.argenton,e.shek}@campus.unimib.it,
fabrizia.mantovani@unimib.it
[2] Department of Sport Sciences, Nutrition and Health, University of Milan,
Via Festa del Perdono, 7, 20122 Milan, Italy
marisa.muzio@unimi.it

Abstract. Networking and team working are becoming the foundations of human performance in educational, organizational and recreational settings. Here, new communities of practice are being established to promote an engagement economy that will be able to foster innovation and success by sustaining collective well-being and group flourishing. Considered as "positive technologies", Serious Games (SGs) can support these processes. By fostering continuous learning experiences blended with entertaining affordances, SGs have in fact been able to shape new opportunities for human psychological training and assessment. However, despite the impressive growth of SGs applications, only a few of them have been tested and scientifically considered from an empirical point of view. Our study tries to address this gap, evaluating the potential of digital game technology compared to paper-based applications not only among individuals, but also among groups. The study, conducted with *Mind the Game*, a multiplayer SG, involved 75 students. Preliminary results showed only minor but fundamental differences between the two experimental conditions. On the one hand, groups who experienced the paper-based condition felt more competent than groups exposed to the digital experience, reporting higher levels of negative feelings too. On the other hand, groups exposed to the digital condition described themselves as more challenged and efficient in a collective way.

1 Introduction

Networking and team working are becoming the foundations of human performance in educational, organizational and recreational settings [1]. Here, new communities of practice are being established to promote an engagement economy that will be able to foster innovation and success by sustaining collective well-being and group flourishing [2, 3]. Serious applications for computer game technologies have become important

© Springer International Publishing Switzerland 2015
A. De Gloria (Ed.): GALA 2014, LNCS 9221, pp. 54–62, 2015.
DOI: 10.1007/978-3-319-22960-7_6

resources to sustain these processes. Therefore, by fostering continuous learning experiences blended with entertaining affordances, SGs have been able to shape new opportunities for human psychological training and assessment.

Further, SGs have been considered as potentially optimal devices of Positive Technology. Positive Technology is an emergent field based on both theoretical and applied research, whose goal is to investigate how Information and Communication Technologies (ICTs) can be used to empower the quality of personal experience [4–6]. Based on Positive Psychology theoretical framework [7, 8], Positive Technology approach claims that technology can increase emotional, psychological and social well-being. Hence, positive technologies can influence both individual and interpersonal experiences by fostering positive emotions, and promoting engagement, as well as enhancing social integration and connectedness. The same can be done by serious games. They can in fact support the creation of socio-technical environments [9] where individuals and groups are empowered through simulative sharing and co-construction of knowledge. However, despite the huge numbers of available SGs, only few of them have addressed group processes and ingroup dynamics.

Among multiplayer games, the main approach is based on the customisation of video games originally created for pure fun. An interesting study realized by Cantamesse et al. [10], for example, examined the effect of playing the online game World of War craft (WoW), both on adolescents' social interaction and on the competence they developed on it. The in-game interactions, and in particular conversational exchanges, turn out to be a collaborative path of the joint definition of identities and social ties, with reflection on in-game processes and out-game relationships. Good examples of specifically designed SGs can be found in the field of organizational management and education. For instance, *Everest V2* (2011), was developed by the Harvard Business School to promote leadership and team working, and *Woodment* (2010) was presented as an educational web-based collaborative multiplayer SG [11]. Another example is *TeamUp* (2013) developed by The Barn in collaboration with the Delft University of Technology and Accenture and winner of the SAGANET Award 2013 [12].

Despite the impressive growth of SGs applications, only a few of them have been tested and scientifically considered from an empirical point of view. Our study goes in the direction of addressing this gap, evaluating the potential of digital game technology compared to paper-based applications not only on individuals, but also among groups. The aim of the present study was to compare paper-based and digital gaming experience, focusing on user experience both at an individual and collective level.

2 Mind the Game: Main Elements

Mind the Game•is a multiplayer decision-making serious game developed to create a socio-technical environment [9] where the interconnection between humans and technology could encourage the emergence of ingroup dynamics.

Embedding the potential of serious gaming, *Mind the Game*•aims to expand the range of resources that groups can access in daily contexts, allowing a greater awareness of the skills possessed both individually and as a whole, and implementing an experiential learning process that supports shared optimal experiences. The serious game generates a virtual environment where groups can express their potential, dealing with a reality that constantly redefines the balance between challenges and skills [6].

2.1 Technology

The interface is primarily textual, enriched multimodally by clips, images, and animated graphics that make the game more interactive (Fig. 1).

Further, *Mind the Game*••emerged as a multiplayer game studied for small groups of 5 people, that provides the facilitator/the researcher with the ability to monitor the progress of the game. The serious game is embedded in a specific website (www. mindthegame.it) that consists of a welcome page, a tutorial, and a questionnaire section to evaluate the game experience.

Fig. 1. The primarily textual interface of *Mind the Game•* is enriched multimodally by clips, images, and animated graphics.

2.2 Sharing Goals and Emotional Experiences: Sport as a Narrative Tool

The narrative framework - especially in technological solutions based on a textual environment is a core element for serious game design. Narratives have to be clear, straightforward, easy to understand and memorable to capture the interest of the user [13, 14].

Therefore, the choice of plots and settings will be decisive to bring the group out of the comfort zone, nurturing the onset of spontaneous behaviors, as well as promoting the emergence of we intentions [15], social presence and ingroup dynamics in multiplayer settings.

Moreover, the underlying potential of narratives can be amplified through the use of peculiar scenarios that have nothing to do with day by day experiences [16]. In this way, it is possible to modulate the impact of prior knowledge of users and to support common cognitive processes and knowledge sharing practices.

According to the aforementioned considerations, we chose a little-known sport that could be used to promote networked flow: gliding. This is a discipline based on soaring flight, where, in the absence of the driving force of an engine, the pilot is required to take advantage of upward motions and movements of air masses [17]. The development of the narrative plot structure on such a discipline can be particularly effective both because of specific reasons.

As a sport, gliding implies competition and collaboration. The first concept is well reflected by the Grand Prix, a race in which pilots directly compete one another. The goal is to go throughout a task a plot delimited by specific turning points that are placed so as to form a polygon in the shortest time. Generally, the Grand Prix is structured among several days, implying different tasks from time to time.

The choice of an individual sport to promote group creativity and of team working may instead appear paradoxical. But it is not: individual excellence is the tip of the iceberg beneath which team effort and coordination always make the difference. The collaborative dimension of gliding is present because, despite the solo flight of the pilot, his/her staff can support each step of the race from the ground. In fact, parameters to be taken into consideration are extremely numerous and they require the intervention of professionals specifically trained. In particular, according to the model described by Brigliadori and Brigliadori [19], six elements are fundamental:

1. *Technical*. Managing an efficient flight and exploiting the energy available in the atmosphere in the best possible way, require specific skills: decision-making, problem-solving, control, and experience. Moreover, the maintenance of security and risk management are the foundation of successful flights.
2. *Strategic*. The ability to take advantage of circumstances involves a process of decision-making able to take into account meteorological aspects. The race is played on the ability to make the most from the opportunities that are revealed during the task.
3. *Psychological*. Control of emotions, stress management, relaxation, high levels of concentration, resilience and self-efficacy are just some of the psychological components that may be decisive during a competition.
4. *Athletic*. Pilots must take great care in athletic training, monitoring nutrition and fatigue management.
5. *Organizational*. The athlete, together with the staff, is expected to prepare the race in every detail, monitoring equipment and logistics practices.
6. *Meteorological*. Climate is a component whose analysis should be careful and meticulous in order to avoid unnecessary risks and make winning choices.

Thus, in the serious game users will not be asked to wear the shoes of gliding pilots: they will be the team members of a female athlete that has to win the World Competition. Each player will in fact be assigned one of the following roles: team manager, strategist, technical expert, meteorologist or doctor. The arrangement by which each character appears to the player is the same and tends to follow the systemic model proposed by Bowman [20, 21]. It is marked by the definition of name, age, nationality, as well as the role played within the team and the tasks he/she has to preside. The user can then discover his/her background. This is realized on three levels, indicating aspects of the past, present and future. At the same time, the user can also view the individual goals of the character. Finally, there is a brief personality description. During the game each player receive specific information according to his/her role that are not seen by his/her teammates.

2.3 Task and Scores

In line with the theory of Steiner [22], each task has been designed according to a *complementary logic*, in an attempt to involve and engage each player in the same manner. Specifically, players have to cope with five tasks:

1. *Object Challenge:* players needs to identify from a list of 15 objects the five most important tools that their pilot has to bring with her on-board.
2. *Medicine Challenge:* according to the information they receive, players have to select to best medicine for the athlete. The task is complicated by the fact that players have conflicting information.
3. *Map Challenge:* after a GPS breakdown, the pilot is not able to identify her position on the map. Players have to chronologically reorder the information they received and to solve subgroups puzzles to point on the map the right position of the glider.
4. *Strategy challenge:* the final part of the race is approaching. Players have to decide whether going for a risky or a conservative strategy.
5. *Weather challenge:* the team has just 10 min to understand the meteorological condition of the race and to support the athlete with the best option.

   Eventually, the team's score is defined as a result of three parameters:

– Score obtained in the race by the athlete;
– The sum of individual scores;
– Time Management as each task it time bounded.

3 An Ongoing Pilot Study

A total of 50 students who attended a postgraduate specialization in sport medicine, divided in 10 groups of 5 people, played Mind the Game. Of the participants 68,1 % were male and the mean age was 27.12 years (SD = 7.745).

While 5 groups played a computer-based version of the game (condition 1), the other half of the sample experienced the game through a paper-based version (condition 2). Groups were created randomly by balancing the presence of females in each team (at least one per team).

3.1   Measures

At the end of the game, subjects had to complete three questionnaires:

1. *Game Experience Questionnaire* (GEQ) [24]. This self report questionnaire has a modular structure and consists of (1) The core questionnaire, (2) The Social Presence Module, (3) The Post-game module. Part 1 is the core part of the GEQ. It assesses game experience as scores on seven components: *Immersion, Flow, Competence, Positive and Negative Affect, Tension, and Challenge.* Part 2, the social presence module, investigates *psychological and behavioural involvement* of the player with other social entities, be they virtual (i.e., in-game characters), mediated (e.g., others playing online), or co-located. Part 3, the Post-game Module, assesses how *players felt* after they had stopped playing.
2. *Team Potency Scale* [25]. This eight-item scale contains items such as "My group has confidence in itself", "My group believes it can become unusually good at producing high-quality work". Group members individually completed the eight items using a 10-point scale (1 = to no extent, 3 = to a limited extent, 5 = to some extent, 7 = to a considerable extent, and 10 = to a great extent). Each individual's score was computed by averaging across the eight items. Then the individual scores were averaged across group members to arrive at a group potency score for each group.
3. *Optimal Group Performance Evaluation Questionnaire* [27]. This questionnaire is made up by 16 items that are focused on two main dimensions: (1) *Group goals*, (2) *Group Resources*, both assessed on a 6- point scale (1 = totally agree, 6 = totally disagree).

Other analyses are still on-going.

3.2   Results

Results were analysed using an independent-samples t-test in order to identify the differences between the computer-based (condition 1) and the paper-based (condition 2) condition. The analysis highlighted only four main differences, displayed in Tables 1 and 2.

On the one hand, there was a significant difference on *Competence* (t (49) = 2.320, p = 0.023). Groups who played the paper-based version of the game scored significantly higher (M = 3.406, SD = 0,6760) than groups who experienced the computer-based version (M = 2.924, SD = 1.0067). Similarly, subjects exposed to the paper condition (M = 1.6571, SD = 0.68949) scored significantly higher on *Negative Feelings* (t (49) = 0.084, p = 0.028) than did people in the first condition (M = 1.5637, SD = 0.35773) on *Negative Feelings* (t (49) = 0.084, p = 0.028).

On the other hand, groups who played the digital version of the game (M = 2.7886, SD = 0.70116) experienced significantly higher levels of *Challenge* (t (49) = 0.113, p = 0.035) than groups in the paper condition (M = 2.4647, SD = 0.53648). The same effect was registered on the team potency scale (t (49) = 0.541, p = 0.009): scores were significantly higher in the digital condition (M = 4.6066, SD = 3.5786) than in the paper-based one (M = 3.5786, SD = 1.74871).

Table 1. Descriptive Statistics

	Condition	N	Mean	Std. deviation	Std. error mean
GEQ(Core) Competence	1	25	2,924	1,0067	,1726
	2	25	3,406	,6760	,1159
GEQ(Core) Challenge	1	25	2,7886	,70116	,11852
	2	25	2,4647	,53648	,09201
GEQ (Core) Negative Affect	1	25	1,4632	,46520	,07978
	2	34	1,8015	,74310	,12744
Team Potency Scale	1	25	4,6066	1,41660	,24294
	2	25	3,5786	1,74871	,29559

Table 2. Independent sample t-test results

		Levene's Test for equality of variances		t-test for Equality of Means					95% Confidence interval of the difference	
		F	Sig.	t	df	Sig. (2-tailed)	Mean difference	Std. Error difference	Lower	Upper
GEQ(Core) Competence	Equal variances assumed	1,895	,173	2,320	49	,023	−,4824	,2080	−,8975	−,0672
	Equal variances not assumed			2,320		,024	−,4824	,2080	−,8987	−,0660
GEQ (Core) Challenge	Equal variances assumed	2,578	,113	2,150	49	,035	,32387	,15062	,02323	,62450
	Equal variances not assumed			2,159		,035	,32387	,15004	,02409	,62364
GEQ (core) Negative affect	Equal variances assumed	3,077	,084	2,250	49	,028	,33824	,15035	,03805	,63842
	Equal variances not assumed			2,250		,028	,33824	,15035	,03697	,63950
Team potency Scale	Equal variances assumed	,377	,541	−2,679	49	,009	−1,02805	,38378	−1,79408	−,26201
	Equal variances not assumed			−2,687		,009	−1,02805	,38261	−1,79219	−,26390

4 Conclusion

The preliminary findings described above suggest that there may be limited, but fundamental differences between digital and paper-based experiences.

Firstly, the lack of numerous differences between the two conditions is supported by the scientific literature. Vahed [27] found that a non-digital board game could help dental students in learning about tooth morphology and Mayer et al. [28] described how a complex, non-digital game helped students to understand the complex issues involved in planning urban networks.

Secondly, subjects who played the paper-based version of the game felt more competent than people who played the digital version of the game. This result seems to highlight the fact that people are still more confident with paper-based tools than with digital experience. However, such a conclusion should be deepened by considering other socio-cultural elements.

Thirdly, groups who played the digital version of the game felt more challenged, and more collectively efficient than others. The use of a digital medium enhances the level of challenges and individual perception of collective efficacy. Moreover, people exposed to the digital condition experienced significantly lower levels of negative emotions. Such findings may be deepened according to the theory of Flow and Networked Flow [18] and the paradigm of Positive Technology [6].

Even more important is the fact that the aforementioned analyses are only preliminary. Moreover, the research and results are highly explorative and indicative. We are aware of significant limitations related to the use of a single game that is still under construction and that has not yet been compared with other digital team games. The fact that the game has a manly textual interface also suggest that further research is needed.

References

1. Barabasi, A.L.: Linked: The New Science of Networks. Perseus Publishing, Cambridge (2002)
2. McGonigal, J.: Reality is Broken. The Penguin Press, New York (2010)
3. Baker, D.P., Day, R., Salas, P.: Teamwork as an essential component of high-reliability organizations. Health Serv. Res. **41**, 1576–1598 (2006)
4. Botella, C., Riva, G., Gaggioli, A., Wiederhold, B.K., Alcaniz, M., Banos, R.M.: The present and future of positive technologies. Cyberpsychol. Behav. Soc. Netw. **15**, 78–84 (2012)
5. Riva, G., Banos, R.M., Botella, C., Wiederhold, B.K., Gaggioli, A.: Positive technology: using interactive technologies to promote positive functioning. Cyberpsychol. Behav. Soc. Netw. **15**, 69–77 (2012)
6. Argenton, L., Triberti, S., Serino, S., Muzio, M., Riva, G.: Serious games as positive technologies for individual and group flourishing. In: Brooks, A., Braham, S., Jain, M. (eds.) Technologies of Inclusive Well-Being. Springer, New York (2014)
7. Seligman, M.E.P.: Positive Psychology: Fundamental Assumptions. The Psychologist. **16**, 26–27 (2003)
8. Seligman, M.E.P., Csikszentmihalyi, M.: Positive psychology: an introduction. Am. Psychol. **55**, 5–14 (2000)
9. Fisher, G., Giaccardi, E., Eden, H., Sugimoto, M., Ye, Y.: Beyond binary choices: integrating individual and social creativity. Int. J. Hum Comput Stud. **12**, 428–512 (2005)
10. Cantamesse, M., Galimberti, C., Giacoma, G.: Interweaving interactions in virtual worlds: a case study. Stud. Health. Technol. Inform. **167**, 189–193 (2011)
11. Wendel, V., Babarinow, M., Hörl, T., Kolmogorov, S., Göbel, S., Steinmetz, R.: Woodment: web-based collaborative multiplayer serious game. In: Pan, Z., Cheok, A.D., Müller, W., Zhang, X., Wong, K. (eds.) Transactions on Edutainment IV. LNCS, vol. 6250, pp. 68–78. Springer, Heidelberg (2010)
12. Mayer, I.S., van Dierendonck, D., van Ruijven, T., Wenzler, I.: Stealth assessment of teams in a digital environment. In: Gala 2013 Conference, pp. 1–13. Springer, Paris (2013)

13. Bateman, C.M.: Game Writing: Narrative Skills For Video Games. Charles River Media, Independence, Boston (2007)
14. McQuiggan, S.W., Robison, J.L., Lester, J.C.: Affective transitions in narrative-centered learning environments. In: Woolf, B.P., Aïmeur, E., Nkambou, R., Lajoie, S. (eds.) ITS 2008. LNCS, vol. 5091, pp. 490–499. Springer, Heidelberg (2008)
15. Searle, J.: Intentionality. Cambridge University Press, Cambridge (1983)
16. Edery, D., Mollick, E.: Changing the Game: How Video Games are Transforming the Future of Business. FT Press, Upper Saddle River (2009)
17. Piggott, D.: Gliding: A Handbook on Soaring Flight. A&C Black, London (2002)
18. Gaggioli, A., Riva, G., Milani, L., Mazzoni, E.: Networked Flow: Towards an understanding of creative networks. Springer, New York (2013)
19. Brigliadori, L., Brigliadori, R.: Competing in Gliders Winning with your mind. Pivetta Partners, Vedano al Lambro (2011)
20. Bowman, S.L.: The functions of role-playing games. How partecipants create community, solve problems and explore identity. McFarland & Copany Inc., London (2010)
21. Myers, I.B.: Introduction to Type: A Description of the Theory and Applications of the Myers-Briggs Type Indicator. Consulting Psychologists Press, Palo Alto (1987)
22. Steiner, I.D.: Group process and productivity. Academic Press, New York (1972)
23. Arrow, H., Mccrath, I.E., Berdhal, J.L.: Small groups as complex systems: fomation, co-ordination, devlopment and adaptation. Sage, Thousand Oaks (2000)
24. IJsselsteijn, W.A., de Kort, Y.A.W, Poels, L., Bellotti, F.: Characterizing and measuring user experiences in digital games. International Conference on Advances in Computer Entertainment Technology 2: 27(2007)
25. Guzzo, R.A., Yost, P.R., Campbell, R.J., Shea, P.J.: Potency in groups: articulating a construct. Br. J. Soc. Psychol. **32**, 87–106 (1993)
26. Chin, W.W., Salisbury, W.D., Pearson, A.W., Stollak, M.J.: Perceived cohesion in small groups: adapting and testing the perceived cohesion scale in small-group setting. Small Group Res. **30**, 751–766 (1999)
27. Vahed, A.: The tooth morphology board game: an innovative strategy in tutoring dental technology learners in combating rote learning. In: Proceedings of the 2nd European Conference on Games-Based Learning (ECGBL), pp. 16–17, October 2008, Barcelona, Spain (2008)
28. Mayer, I.S., Carton, L., de Jong, M., Leijten, M., Dammers, E.: Gaming the future of an urban network. Futures **36**, 143 (2004)

Designing a Serious Game as a Diagnostic Tool

Pongpanote Gongsook[1,3(✉)], Janneke Peijnenborgh[2],
Erik van der Spek[1], Jun Hu[1], Francesco Bellotti[3], Riccardo Berta[3],
Alessandro de Gloria[3], Francesco Curatelli[3], Chiara Martinengo[4],
Matthias Rauterberg[1], and Jos Hendriksen[2]

[1] Department of Industrial Design, Eindhoven University of Technology,
5600 Eindhoven, MB, The Netherlands
{p.gongsook,e.d.v.d.spek,j.hu,G.W.M.Rauterberg}@tue.nl
[2] Kempenhaeghe, Center for Neurological Learning Disabilities,
5591 Heeze, VE, The Netherlands
{PeijnenborghJ,HendriksenJ}@kempenhaeghe.nl
[3] ELIOS Lab – DITEN, University of Genova,
Via Opera Pia 11/a, 16145 Genova, Italy
{franz,berta,adg}@elios.unige.it, Curatelli@unige.it
[4] DIMA – University of Genova, Via Dodecaneso, 35, 16145 Genova, Italy
martinen@dima.unige.it

Abstract. Serious games offer the potential to not only entertain and educate, but can also operate as a diagnostic tool. While designing a game with the goal of a diagnostic tool, we faced many challenges. In this paper, we share our experiences in dealing with these challenges in the iterations of designing, implementing, and evaluating such a tool.

Keywords: Serious game · Diagnostic tool · Game design

1 Introduction

Computer games offer players rich actions, immediate rewards, challenge, and appealing stories, which seem to be things we hardly get from the everyday life [1]. Next to entertainment however, games can also afford a wide variety of other applications (so-called serious games), such as learning, physical exercise, advertisement and attitude change [2]. In this paper, we describe the development of another type of serious game, namely a game that functions as a diagnostic tool. A problem with clinical assessments is that the patient is often aware of being assessed, leading to nonspecific effects such as subject-expectancy or Hawthorne effects [3]. Conversely, games offer immersion to such an extent that players forget their surroundings [4], as well as the possibility for stealth assessment [5]. Using a game could therefore improve the ecological validity of a diagnosis.

Creating a game needs more than having an individual passion. It requires collaboration of people from different disciplines working as a team, which is a common practice that most of the game companies adhere to nowadays [6]. Therefore, in addition to individual passion, effective team communication and synchronization are

© Springer International Publishing Switzerland 2015
A. De Gloria (Ed.): GALA 2014, LNCS 9221, pp. 63–72, 2015.
DOI: 10.1007/978-3-319-22960-7_7

needed. In this paper, we would like to illustrate the steps taken and share our experience in developing a game as a diagnostic tool.

2   Development Process

The diagnostic tool we are developing strives to collect data, and thereby enhance a psychological diagnosis. Example computer games designed for a similar purpose are IntegNeuro, and Groundskeeper [7, 8]. In order to create our diagnosis game, we had the following requirements:

1. The game should be usable by children aged between 4-8 years old.
2. It should be a single player game in first person perspective.
3. The game should have a controlled linear story to ensure that every player will have the same storyline.
4. The user interaction in the game is based on mouse clicks, or finger touches on a touch screen.
5. The game should be able to record user interactions.
6. It should have more than one mini-game.
7. It should be easy to modify game parameters without the need of a technical expert, in order for the diagnostic process to be conducted by non technical experts.

Our development stages of the game were separated into three iterative phases: Design, Implementation, and Evaluation (see Fig. 1). Each phase had micro iterations in the similar manner as a spiral model [9, 10].

2.1   Design Phase

We aimed to create a game for children aged between 4–8 years old. There is no game that fits all age groups [11]. Doing research by gathering data from existing games in the market can give us a hint of which kind of game children may like. To get deeper and a more direct insight, we applied the participatory design model (PD) and a user-centred design approach (UCD) during the design phase [12, 13]. Children had been invited to our design process. Similar to 'Child's Own Studio', 'Draw Your Toy', and 'Make with Grace', custom made soft toys were used based on the children's own drawings [14–16]. We encouraged the children to express their thoughts by drawing what they thought a character would look like with provided outlines of visual elements in the game (see Fig. 2). This method provided us with a source of ideas for designing characters for the game, increasing the likelihood that the characters we designed would be accepted by children.

The game consists of multiple mini-games, designed to retain interest of the child for a single play session of roughly 30 min. The use of more than one mini-game additionally gives us the possibility to apply more than one diagnostic instrument; that is, one for each mini-game. Books were used to give us ideas when designing mini-games [17, 18]. However, having more than one mini-game did present us with a problem: if the player is able to choose the order of the mini-games, this could result in an incoherent storyline, which could in turn lower engagement and attenuate the

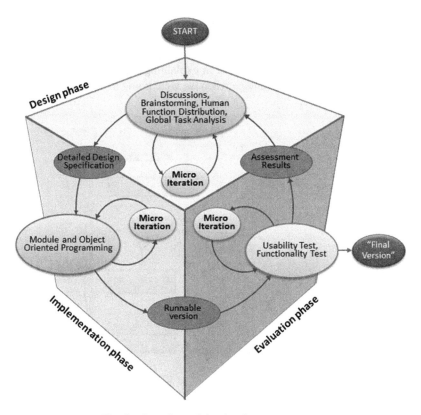

Fig. 1. Overview of the development process

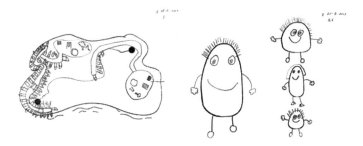

Fig. 2. Sample design of the game setting and characters by a child

internal validity benefits of using a game in the first place. To solve this problem, instead of first thinking about the whole concrete story of the game all at once, we used the theme of the game more as a loose framework. Then we designed each mini-game to serve a diagnostic purpose and tailored it into a single story line. This process needs sub-iterations to fine tune each mini-game to work with the other mini-games. To create a good story, the book by C.H Miller, 'Digital storytelling: a creator's guide to interactive entertainment' is found to be useful [19].

After the mini-games were designed, we needed to transfer the abstract ideas of mini-games to the team members. Visual communication was found to be more efficient than verbal communication [20]. We chose to present the game with a simple flow chart (see Fig. 3). This was not only better in explaining the flow of game to the team members, but also gave us an advantage when we were going to implement the abstract game with a game engine.

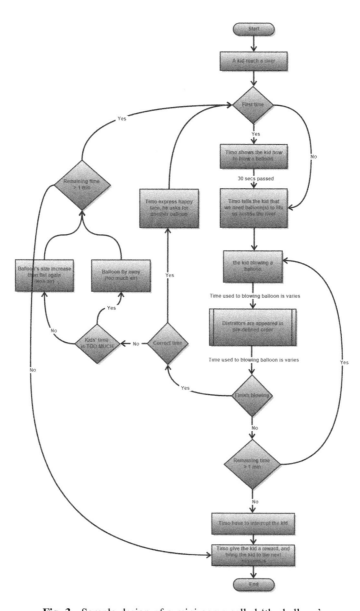

Fig. 3. Sample design of a mini-game called 'the balloon'

2.2   Implementation Phase

The implementation phase focused on the implementation techniques of the game. We selected Unity[1] for our game engine.. The game is written in C# in MonoDeveloper; Unity's native integrated development environment (IDE). In fact, one can use three different languages: C#, JavaScript, or Boo. We choose C# because of its strict syntax. One may think that this makes coding harder, but we think that this help us with more robustness.

Concerning the reusability, each mini-game is broken down into a number of modules according to their functionality (see Fig. 4). The core module is the 'Gameplay Manager' that controls the flow of game play in each mini-game. Since each mini-game is unique it has its own 'Intro Manager' and 'Ending Manager', with which we can program an introduction and an ending respectively. There are common shared modules; 'Database Manager' to connect with a SQLite database file, 'Interaction Manager' to record user interaction, 'File Manager' to handle read/write log files, and 'Scene Transition Manager' to control the game's camera movement. The order of execution is shown in Fig. 4.

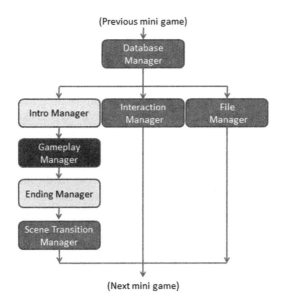

Fig. 4. Modules in each mini-game

1. 'Database Manager' has the responsibility to make a connection to a SQLite database file. It retrieves a dataset and puts this into an ArrayList in order to prepare the game variables before they can be accessed by the 'Gameplay Manager'.

---

[1] Unity3D Game Engine, http://unity3d.com/.

2. The 'Intro Manager' is called to play an introduction, and since each mini-game is unique, it demonstrates how to play a mini-game before the children start playing the game.
3. Meanwhile an 'Interaction Manager' is prepared to gather all the clicking data and to send these to a 'File Manager' in the form of a chunk of strings, before being periodically written to a log file.
4. The 'Gameplay Manager' is executed after the introduction. The children play the game without knowing that they are being observed and their clicking data are being logged.
5. After the game is finished, the 'Ending manager' is called. A map of the overall game is shown so children know how many mini-games are left. This module plays the ending cinematics to ensure that children know that the current mini-game is over and that they should get ready for the next mini-game.
6. A 'Scene Transition Manager' is called at last, to bring children to the next mini-game in a first person perspective and two and a half dimensional game environment.

There were many 3D computer models in the game. All of them were made using Blender[2], a polygonal mesh object modeling program. Unity and Blender can seamlessly work together. We can create a model in Blender and save it as a blend file and place it directly into the Unity game folder. Unity is smart enough to detect the file and import it into the game as an asset which we can select and use in the game. If any modification is needed, we just select the imported model and open it again in Blender, make the modification, then overwrite the old file. Unity will automatically re-import the model,. The process is very convenient and productive. Many tutorials about Blender on YouTube are available, but attention needs to be paid to the correct version, because Blender is open source, a different version has a slightly different user interface and this may cause some confusion.

The other requirement was that the game should be able to have its parameters modified without the need of a technical expertise. If we hard code parameters inside the game, we must re-compile the game every time when a modification is made. Therefore, our game is designed to read a property file when the game is launched. The property file is merely a text file with tab separated values. The game will configure the values with shared global variables, like a lookup table, where each mini-game can have access to. This process is done quickly while the game is launched with the title screen. Hard coding of default values is still needed in order to secure that the game can run even without the property file.

2.3 Evaluation Phase

In the evaluation phase, an approval from medical ethical committees is needed before conducting tests. It normally takes several months to get the approval. To get the feedback earlier, we asked children from our colleagues to volunteer instead. The

---

[2] Blender 3D Modeling tool, http://www.blender.org/.

parents of the children were well informed about the game and gave us consent for the user test, as well as consent to video record the test. The recorded video was for the research purpose of the game development team only and won't be publicly published. Every volunteer was given a small incentive.

The characteristics of a participant were noted down with an anonymous user persona. For example, "Busko is in her first grade. She likes going to school, she has some nice friends and she likes that she finally learns to read. Mathematics, however, is more difficult for her, but with hard work she manages. Her favorite activity at school is drawing or gymnastics.

She lives at home with her mom and dad, and a 4 year old younger sister. In her free time she plays with her sister. Although she likes to play with her sister, they sometimes argue. It is no problem for her to keep herself busy. She has a lot of interests and can play for hours. She likes playing with Barbies, and taking stories with Barbies. Furthermore, Busko is a member of the local judo club. The parents are proud of the fact that she is self-reliant. She can make her own sandwich in the morning. They don't have any big concerns about Busko."

The test environment was set in a room with two desks, and a few chairs. The game was installed on a computer with a 23 inch LCD touch screen, being placed at 15 cm from the edge of the desk in front of the child. We put the keyboard away from the reach of the child. We covered any wall decorating pictures and book shelves with a white canvas to prevent them from being distracted while playing the game. The window blinds were put down, to prevent light from outside. There were only a psychologist and the child in the room. The parent(s) were not allowed inside, but waiting outside the room. The test started with a brief introduction by the psychologist. The child was informed that he/she is going to play a game, and was asked a few questions. The psychologist asked the child whether he/she wanted to go to a toilet before the game started. If everything was set, then the test begun. The test took around 30 min.

The psychologist observed the child's behavior and took notes. It was deemed important to make sure that the child felt comfortable and did not feel lonely or anxious. However, the psychologist wasn't allowed in any way to help the child complete the game. If the child got stuck on something, the psychologist noted down a remark, because this could be valuable feedback for improvement in the next iteration. The behaviors of the child mco were video recorded, and the game itself logged the user interaction.

2.4   Micro Iterations

There were iterations at a level under the whole development cycle within each phase, adapted from 'an iterative-cyclic software process model' [21], so called 'micro iterations'. The purpose of a micro iteration is not solely a small iterative version of the containing phase, but focusing more on a collaborative process of synchronizing and scheduling. It is to optimize on time and human resources, make a concept clear, enable dynamic changes, and catch unwanted defects before they are passed on to the higher development phase.

In the design phase, children were not the only users of the game, the participatory design model was also applied to psychologists who would use our game as a diagnostic tool. The participation included gathering requirements, implementing them, communicating and presenting them to the team members, getting their feedback and reconciling in open discussions. We modified the design according to the team feedback and comments. The aforementioned tasks were iterated until all team members agreed, before starting on the next phase.

In the implementation phase the programmer was encouraged to present a playable mini-game to the team, using rapid prototyping. The team was aware that the prototypes were not the final versions, so the micro iterations were not to find programming defects, but rather to present a proof of concept, and to discuss a solution in case that any limitation arose. The programmer could introduce additional elements that were not stated in the design, if they contributed to the design.

In the evaluation phase, we followed a user's perspective. The game must meet user requirements, and many times we found that we needed to make new improvements. For example, we added more game visual elements, smoothed the scene change, and improved the textures of game objects. Of course, this would bring us back to the design phase and implementation phase. But considering the completeness and usefulness of the game this also necessary. Every micro iteration was well documented for later reference in case of inconsistency and misunderstanding.

3 Conclusion and Future Work

In this paper, we present our experience in designing a diagnostic game. User requirements are presented to show what the final goal is, as well as the iteration phases. The iterative process can prevent problems from slipping though during the development. It helps incremental development of the game and allows changes during the development.

Design needs lots of creativity and time. And still this does not preclude the terrifying moment for a designer that at the end of the day the work can be rejected by the end user. In order to increase the level of acceptance from the user perspective, we followed the design process of participatory design and user-centred design. We have seen that the children who we invited to participate in our design really loved to express their thoughts.

We implemented the game in the Unity game engine, and modeled the 3D models in Blender. One can program in C#, JavaScript, or Boo. C# was our preferred programming language because of its stick syntax. When the game becomes huge, only one module to do all the tasks is not enough. We applied a divide-and-conquer strategy of dividing it into sub modules, depending on its functionality, and grouping modules that had similar functionalities later. This enabled the usability of those modules, and it was easier to add more functionality. Unity supports running modules in parallel as long as it has been enabled and it is attached to a GameObject. We control the order of execution, disabling others modules and enabling them when needed.

The ideas acquired from each phase must be shared by every team member with different expertise and backgrounds. Micro iterations may help in sharing thoughts and synchronizing the actions. We found that visual communication worked better than verbal communication.

At the time of writing, we are currently conducting a full scale experiment. From the evaluation feedback so far we consider that the process we followed worked well for its purpose.

Acknowledgement. This work was supported by the Erasmus Mundus Joint Doctorate in Interactive and Cognitive Environments (ICE), which is funded by the EACEA Agency of the European Commission under EMJD ICE FPA n 2010-0012. We are also very grateful for the collaboration with {Dr. Jos Hendriksen, Prof. Dr. Hans Vles, Prof. Dr. Bert Aldenkamp, and Janneke Peijnenborgh MSc.} from Kempenhaeghe, Center for Neurological Learning Disabilities, and Christian Sallustro from Eindhoven University of Technology. This work also is co-funded by the EU under the FP7, in the Games and Learning Alliance (GaLA) Network of Excellence, Grant Agreement nr. 258169.

References

1. Bioulac, S., Arfi, L., Bouvard, M.P.: Attention deficit/hyperactivity disorder and video games: a comparative study of hyperactive and control children. Eur. Psychiatry. **23**, 134–141 (2008)
2. Bellotti, F., Berta, R., De Gloria, A.: Designing effective serious games: opportunities and challenges for research. Int. J. Emerg. Technol. Learn. **5**, 22–35 (2010)
3. McCarney, R., Warner, J., Iliffe, S., van Haselen, R., Griffin, M., Fisher, P.: The hawthorne effect: a randomised, controlled trial. BMC Med. Res. Methodol. **7**, 30 (2007)
4. Chen, J.: Flow in games (and everything else). Commun. ACM **50**, 31–34 (2007)
5. Shute, V.J., Ventura, M., Bauer, M., Zapata-Rivera, D.: Melding the power of serious games and embedded assessment to monitor and foster learning. Serious Games Mech. Eff. **2**, 295–321 (2009)
6. Fullerton, T.: Game Design Workshop: A Playcentric Approach to Creating Innovative Games. CRC Press, Boca Raton (2008)
7. New breakthrough in diagnosis of ADHD. http://sydney.edu.au/news/84.html?newsstoryid=4501
8. Montini, L.: CogCubed Is Using Games to Help Diagnose ADHD. http://www.health2con.com/news/2013/04/16/cogcubed-is-using-games-to-diagnose-adhd/
9. Boehm, B.: A spiral model of software development and enhancement. Computer (Long. Beach. Calif). **21**, 61–72 (1988)
10. Rauterberg, M., Strohm, O., Kirsch, C.: Benefits of user-oriented software development based on an iterative cyclic process model for simultaneous engineering. Int. J. Ind. Ergon. **16**, 391–410 (1995)
11. Greenberg, B.S., Sherry, J., Lachlan, K., Lucas, K., Holmstrom, A.: Orientations to video games among gender and age groups. Simul. Gaming. **41**, 238–259 (2010)
12. Read, J., Gregory, P., Macfarlane, S., Mcmanus, B., Gray, P.: An investigation of participatory design with children – informant, balanced and facilitated design. Interaction Design and Children, pp. 53–64 (2002)
13. Rauterberg, M.: User centered design : what, why, and when. In: Graefe, E. (ed.) tekom Jahrestagung, pp. 175–178. Gesellschaft fuer technische Kommunikation e.V, Wiesbaden, Germany (2003)

14. Tsao, W.: Child's Own Studio. http://www.childsown.com/
15. Adey, M.: Make with Grace. http://makewithgrace.com/
16. Draw Your Toy. http://drawyourtoy.blogspot.it/
17. Trefry, G.: Casual Game Design: Designing Play for the Gamer in All of Us. CRC Press, Boca Raton (2010)
18. Salen, K., Zimmerman, E.: Rules of play : game design fundamentals. MIT Press, Cambridge (2003)
19. Miller, C.H.: Digital Storytelling: A Creator's Guide to Interactive Entertainment. Focal Press/Elsevier, Burlington (2008)
20. Larkin, J., Simon, H.: Why a diagram is (sometimes) worth ten thousand words. Cogn. Sci. **99**, 65–99 (1987)
21. Rauterberg, M.: An iterative-cyclic software process model. In: Proceedings of the Fourth International Conference on Software Engineering and Knowledge Engineering, pp. 600–607 (1992)

Gamification in a Smart City Context.
An Analysis and a Proposal for Its Application
in Co-design Processes

Antonio Opromolla[1,4(✉)], Andrea Ingrosso[2], Valentina Volpi[1,4],
Carlo Maria Medaglia[3], Mauro Palatucci[1], and Mariarosaria Pazzola[1]

[1] ISIA Roma Design, Piazza della Maddalena 53, 00196 Rome, Italy
{anto.opro,valentina.volpi84,mauro.palatucci,
m.pazzola14}@gmail.com
[2] CORIS, Sapienza Università di Roma, Via Salaria 113, 00198 Rome, Italy
andrea.ingrosso@uniroma1.it
[3] DIAG, Sapienza Università di Roma, Piazzale Aldo Moro 5, 00185 Rome, Italy
carlomaria.medaglia@uniroma1.it
[4] Link Campus University, Via Nomentana 335, 00162 Rome, Italy

Abstract. In the academic debate on smart city definition, the "human" part of the city is gaining a prominent position as a decisive factor in good city policies. So, Public Administrations (PAs) are looking for the citizen involvement in the decision-making processes, in order to create products and services really meeting the city needs. In this context, gamification principles are more and more employed as facilitator of the citizen engagement process. In this paper, we intend to show the main findings of our analysis on the literary review about application of gamification principles in the smart city context, providing some considerations about their possible application in public policies co-design.

1 Introduction

In the last years, the academic literature gave several definitions and visions of the concept of "smart city", setting some common multidimensional components related to three main categories: technology, people, and institutions [1]. According to Hollands [7], who provided a preliminary critical polemic against some of the more rhetorical aspects of smart city, each of these definitions is strictly related to the field of study of the single researcher who delivers it.

Generally, in the vision of smart city the use of ICT is emphasized, but recently into the academic debate on smart cities people became the center of the urban smartness. The Human Smart Cities Manifesto [3] is emblematic of this vision. In detail, "Human Smart Cities are those where governments engage citizens by being open to be engaged by citizens, supporting the co-design of technical and social innovation processes through a peer-to-peer relationship based on reciprocal trust and collaboration. [...] A Human Smart City adopts services that are born from people's real needs and have

© Springer International Publishing Switzerland 2015
A. De Gloria (Ed.): GALA 2014, LNCS 9221, pp. 73–82, 2015.
DOI: 10.1007/978-3-319-22960-7_8

been co-designed through interactive, dialogic, and collaborative processes. In a Human Smart City, people […] are encouraged to compose their own services using available technologies in simple, often frugal solutions". We agreed with this "human" vision of the smart city. Moreover, we suppose that the use of gamification principles can support citizen engagement in the smart city co-design process. In detail, we deem the game mechanisms and dynamics can produce socially virtuous behaviour, by improving the world understanding and by making some actions more enjoyable [5].

In this paper, we intend to show the main findings of our analysis on the literary review about application of gamification principles in the smart city context, providing some considerations about their possible application in public policies co-design. In detail: in the next section we will define the gamification and co-design methodologies, focusing on their integration in order to involve citizens in city issues; in the third one we will analyse the academic literature about application of gamification principles in the smart city context; in the fourth section we will discuss the findings of our analysis; in the fifth one the conclusions and future work.

2   Citizen Engagement in Gamification and Co-design Processes

Nowadays, Public Administrations (hereafter PAs) are opening to a larger citizen engagement in decision-making processes concerning local public policies activities [24], aware of the importance to really meet the citizen needs in the design of new services or products [2, 3]. This attitude is consistent with the increasing joint involvement by citizens aiming to actively influence the decisions of the PAs (*bottom-up* approach), or even aiming to work together by organizing themselves without PA presence (*crowdsourcing* approach). Anyway, it is the duty of the PA trying to involve as much as possible all citizens interested by a given action.

Co-design is a practice very useful for citizen involvement in PA-driven decision-making processes [40]. It is particularly suited to bring citizens to the city issues and to make them more satisfied, since it helps to provide a vision shared between the different stakeholders living in the smart city environment [25] and to meet people effective needs. In co-design process designers encourage and guide users to develop solutions (i.e. new products and services) for themselves, attempting to actively involve all the stakeholders, and not limiting participation to a selected group of people (*lead user* approach). As for other similar approaches, like co-creation (i.e. creativity that is shared by two or more people) and participatory design (i.e. user participation in system design), the user is considered as a partner [25], not as a subject to be studied, but in co-design all the players (i.e. designers, researchers, and users) have the same importance in the system design.

In the report of the Smart Cities project [40], the co-design process is implemented following the five stages design thinking process (i.e. the design-specific cognitive activities that designers apply during the process of designing [4]), that includes: problem statement (with the identification of user needs), immersion and empathy (in the specific problem), synthesis (of the emerged ideas), ideation (of new products or services), prototyping (of a model quickly showing citizens and users what their inputs have produced). By actively collaborate into the design process, the user results to be involved in that particular matter, but the *intensity of the engagement* [40] (i.e. if the engagement is simply a case of fact-finding, or people are able to shape the outcome together) changed depending on those in charge for delivery of the service or product.

From the point of view of a PA opening to a larger citizen engagement in decision-making processes, the intensity of engagement have to reach the higher level and the larger number of people involved. In this regard, the *gamification approach*, whose main purpose is to engage people through innovative modes, could help in actively involving citizens during the design activities. In detail, according to Deterding et al. [36], "gamification" is *"the use of game design elements in non-game contexts"*. It differs both from "playful interactions" (in which there are no rules, competition, and goals), and "serious games" (in which complete game for non-entertainment purposes are used). Gamification can be used to make more attractive task and activities in different areas of application, therefore improving the participation and the motivation of people who have to perform them [6]. So, we deem that gamification and co-design can be joint together to enhance citizens engagement in the smart city context.

3 A Literature Review of Gamification in a Smart City Context

Only recently, in the academic debate, the city has been investigated as an area of application of gamification principles. In this paragraph, we will introduce a brief literature review regarding the application of gamification in a smart city context. The use of these principles can be analysed from different points of view. So, we will focus on the gamification modes for engaging citizens in the city issues. On this basis, we will consider people as "citizens" and "players" at the same time.

The most part of the scientific contributions on gamification applied in a smart city context concerns the design and the development of web and mobile applications (or proofs of concept) addressed to the citizens. In this work, we analyse 24 game applications (or proofs of concept) applied in a smart city context. Since our focus is the citizen engagement through gamification, we consider three main elements: the *playing area*, the *user interaction modes*, and the *roles performed by the citizens* while using a certain application.

In particular, the "playing areas" aspect allows us to investigate the main environments and matters affected by game applications, as well as the places and the topics *where* citizens are involved. The "interaction modes" are important for the identification of the actions performed by users in the smart city context, showing *how* citizens are involved. Finally, the "roles" aspect permits us to identify the kind of activity that citizens perform in the smart city context, to figure out *what* effect the engagement produces. Below, the main findings of our literature review.

3.1 The Playing Areas of Game Applications in the Smart City Context

As "playing area", we mean both the places where citizens are engaged through gamification, and the topics on which they are involved. In the considered applications, the main playing area is the physical environment of the city. As a consequence, most part of these applications are *mobile* and they mainly affect the *mobility* and *environment* issues. In particular, their main aim is to prompt citizens to do more eco-friendly activities. For example: to reduce the CO_2 emissions [9, 18, 29]; to choose sustainable means of transportation [10, 18, 30]; to promote collaborative riding [35]; to recycle [10, 14]; to check noise pollution [12]; to foster sustainable communities [16, 39]; to foster healthy climate [16]; and to educate in energy conservation [31].

In addition to the mobility and environment fields, we found that the gamification principles are used also into the *touristic field*. For example, Gordillo et al. [8] propose a new way of visiting a city by employing a "treasure hunt", in order to provide people some information about the cultural heritage. Moreover, in [20] Lorenzi et al. describe a mobile application based on QR Code technology with the aim to incentivize the use of a National Park.

Another important field of application of gamification in a smart city context concerns the *relationship among people*. In [13], for example, Laureyssens et al. describe a public game designed with the only aim of augmenting the community cohesiveness, as well as in [19]. Moreover, in [32] Bista et al. propose an online community in which some users can give support to others relying on their previous experiences in specific matters.

In other cases, the applications affect *a large number* of playing areas. In this regard, in [11] Crowley et al. present a mobile application designed with the aim to prompt citizens to report on issues about the whole city context, i.e. mobility, environment, living, government, etc. Also Lehner et al., in [23], propose a mobile application in which citizens can share personal ideas or opinions about all the issues concerning the city.

3.2   The User Interaction Modes of Game Applications in the Smart City Context

The applications we analysed have different user interaction modes. As "user interaction mode", we refer to the main actions that user needs to perform in order to progress in the game. So, it is related to the modes of citizen engagement in the game applications. By analysing them, we have identified the following user interaction modes:

1. *The user acts and the system records the user actions and/or data about user actions*. According to this interaction mode, user is free to perform actions in the real environment; the system automatically records these actions or the data about them. This is the case of the application described in [12]: citizens go through the city and the system records data on the city noise. Moreover, the application of Kuramoto et al. [15] records data about the citizen behaviour in public means of transportation, while in [17] Gnauk et al. design an application that registers the citizen data consumption.

2. *The user self-reports the performed actions and/or data about them*. In this case, user performs actions in the real environment and he/she autonomously reports his/her actions and/or data about them on the application. In [9], Liu et al. design an application in which user needs to indicate the performed actions in the sustainability field. Only after doing this, the system is able to indicate if these actions lead the users to progress in the game or not. The application of Vara et al. [10] provides the

user the typologies of actions among which he/she can indicate the performed action (e.g. "walking", "biking", etc.), while in [11] Crowley et al. design an application in which users can share the problems encountered in the city context.

3. *The user completes missions.* In this case, the system gives some goals to the user and the latter performs actions in order to achieve them. In [16], for example, Lee et al. describe an application that gives communities some missions concerning the respect for the environment, while the application of Jylhä et al. [18] gives people missions about the sustainable mobility.

4. *The user shares user-generated contents.* According to this interaction mode, user can share personal contents in order to progress in the game. For example, in [23], Lehner et al. propose a mobile application in which citizens can share contributions about the city environment (e.g. ideas, opinions, etc.) in order to strengthen his/her participation in the city issues. Similarly, in [32] Bista et al. propose a mobile application in which citizens can share their experiences in order to support other people in similar situations.

5. *The user explores locations.* This interaction mode foresees to explore the city and to find specific places in order to progress in the game. For example, in [8], Gordillo et al. consider the city as a "learning gamified platform", with specific "Learning Points of Interest" to be discovered. Moreover, in [22], Chan proposes a game application with the aim to prompt people to explore alternative routes for their commute, in order to reduce the traffic congestion.

6. *The user simulates a situation.* In this case the game strengthens the user's skills in a simulated environment. For example, in [33] Schoech et al. develop a violence prevention game for youths, by putting them within some possible real-life situations. The youth civic education purpose is present in [34] too, where Barthel designs a video game in order to provide young people with knowledge about the governmental processes.

3.3 The Roles of Citizens Using Game Applications in the Smart City Context

Finally, as "role" we intend the kind of activity that citizens perform in the smart city context. The main roles of the citizen using the game applications are:

1. *Learner*: the citizen learns something in order to improve the quality of his/her life or to change his/her lifestyle. He/She can assimilate contents (e.g. in [8], Gordillo et al. consider the city as the place in which citizen can play and learn something about its history) or behaviours (e.g. in [21] the application aims to encourage students to increase the physical activities; the application described in [30] aims to encourage cycling). In some cases the target of the applications is young people (e.g. [33, 34]).

2. *Examinee*: in this case, it is examined whether or not the citizen performs the correct behaviour. Therefore, the citizen is not a "learner", but the application only evaluates his/her behaviour. For example, in [9], Liu et al. design an application aiming to evaluate if user do eco-friendly activities. He/She knows the correct behaviour, and he/she needs only to put it into practice.

3. *Teacher*: the citizen "evaluates" and monitors the city and its elements. For example, Crowley et al. [11] design an application in which the user has to report the problems about the city. In this case, the citizen is not a "learner", nor an "examinee", but he/she acts on the basis of a prior knowledge. The same thing occurs in [23], where the described game application is based on the contributions of the citizen: he/she can share his/her ideas or opinions about the city context. The "teacher" role is particularly emphasized in [32], where Bista et al. propose an online community in which people can give support to others, through advices and opinions.

4. *Sensor*: the citizen collects data and information on the environment that PAs can use for specific analysis on the urban context. This is the case of the applications described by Garcia Marti et al. in [12], in which the "crowdsourcing approach" allows the collection of data about the noise pollution, and by Gnauk et al. in [17], where the aim of the application is to collect data about energy consumption.

4 Discussion

The game applications we analysed engage citizens according to different degrees. The analysis of the user interaction modes (Sect. 3.2) points out that the game mechanisms can be more captivating (e.g. the user interaction mode "Share user-generated contents"), or less (e.g. the user interaction mode "The user acts and the system records the user actions and/or data about user actions"). The analysis of citizen roles (Sect. 3.3) shows that these applications generally aim to prompt people to assume a good behaviour in living the city. The most affected fields are mobility and environment (Sect. 3.1).

However, in these game applications, the citizen engagement settles on medium degrees of intensity. Indeed, only in very few cases the contributions of the citizens are the core of the applications. We refer in particular to the work of Crowley et al. [11], where citizens can report on issues about the city context, and to the work of Lehner et al. [23], where citizens can share ideas and opinions on how to solve city problems.

On the contrary, we assert that the degree of intensity of citizen engagement through gamification can further increase. Consequently, *citizens would be required to collaborate and participate, in a gamification context, during the decision-making processes concerning the smart city issues* and *to take part during the co-design of new services and products in the urban context*. According to this consideration, we assert that the areas of *gamification* and *co-design* can be profitably integrated. Below, a no complete list of the meeting points of these two areas:

1. *Improvement*. On the one hand, co-design results lead to the improvement of quality of life (through the realization of new services and products). On the other hand, the commitment in the game applications leads to the progress of the player (through new levels, new powers, etc.).

2. *Several roles and Empathy*. On the one hand, in co-design processes different stakeholders with specific needs work together and collaborate to design products and services for themselves. The people involved are asked to fully "play" the role they

have (for example, one of the main tools used during a co-design process is the customer journey mapping, in which stakeholders indicate their own habits and daily activities). On the other hand, during a gamification process player plays a role, with specific characteristics, and different players can play different roles.

3. *Story*. On the one hand, co-design process is a developmental process: it "tells a story", that the involved stakeholders will lead to a "happy ending" (to design a product or service). On the other hand, one of the "affordances" that can be used during a gamification process is the "story", in which the narrative elements play a central role. The "story" elements are closely related to the "roles".

4. *Human aspects*. On the one hand, co-design processes count on people (with their specific wants and needs) as designers. On the other hand, according to [36] in gamification processes, HCI (Human Computer Interaction) field is not related to the technological aspects, but to the user interaction ones.

5. *Creativity*. On the one hand, in co-design process a point of strength is to find innovative solutions to new or traditional problems. On the other hand, imagination and creativity are fundamental elements of the games. In general, creativity supports problem solving.

6. *Results orientation*. On the one hand, all the steps of a co-design process are oriented to the design and prototyping of a product or service that citizens can use. On the other hand, during a gamification process players intend to achieve specific aims (points, badges, to win a competition). The achievement of the results gives satisfaction.

7. *Rules*. On the one hand, a co-design session has rules that participants must follow. On the other hand, during a game, players can achieve specific aims only if they follow the given rules.

Considering these common points, we argue that gamification techniques and principles can be applied during the co-design processes, in order to improve citizen engagement and participation in the realization of new products and services in the smart city context. In the academic debate, some authors have begun to explore the contact area between co-design and gamification. Their works concern two main fields of application: the collaborative working environments (e.g. in [37] Fernández-Luna et al. focus on CIS - Collaborative Information Seeking systems; in [38] Moradian et al. focus on brainstorming systems) and the learning context (e.g. in [26] Dodero et al. present a study in which co-design is blended with gamification and collaborative learning). Nowadays, the contact area of gamification and co-design in the smart city context is still an unexplored area.

5   Conclusions and Future Work

Following a "human approach" to the smart city services and products design, we investigated how gamification principles were applied in a city context in order to engage citizens. We found that despite the aim of gamification is the involvement of people, nowadays its application is underestimated by the PAs looking for a deeper involvement of citizens in the city issues. On the contrary, we argue that gamification is really suitable to be used in decision-making processes and during the co-design of new services and products in order to motivate citizen to actively participate.

On the basis of this preliminary analysis, our future work will be addressed to the implementation of the gamification principles in co-design processes, by focusing on the identification of the more suitable game patterns [27], affordances, models and methods in accordance with the specific city context. In so doing, we will evaluate in which degree gamification increases the intrinsic and extrinsic motivations [28] of citizens at participating in city development.

References

1. Nam, T., Pardo, Theresa A.: Conceptualizing smart city with dimensions of technology, people, and institutions. In: 12th Annual International Digital Government Research Conference: Digital Government Innovation in Challenging Times, pp. 282–291. ACM, New York (2011)
2. Puerari, E., Concilio, G., Longo, A., Rizzo, F.: Innovating public services in urban environments: a SOC inspired strategy proposal. In: International Forum on Knowledge Asset Dynamics (IFKAD), pp.987–1007 (2013)
3. The human smart cities manifesto. http://www.peripheria.eu/blog/human-smart-cities-manifesto
4. Visser, W.: The Cognitive Artifacts of Designing. Lawrence Erlbaum Associates, New York (2006)
5. McGonigal, J.: Reality Is Broken: Why Games Make Us Better and How They Can Change the World. Penguin Group, New York (2011)
6. Aparicio, A.F., Vela, F.L.G., Sánchez, J.L.G., Montes, J.L.I.: Analysis and application of gamification. In: 13th International Conference on Interacción Persona-Ordenador, INTERACCION 2012, 2 P, Article 17. ACM, New York (2012)
7. Hollands, R.G.: Will the real smart city please stand up? City **12**(3), 303–320 (2008)
8. Gordillo, A., Gallego, D., Barra, E., Quemada, J.: The city as a learning gamified platform. In: Frontiers in Education Conference, pp. 372–378. IEEE (2013)
9. Liu, Y., Alexandrova, T., Nakajima, T.: Gamifying intelligent environments. In: International ACM workshop on Ubiquitous Meta User Interfaces (Ubi-MUI 2011), pp. 7–12. ACM, New York (2011)
10. Vara, D., Macias, E., Gracia, S., Torrents, A., Lee, S.: Meeco: gamifying ecology through a social networking platform. In: IEEE International Conference on Multimedia and Expo (ICME), pp. 1–6 (2011)
11. Crowley, D.N., Breslin, J.G., Corcoran, P., Young, K.: Gamification of citizen sensing through mobile social reporting. In: IEEE International Games Innovation Conference (IGIC), pp. 1–5 (2012)
12. Martí, I.G., Rodríguez, L.E., Benedito, M., Trilles, S., Beltrán, A., Díaz, L., Huerta, J.: Mobile application for noise pollution monitoring through gamification techniques. In: Herrlich, M., Malaka, R., Masuch, M. (eds.) ICEC 2012. LNCS, vol. 7522, pp. 562–571. Springer, Heidelberg (2012)
13. Laureyssens, T., Coenen, T., Claeys, L., Mechant, P., Criel, J., Vande Moere. A.: ZWERM: a modular component network approach for an urban participation game. In: 32nd annual ACM conference on Human factors in computing systems (CHI) 2014, pp. 3259–3268. ACM, New York (2014)

14. Berengueres, J., Alsuwairi, F., Zaki, N., Ng, T: Gamification of a recycle bin with emoticons. In: 8th ACM/IEEE International Conference on Human-robot interaction (HRI 2013), pp. 83–84. IEEE Press, Piscataway (2013)
15. Kuramoto, I., Ishibashi, T., Yamamoto, K., Tsujino, Y.: Stand up, heroes! : gamification for standing people on crowded public transportation. In: Marcus, A. (ed.) DUXU/HCII 2013, Part II. LNCS, vol. 8013, pp. 538–547. Springer, Heidelberg (2013)
16. Lee, J.J., Matamoros, E., Kern, R., Marks, J., de Luna, C., Jordan-Cooley W.: Greenify: fostering sustainable communities via gamification. In: Extended Abstracts on Human Factors in Computing Systems, CHI EA 2013, pp. 1497–1502. ACM, New York (2013)
17. Gnauk, B., Dannecker, L., Hahmann, M.: Leveraging gamification in demand dispatch systems. In: Srivastava, D., Ari, I. (eds.) Joint EDBT/ICDT Workshops, EDBT-ICDT 2012, pp. 103–110. ACM, New York (2012)
18. Jylhä, A., Nurmi, P., Sirén, M., Hemminki, S., Jacucci, G.: MatkaHupi: a persuasive mobile application for sustainable mobility. In: ACM conference on Pervasive and ubiquitous computing adjunct publication, UbiComp 2013, pp. 227–230. ACM, New York (2013)
19. Zarzycki, A: Urban games: application of augmented reality. In: IGGRAPH Asia 2012 Symposium on Apps (SA), 1. P, Article 8. ACM, New York (2012)
20. Lorenzi, D., Shafiq, B., Vaidya, J., Nabi, G., Chun, S., Atluri V.: Using QR codes for enhancing the scope of digital government services. In: 13th Annual International Conference on Digital Government Research (dg.o 2012), pp. 21–29. ACM, New York (2012)
21. Xu, Y., Shehan Poole, E., Miller, A.D., Eiriksdottir, E., Catrambone, R., Mynatt, E.D., Designing pervasive health games for sustainability, adaptability and sociability. In: International Conference on the Foundations of Digital Games (FDG), pp. 49–56. ACM, New York (2012)
22. Chan, K.: Visual ethnography in game design: a case study of user-centric concept for a mobile social traffic game. In: 15th International Academic MindTrek Conference: Envisioning Future Media Environments, MindTrek 2011, pp. 75–82. ACM, New York (2011)
23. Lehner, U., Baldauf, M., Eranti, V., Reitberger, W., Fröhlich, P.: Civic engagement meets pervasive gaming: towards long-term mobile participation. In: Extended Abstracts on Human Factors in Computing Systems, CHI EA 2014, pp. 1483–1488. ACM, New York (2014)
24. European eGovernment Action Plan 2011–2015. http://ec.europa.eu/digital-agenda/en/european-egovernment-action-plan-2011-2015
25. Sanders, E.B.-N., Stappers, P.J.: Co-creation and the new landscapes of design. Co-Design 4(1), 5–18 (2008)
26. Dodero, G., Gennari, R., Melonio, A., Torello, S.: Gamified co-design with cooperative learning. In: Extended Abstracts on Human Factors in Computing Systems, CHI EA 2014, pp. 707–718. ACM, New York (2014)
27. Bjork, S., Holopainen, J.: Patterns in Game Design. Charles River Media, Boston (2005)
28. Deci, E.L., Ryan, M.R.: Self-determination theory: a macrotheory of human motivation, development, and health. Can. Psychol. 49(10), 182–185 (2008)
29. Prost, S., Schrammel, J., Tscheligi, M.: Sometimes it's the weather's fault: sustainable HCI & political activism. In: Extended Abstracts on Human Factors in Computing Systems, CHI EA 2014, pp. 2005–2010. ACM, New York (2014)
30. Navarro, K.F., Gay, V., Golliard, L., Johnston, B., Leijdekkers, P., Vaughan, E., Xun Wang, Williams, M.-A.: SocialCycle what can a mobile app do to encourage cycling? In: IEEE 38th Conference on Local Computer Networks Workshops, LCN Workshops 2013, pp. 24–30 (2013)

31. Marques, B., Nixon, K.: The gamified grid: possibilities for utilising game-based motivational psychology to empower the Smart Social Grid. In: AFRICON 2013, pp. 1–5 (2013)

32. Bista, S.K., Nepal, S., Paris, C.: Data abstraction and visualisation in next step: experiences from a government services delivery trial. In: IEEE International Congress on Big Data, BigData Congress 2013, pp. 263–270. IEEE Computer Society (2013)

33. Schoech, D., Boyas, J.F., Black, B.M., Elias-Lambert, N.: Gamification for Behavior Change: Lessons from Developing a Social, Multiuser, Web-tablet based prevention game for youths. J. Technol. Hum. Ser. **31**(3), 197–217 (2013)

34. Barthel, M.L.: President for a day. video games as youth civic education. Inf. Commun. Soc. **16**(1), 28–42 (2013)

35. Vieira, V., Fialho, A., Martinez, V., Brito, J., Brito, L., Duran, A.: An exploratory study on the use of collaborative riding based on gamification as a support to public transportation. In: Brazilian Symposium on Collaborative Systems, SBSC 2012, pp. 84–93 (2012)

36. Deterding, S., Khaled, R., Nacke, L.E., Dixon, D.: Gamification: toward a definition. In: CHI 2011 Gamification Workshop, pp. 1–4, Vancouver, Canada (2011)

37. Fernández-Luna, J.M, Huete, J.F., Rodríguez-Avila H., Rodríguez-Cano, J.C.: Enhancing collaborative search systems engagement through gamification. In: First International Workshop on Gamification for Information Retrieval, GamifIR 2014, pp. 42–45. ACM, New York (2014)

38. Moradian, A., Nasir, M., Lyons, K., Leung, R., Sim. S.E.: Gamification of collaborative idea generation and convergence. In: Extended Abstracts on Human Factors in Computing Systems, CHI EA 2014, pp. 1459–1464. ACM, New York (2014)

39. Massung, M., Coyle, D., Cater, K.F., Jay, M., Preist, P.: Using crowdsourcing to support pro-environmental community activism. In: SIGCHI Conference on Human Factors in Computing Systems, CHI 2013, pp. 371–380. ACM, New York (2013)

40. Smart cities: Co-design in smart cities. A guide for municipalities from smart cities (2011). http://www.smartcities.info/files/Co-Design%20in%20Smart%20Cities.pdf

A Conceptual Model Towards the Scaffolding of Learning Experience

Sylvester Arnab[1(✉)], Pablo Moreno Ger[2], Theodore Lim[3], Petros Lameras[4], Maurice Hendrix[5], Kristian Kiili[6], Jannicke Baalsrud Hauge[7], Manuel Ninaus[8], Sara de Freitas[9], Alessandro Mazzetti[10], Anders Dahlbom[11], Cristiana Degano[10], Ioana Stanescu[12], and Maria Riveiro[11]

[1] Disruptive Media Learning Lab, Coventry University, Coventry, UK
s.arnab@coventry.ac.uk
[2] Universidad Complutense de Madrid, 28040 Madrid, Spain
pablom@fdi.ucm.es
[3] Herriot-Watt University, Edinburgh, EH14 5SJ, UK
T.Lim@hw.ac.uk
[4] Serious Games Institute, Coventry University, Coventry, UK
PLameras@cad.coventry.ac.uk
[5] School of Science and Technology, University of Northampton, Northampton, NN2 6JB, UK
Maurice.hendrix@northampton.ac.uk
[6] Tampere University of Technology, P.O. Box 300 28101 Pori, Finland
kristian.kiili@tut.fi
[7] Bremer Institut für Produktion und Logistik, Hochschulring 20, 28359 Bremen, Germany
baa@biba.uni-bremen.de
[8] University of Graz, Universitätsplatz 2/III, 8010 Graz, Austria
manuel.ninaus@uni-graz.at
[9] Curtin University, Kent St., Bentley, WA 6102, Australia
Sara.deFreitas@curtin.edu.au
[10] Gruppo SIGLA S.r.l, Via Finocchiaro Aprile 31 - 16129, Genoa, Italy
{alessandro.mazzetti,cristiana.degano}@grupposigla.it
[11] Högskolan i Skövde, Box 408 541 28 Skövde, Sweden
{andreas.dahlbom,maria.riveiro}@his.se
[12] "Carol I" National Defence University, 68-72 Panduri Street, Bucharest, Romania
ioana.stanescu@aldnet.ro

Abstract. The challenge of delivering personalized learning experiences is amplified by the size of classrooms and of online learning communities. In turn, serious games are increasingly recognized for their potential to improve education, but a typical requirement from instructors is to gain insight into how the students are playing. When we bring games into the rapidly growing online learning communities, the challenges multiply and hinder the potential effectiveness of serious games. There is a need to deliver a comprehensive, flexible and intelligent learning framework that facilitates better understanding of learners' knowledge, effective assessment of their progress and continuous evaluation and optimization of the environments in which they learn. This paper aims to explore the potential in the use of games and learning analytics towards scaffolding and supporting teaching and learning experience. The conceptual model discussed

© Springer International Publishing Switzerland 2015
A. De Gloria (Ed.): GALA 2014, LNCS 9221, pp. 83–96, 2015.
DOI: 10.1007/978-3-319-22960-7_9

aims to highlight key considerations that may advance the current state of learning analytics, adaptive learning and serious games, by leveraging serious games as an ideal medium for gathering data and performing adaptations. This opportunity has the potential to affect the design and deployment of education and training in the future.

1 Introduction

The EU Education and Training 2020 (ET2020 [1]) identified that a major challenge for improving the quality and efficiency of formal education (K12) is to enable the acquisition of 21st century skills as means to develop excellence and allow Europe to retain a strong global role. The 21st century is perceived as the beginning of a digital age with an unprecedented growth in technology. Technology may be used for enhancing education, where it offers unprecedented opportunities to improve quality, access and equity in education and training. There is also an emergence of new ways of learning characterized by personalization, engagement, use of digital media, collaboration, bottom-up practices and learner/teacher as a creator of the learning content. To effectively support the acquisition of 21st century skills, both teachers and students need to receive better and more personalized support in conjunction with effective deployment of technology-assisted approaches.

This is in line with a number of research studies and policy reports that have emerged over the past decade [2–6] that emphasize how students can apply knowledge rather than how much knowledge they have attained. This presents a challenge in effective tracking and analysis of the right parameters related to students' progress and it should be more than just a grading system based on traditional methods, emphasizing more on how to monitor and assess quality of education and learning, as well as exploiting innovative technology-enabled disciplines such as social learning analytics.

The quality of delivery of and engagement with a learning process is key in ensuring and maximizing the effectiveness of a learning process.

The quality and efficacy of a learning process is indeed influenced by the quality of teaching, learning support and environment. How can learners' needs and performance be effectively monitored and exploited so that the right support is provided? Considered to be one of the most effective approaches to instruction, the Vygotskian scaffolding concept [7, 8] can be adapted. This concept allows individual learners to be given tailored support during the learning process, personalized to their individual needs. Understanding how the different learning preferences influence how learners learn most efficiently [9, 10] is essential to maximizing the impact of a teaching and learning process.

ICT solutions deployed in educational and training institutions should consume less resources and enable wider applicability and interoperability within the existing infrastructure of these institutions. This includes improvements in human computer interaction such as increased user friendliness and greater user adaptivity to maximize the use and scalability of the solution. Existing and emerging trends, such as the increased use of Learning Management Systems (LMS) in both schools and training courses, the deployment of online courses on a large scale (Massive Open Online Courses or

MOOCs) and the ability of a game-based platform to engage large numbers of players for long periods of time, provide an opportunity for a real wealth of data about students and their learning to be collected and utilized towards personalizing effective learner support in real-time interactions.

The challenge is how to best collect, measure and analyze these big datasets and utilize the analysis to predict the best teaching approach for the individual learners and adapt their experience, whether within a virtual learning environment or the actual physical delivery/deployment. With this perspective, this paper introduces a conceptual model (ecosystem and architecture) that can potentially support the scaffolding of teaching and learning experience within a formal setting. Towards this end, Sect. 2 discusses the related concepts followed by Sect. 3, where the overview of the proposed conceptual ecosystem is described. Section 4 explores the conceptual architecture that can be developed and Sect. 5 concludes the paper with the future research and development requirements for implementing the system and architecture in practice.

2   Related Concepts

The 2013 Horizon Report places emphasis on both games and learning analytics as the technologies to be adopted over the next two to three years, which presents an opportunity for the benefits of both technologies to be exploited.

2.1   Capitalizing on Serious Games as a Platform to Engage and Sustain Participation

We recognize games technologies as 'the innovation catalyst of information technology' [14]. Serious games (SG) are attractive tools for learning, but such tools also provide an opportunity for vital educational data to be recorded, monitored and analyzed (e.g. Buckingham Shum et al. [15]). The power of games to immerse and motivate [16, 17] and the capabilities of games to change perceptions and views [18, 23] have created a more positive approach to games and new game genres. More use of games in non-entertainment contexts such as learning and training [19] are transforming everyday lives and multiplayer and social games communities are changing social interactions, leading to greater capabilities for social learning and importantly more fun in everyday contexts [20].

The first pragmatic controlled trial showed how game-based approaches were found to be more effective than traditional learning in triage training (Triage Trainer [21]). Kato et al. [22] showed how game-based approaches in Re-Mission could support medication adherence in children with cancer. The study by Rebolledo-Mendez et al. on FloodSim [23] likewise showed how awareness raising of flooding policy could be supported by game-based approaches. Arnab et al. [24] demonstrated that game-based learning platform when deployed within a classroom setting promotes knowledge transfer and encourage communal discourse on sensitive issues.

2.2   The Potential of Learning Analytics and Big Data

In traditional formal education scenarios, the main evaluation method of both the students and the course itself is based on written examination. The amount of data available through this evaluation method is limited, and it is usually restricted to students and educators subjective perceptions. Moreover, this data usually becomes available when the activity is finished or when it is too late to make an intervention, improvement or correction in the ongoing action. Therefore, powerful insights could be extracted from data gathered from learning process and experience that is broken down into measureable steps/stages in order to assess preliminary and intermediate knowledge transfer at a discreet scale.

e-learning tools like LMSs offers the possibility to collect and analyze the learners' interaction with the different learning resources not only to improve the evaluation methods, but also to obtain real-time feedback about the progress of any educational activity, enabling educators to predict results and react to that progress. This kind of analysis is not new in other domains like Business, where all of these analysis and techniques are under the umbrella of the term Business Intelligence (BI) [25].

Until now, the available set of parameters to analyze educational outcome has not been enough to establish the conditions of success or failure in the different educational processes. Nowadays, mainly due to new mobile technologies expansion, students interact with varied and increasingly interactive educational resources coming from multiple sources and platforms, producing great amounts of interaction data that can be collected and analyzed. Therefore, the amount of available data has increased significantly. This fact, coupled with the evolution and improvement of analysis techniques, as well as with the current processing power of computers, favours the potential impact of Learning Analytics Systems.

The Learning Analytics discipline [11, 12] consolidates its impact within Technology Enhanced Learning as a methodology to determine how data collected from learners can help to improve any of the many aspects of the educational process. Despite being a relatively new discipline, research about Learning Analytics has resulted in solutions such as LOCO-Analyst or SNAPP [13], where analyses on learing are based on the notion of Learning Object Context (LOC) capturing student (or a group of students) interaction with a learning content by performing certain activity (e.g. reading, quizzing, chatting). Most of this research is focused in the interactions performed by the students within the LMS. Brown [36] emphasises that the most effective learning analytics programs should be institution-wide efforts, taking advantage of a wide range of resources that would enhance analysis of the learinbg process. Greller and Drachsler [38highlight the importance to consider these entities when designing a learning analytics framework for an institution: stakeholders, objectives, data, instruments, external constraints, and internal limitations.

The increasing acceptance of SGs leads to teachers from different areas and levels to use games (or game-like activities) to engage their students. However, most of these activities do not have an important weight on the final student evaluation, because most games and simulations lack an appropriate assessment system able to generate rigorous and reliable feedback on student results. Therefore, while games promise to teach in innovative ways, the assessment of their effectiveness tends to gravitate back to written examinations or debriefing sessions [24, 26]. This has caused an increasing gap between the purportedly deep learning that can be conveyed by educational games and the shallow techniques used to assess learners' performance.

Different solutions and techniques have been proposed to fill this gap, including using the games themselves to assess the performance. The field of implicit in-game evaluation (also called stealth assessment [27]), offers rich opportunities: since games are highly interactive and complex software artifacts, they can produce a great amount of data on how the user is playing, which is readily available for assessment purposes. However, the best methods and techniques for utilizing all this data to measure learning effectiveness and assessing learners most effectively remains an open research and development challenge. It is therefore useful to scope the current applications and refinements of Learning Analytics techniques, adapting them to the specific context of SGs, in order to leverage the vast amount of trace data that games can generate to provide rich learner-based assessment information.

3 The Conceptual Ecosystem

Bringing together SGs and Learning Analytics to facilitate the understanding and support of engaged learners opened he possibility to create an intelligent and interoperable learning framework capitalizing on learning analytics tools that can be implemented and integrated onto a LMS, a game engine and a game editor to provide a wide range of scaffolded support for learners and teachers/instructors within a formal setting.

Participatory approach is of key importance to the teaching and learning ecosystem, where the metrics and performance indicators specific to the stakeholders can be specified and included in the design of the intelligent learning environment. The ecosystem, as illustrated in Fig. 1, aims to support the capture and reasoning of large-scale educational data from engaging sources to better understand learners' knowledge, assess their progress and provide actionable feedback, which will be relevant to the stakeholders involved. Non-scientific users as stakeholders, such as learners, teachers, parents, school administrators and state/regional bodies could be supported and they will be able to engage with and exploit large datasets. The ecosystem reflects the importance of stakeholders, data and instruments to assist in the capturing and analysis of the learning process.

The potential benefits to the stakeholders are at four levels

- **Course-Level:** Learners and teachers/instructors will obtain a better perspective of the educational process and its results, which will help individual learners to reach their learning goals and the teachers/instructors to provide the right support to their pupils/trainees. For e.g. learners will benefit from actionable feedbacks related to the specific course and will allow teachers to optimise solutions and face-to-face intervention related to the insights provided at the course-level.
- **Course-Aggregated Level:** Predictive models and success/failure patterns can be correlated in the analyzed data based on the specific measures and metrics, which can be used to design actionable solutions to overcome the weakness of the teaching and learning strategy;

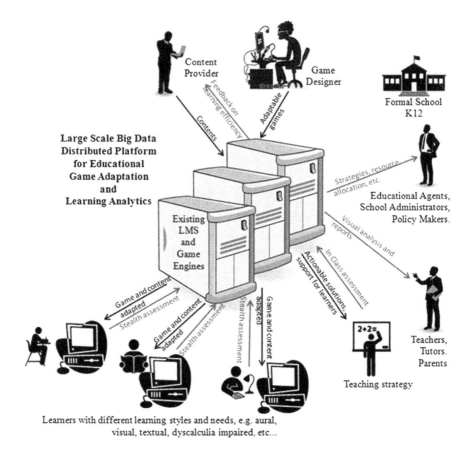

Content Provider

Game Designer

Formal School K12

Large Scale Big Data Distributed Platform for Educational Game Adaptation and Learning Analytics

Existing LMS and Game Engines

Feedback on learning efficiency

Contents

Adaptable games

Strategies, resource allocation, etc.

Educational Agents, School Administrators, Policy Makers.

Visual analysis and reports

In Class assessment

Actionable solutions, support for learners

Game and content adapted

Stealth assessment

Game and content adapted

Stealth assessment

Stealth assessment

Game and content adapted

2+2=

Teachers, Tutors. Parents

Teaching strategy

Learners with different learning styles and needs, e.g. aural, visual, textual, dyscalculia impaired, etc...

Fig. 1. A conceptual ecosystem

- **Administration-Level:** More detailed statistics can be obtained for groups of students or/and schools in order to, for example, improve resources allocation, change of instructional strategy. Student groups can be based on the specific courses, modules and classes to allow identification of practical needs in terms of funding and equipment for instance;

- **Regional/State Level:** Analysis carried out for various schools or faculties can be compared, which may influence how education strategy and policy is developed. The potential is endless, which includes identifying the right practical support for schools in various geographical and cultural contexts, understanding students and teachers' expectation in terms for digital resources for instance and designing education strategy and policy to support personalised requirements.

The ecosystem should embrace adaptivity, enabling the game environment be adapted to specific learner profiling. This will allow longitudinal and continuous studies of how the learning experience evolve with time and with respect to the change of teaching and learning strategy to respond to the learners' specific needs.

4   The Conceptual Architecture

The capture, analyse and feedback loop is iterative and this requires an architecture that will supports these key activities. Based on the context of using games to support analytics, Fig. 2(a) illustrates a continuous embedded stealth assessment (in-game measures) that will provide useful feedback and analysis to the primary stakeholders (learners, teachers and schools) and other relevant stakeholders (such as parents, who would be able to provide support to their children outside of the formal setting, and the school management and policy maker who can assess their education strategy) based on the agreed metrics or Key Performance Indicators (KPIs) for the specific educational institutions. This reflects the need to support the stakeholders illustrated in the ecosystem Fig. 1. In order to support the stealth loop, we identify that a learning analytics model should be linked with user models, adaptive model and visual analytics to support personalisation. These modelling and the in-game measures should be pedagogically driven to ensure that the right discreet steps within the game will allow learning traces are captured. Figure 2(b) highlights the key components and how outcomes from these components can feed into an iterative analytic process involving the stakeholders as part of the process.

Games are highly interactive and produce a vast number of interactions per game session, which leads to the challenges such as: (i) What variables should user models for Serious Games include? How do these depend on learning goals? And what techniques can be used to capture and analyze the required information about a user? (ii) How and what can we adapt inside a serious game? and (iii) How will the adaptation enhance the user's experience? Meaningful interaction and engagement from a learning perspective need be defined and, correctly and ethically captured (using opt in and opt out user consent). Therefore, the theoretical construct structured by the pedagogical patterns related to game design patterns provides the relationship between game and learning contents. This provides a more effective way to data mine the relevant data, extract meaningful learning interactions and gain insight on how learning can be scaffolded.

Learners are an important entity in the definition of the relationship between engagement with game and learning contents during the actual game play. It is important to understand players' and learners' preferences to allow learning and playing patterns to be analyzed and adapted. In order to adapt to different learning preferences, we need to be able to conceptualize the user in terms of their learning capabilities and learning progress by investigating what parameters would more accurately characterize the user - and how do these map to specific player categories.

Capturing players' activity during game play can help measure these parameters as well as the flow characteristics required for an immersive learning experience [28]. In terms of flow analysis, more usable, generalizable and valid methods for assessing flow in a learning process (during game play) in a non-intrusive way have to be developed and tested. This will require an algorithm linked to and formulated within the learning analytics as illustrated in Fig. 2.

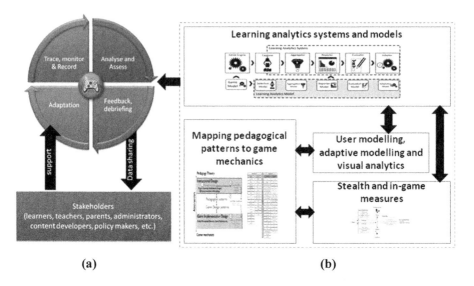

(a)   (b)

Fig. 2. (a) The iterative and continuous process of monitoring and analysing data based on the metrics and KPIs specific to the stakeholders, supported by (b) the key technical components to support a pedagogically-driven learning analytics and adaptive platform

Analysis from this real-time data can be used to build the relevant user models, which could be included in the feedback, reporting and adaption model. The visualization of the analyzed data is important to maximize the impact of the correlated and fused information about the learners. These immediate findings (feedback, reports and models) can be subsequently **validated** by *(i) iteratively adapting a game environment to match the individual learners' model and track the performance continuously, and (ii) evaluating the resulting intervention within a classroom setting*, where teachers will be able to design their teaching strategy based on these findings.

4.1 Tracking Learners/Players Using a Serious Games-Tailored Learning Analytics

Unlike educational data mining, which emphasizes system-generated and automated responses to students, Learning Analytics enables human tailoring of responses, such as through adapting instructional content, intervening with at-risk students, and providing feedback [29].

With this perspective, existing tools, such as the Games and LEarning ANalytics for Educational Research (GLEANER, see Fig. 3) can be implemented to support the tracking or learners and analyze their in-game activities. Gleaner, developed as part of the R&D activity under the GALA network comprises both an abstract framework and an implementation to support the Learning Analytics approach [30].

GLEANER is composed of a Learning Analytics Model (LAM) that defines all the information required for every step, and a Learning Analytics System (LAS) comprises all the processing power required by the model (see Fig. 3). In our approach, the LAS component has been considered as a separate system that is in continuous communication with the game engine. The LAS also has access to the game description and the LAM. The LAM is in turn defined by a set of sub-models, which are directly related to the different modules contained by the LAS.

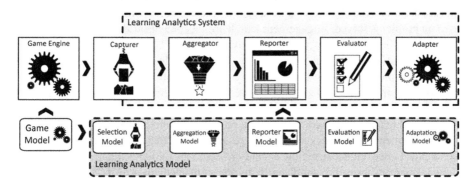

Fig. 3. Main components of GLEANER, and their relationship with the game engine- from capturing and measuring data to reporting the analysis and adapting the existing environment to respond.

Key part of activities proposed by GLEANER, such as the reporting and adapting modules, use visual analytics as analytical reasoning supported by highly interactive visual interfaces. For instance, it is important to provide a user-friendly infrastructure as illustrated in Fig. 4 - personalized dashboards to provide personalized feedback, summaries and actionable steps (a simplistic infrastructure loosely based on adaptive learning systems [31]). The system allows key players (teachers, administrators) to be involved in the adaptation of the content based on the analysis of the learners' progress.

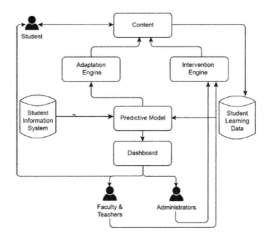

Fig. 4. Adaptive learning system [31]

4.2   Optimizing Stealth and In-game Measures

The engagement with the learning content can be tracked using in-game measurement identifying the exploratory path taken during game-play and the specific content accessed by the players. Recorded information can be the number of times tutorials and hints are accessed, the amount of time spent on problem-solving mini games, the scores based on problems solved. Engagement with learning contents also links to the learning curve and performance assessment (e.g. knowledge gain). Ultimately, positive engagement with learning content is measured by the level of learning outcomes achieved, which can be measured using the in-game scoring and testing and/or post-intervention self-reporting or debriefing. In general, it is crucial to understand that engagement with game play must be established before effective learning experiences can be measured and achieved [32]. Flow theory for instance provides a useful starting point for considering engagement in SGs, because previous research states that flow works in wide range of contexts. However, because flow actually refers to the extreme and momentary form of engagement it has to be completed with other engagement aspects. Engagement is seen as a multifaceted phenomenon [33] that consists of three dimensions: behavioural engagement (involvement with activities), emotional engagement (positive and negative reactions to activities and actors) and cognitive engagement (investment). Within these dimensions, engagement can vary in intensity and duration.

4.3   Pedagogical Modelling

Tracking learner interaction during game play provides vital information that will allow learning style and requirements to be analyzed and game play and content to be adapted. The reasoning of in-game interactions pertaining to learning has to be pedagogically driven by extracting the relationship between games and learning mechanics at the abstract and concrete level- the fundamentals behind what links a game design pattern to a pedagogical pattern. The Learning-Game Mechanics mapping (LM-GM) framework [34] provides a basis to construct use-case models which has been validated using two comparative user tests demonstrating the advantages of the proposed model with respect to a similar state-of-the-art framework. This mapping has also been used by Arnab et al. [24] to validate the relationship between the learning mechanics and game mechanics implemented in the PREPARe game, which has undergone a cluster randomized control trial that concluded positive learning outcomes. The mapping framework considers pedagogical elements as an abstract interface while game elements are deemed as a concrete interface of SGs. Clear definition of such relationship will allow meaningful learning engagement during game play to be correctly tracked and assessed. This definition will contribute towards the definition of data to be tracked and processed by the LAM in Fig. 3.

4.4   User Modelling and Adaptive Modelling

User modelling will include cognitive models, prior knowledge and learning preferences, while adaptive modelling will involve adapting content, mechanics, dynamics, and aesthetics with regards to the specific user profiling. By understanding the relationship between learning preferences and the learning content presented within the game environment, we could advance a more personalized solution. The need to personalize and adapt learning experiences to different learning abilities, and preferences at user level necessitates the development of user models that encompass the specificities of each learner and provide critical input for engagement strategies.

User models abstract the distinctive features of a user, so that they can be continuously updated by the game-based environment while giving input to a personalization engine, which adapts the contents and their provision modalities to the elicited requirements. User model methods have been widely employed in the context of Intelligent Tutoring Systems, Adaptive Hypermedia Systems, which can be adapted to support user modelling in games for learning in conjunction with the GLEANER framework (Fig. 3). The major example of SG using user modelling for interactive learning has been implemented in the Travel in Europe (TiE) and SeaGame projects [35]. User models abstract the distinctive features of a user, so that it can be continuously updated by the game-based environment while giving input to a personalization engine, which adapts the contents and their provision modalities to the elicited requirements. User model methods have been widely used in the context of Intelligent Tutoring Systems, Adaptive Hypermedia Systems, which can be adapted to support user modelling in games for learning in conjunction with the GLEANER framework (Fig. 3). The major example of SG using user modelling for interactive learning has been implemented in the Travel in Europe (TiE) and SeaGame projects [35].

5   Conclusions and Future Work

ICT solutions such as learning management systems (LMSs), e-learning and game-based learning platforms are widely being deployed in schools, universities and training institutions. The efficient use of ICT should enable the use of less resources, while providing a wider applicability and interoperability within the existing infrastructure. The ICT solution should also be user friendly and adaptive to maximize the use and scalability of the solution. And most importantly, the use of such solution should be evidence-based, where performance can be effectively monitored and personalization could be carried out to support the needs of the users.

ICT should not only be a platform for learning, but also to support strategic evaluation and monitoring of the needs of both learners and teachers/instructors. With the use of Learning Analytics, the proposed model aims to optimize ICT learning platforms and maximize usability and impact on the existing teaching and learning system. Learning Analytics emphasizes on the measurement and data collection as activities that educational organizations need to undertake and understand, focuses on the analysis and reporting of the data, which will subsequently allow actionable steps and measures to be designed to overcome potential issues or weaknesses. The use of a visual representation of analytics is critical to generate actionable analyses and information represented in an easily digestible form. Strengths of the existing teaching and learning could also be highlighted, serving as a great incentive to the organizations involved.

The proposed model answers to the challenge of how to best collect, measure and analyze dynamic datasets and utilize the analysis to predict the best teaching approach for the individual learners and adapt their experience, whether within a virtual learning environment or the actual physical delivery/deployment. The implementation of such a model will present an opportunity for future evaluation of how the analytics and adaptation affects the learning experience in a user study by comparing the adapted learning experience with a control group using a default non-adapted version of the teaching and learning strategy or of the same serious game. The potential deployment evaluations will include empirical studies, such as cluster randomized control trials (c-RCT) – with intervention and without intervention for both scenarios: game-based learning environment and the classroom teaching environment (pre and post surveys, questionnaires, analysis of in-game data, analysis of classroom performance, etc.)). Intervention in this case will be the scaffolded support based on the proposed model. In addition to experimental or quasi-experimental impact analysis, the evaluation could adopt a mixed method approach to explore changes in other important dimensions that may result from the engagement with the ecosystem, including but not limited to: (i) Changes in teaching practices, including changes in subject-specific and cross-curricular pedagogic approaches; (ii) Changes in patterns of homework/schoolwork among students, (iii) Changes in school-level approaches to curriculum design and implementation; and (iv) Changes in perceptions and attitudes among students in relation to interests and aspirations.

This opportunity will potentially affect the design and deployment of education and training in the future. The vast amount of data that is being collected about students also has policy implications in addition to technical ones. The investigation of how the collection and analysis of this educational data fits current institutional policies as well as European guidelines and ethical procedures can also be carried out. The availability of this type of data in different countries presents a unique opportunity. Not only will it be possible to investigate differences between countries and more accurately map and translate qualifications between countries, it will also have the potential to reveal differences between educational institutions and countries in terms of effectiveness. While beyond the scope of this paper, the potential impact could include the raising and harmonizing of the quality of education among different member states by sharing best practices scientifically supported by empirical statistical evidence of their effectiveness.

Acknowledgments. This work has been co-funded by the EU under the FP7, in the Games and Learning Alliance (GALA) Network of Excellence, Grant Agreement nr. 258169, and the SCAFFOLD consortium.

References

1. ET 2020. http://europa.eu/legislation_summaries/education_training_youth/general_framework/ef0016_en.htm
2. Silva, E.: Measuring skills for 21st-century learning. Phi Delta Kappan **90**(9), 630–634 (2009)

3. Ananiadou, K., Claro, M.: 21st Century Skills and Competencies for New Millennium Learners in OECD Countries (2009). http://www.oecd-ilibrary.org/education/21st-century-skills-and-competences-for-new-millennium-learners-in-oecd-countries_218525261154. Accessed 16 March 2013
4. Salpeter, J.: 21st Century Skills: Will our students be prepared? (2008). http://dca1to1.pbworks.com/f/21st+Century+-+will+our+students+be+prepared.pdf. Accessed 15 March 2013
5. Dede, C.: Comparing frameworks for 21st Century Skills (2009). http://dca1to1.pbworks.com/f/21st+Century+-+will+our+students+be+prepared.pdf. Accessed 15 March 2013
6. Eurydice Report. Developing Key Competencies at School in Europe: Challenges and Opportunities for Policy (2012). http://eacea.ec.europa.eu/education/eurydice/documents/thematic_reports/145EN.pdf. Accessed 17 March 2013
7. Wood, D., Brunet, J., Ross, G.: The role of tutoring in problem solving. J. Child Psychol. Psychiatry Allied Disciplines **17**, 89–100 (1976)
8. Vygotsky, L.S.: Mind in society: the development of higher mental processes. In: Cole, M., John-Steiner, V., Scribner, S., Soubeman, E. (eds.). Harvard University Press, Cambridge (1978)
9. Kolb, D.A.: Experiential Learning: Experience as the Source of Learning and Development. Prentice-Hall, Englewood Cliffs (1984)
10. Coffield, F.: Learning styles and pedagogy in post-16 learning: a systematic and critical review (2004)
11. Ferguson, R.: The state of learning analytics in 2012: a review and future challenges. Technical report KMI-12-01, Knowledge Media Institute, The Open University, UK (2012)
12. Ali, L., Hatala, M., Gašević, D., Jovanović, E.: A qualitative evaluation of evolution of a learning analytics tool. Comput. Educ. **58**(1), 470–489 (2012)
13. Dawson, S., Bakharia, A., Heathcate, E.: SNAPP: realising the affordance of real-time SNA within networked learning. In: Proceedings of the 7th International Conference on Networked Learning, Aalborg, Denmark, pp. 125–133 (2012)
14. The JRC Scientific and Technical Report Born Digital/Grown Digital: Assessing the Future Competitiveness of the EU Video Games Software Industry, EUR 24555 En-2010
15. Buckingham Shum, S., Ferguson, R.: Social learning analytics. Educ. Technol. Soc. **15**(3), 3–26 (2012)
16. Garris, R., Ahlers, R., Driskell, J.E.: Games, Motivation, and Learning: A Research and Practice Model. Simul. Gaming **33**, 441–467 (2002)
17. Panzoli, D., Qureshi, A., Dunwell, I., Petridis, P., de Freitas, S., Rebolledo-Mendez, G.: Levels of interaction (LoI): a model for scaffolding learner engagement in an immersive environment. In: Aleven, V., Kay, J., Mostow, J. (eds.) ITS 2010, Part II. LNCS, vol. 6095, pp. 393–395. Springer, Heidelberg (2010)
18. de Freitas, S.: Game for change. Nature **470**(7334), 330–331 (2011)
19. Mautone, P.D., Spiker, V.A., Karp, M.R.: Using serious game technology to improve aircrew training. In: Proceedings of the Interservice/Industry Training, Simulation and Education Conference (IITSEC) (2008)
20. McGonigal, J.: Reality is Broken: Why Games Make us Better and How They can Change the World. Jonathan Cape, London (2008)
21. Knight, J., Carly, S., Tregunna, B., Jarvis, S., Smithies, R., de Freitas, S., Mackway-Jones, K., Dunwell, I.: Serious gaming technology in major incident triage training: a pragmatic controlled trial. Resuscitation J. **81**(9), 1174–1179 (2010)
22. Kato, P.M., Cole, S.W., et al.: A video game improves behavioral outcomes in adolescents and young adults with cancer: a randomized trial. Pediatrics **122**(2), 305–317 (2008)

23. Rebolledo-Mendez, G., Avramides, K., de Freitas, S., Memarzia, K.: Societal impact of a serious game on raising public awareness: the case of FloodSim. In: Proceedings of the 2009 ACM SIGGRAPH Symposium on Video Games, New Orleans, Louisiana, pp. 15–22 (2009)
24. Arnab, S., Brown, K., Clarke, S., Dunwell, I., Lim, T., Suttie, N., Louchart, S., Hendrix, M., de Freitas, S.: The development approach of a pedagogically-driven serious game to support relationship and sex education (RSE) within a classroom setting. Comput. Educ. **69**, 15–30 (2013)
25. Davenport, T.H.: Competing on analytics. Harvard Bus. Rev. **84**(1), 98–107 (2008)
26. Peters, V.A.M., Vissers, G.A.N.: A simple classification model for debriefing simulation games. Simul. Gaming **35**(1), 70–84 (2008)
27. Shute, V.J.: Stealth assessment in computer-based games to support learning. In: Tobias, S., Fletcher, J.D. (eds.) Computer Games and Instruction, pp. 503–523. Information Age Publishers, Charlotte (2011)
28. Kiili, K., de Freitas, S., Arnab, S., Lainema, T.: The design principles for flow experience in educational games. Procedia Comput. Sci. **15**, 78–91 (2012)
29. Bienkowski, M., Feng, M., Means, B.: Enhancing Teaching and Learning Through Educational Data Mining and Learning Analytics: An Issue Brief, pp. 1–57. Office of Educational Technology, U.S. Department of Education, Washington, DC (2012)
30. Serrano-Laguna, Á., Marchiori, E.J., et al.: A framework to improve evaluation in educational games. In: Proceedings of the IEEE Engineering Education Conference (EDUCON), Marrakesh, Morocco, April 2011
31. Keim, D.A., Andrienko, G., Fekete, J.-D., Görg, C., Kohlhammer, J., Melançon, G.: Visual analytics: definition, process, and challenges. In: Kerren, A., Stasko, J.T., Fekete, J.-D., North, C. (eds.) Information Visualization. LNCS, vol. 4950, pp. 154–175. Springer, Heidelberg (2008)
32. Whitton, N.: Game engagement theory and adult learning. Simul. Gaming **42**(5), 596–609 (2011)
33. Fredricks, J.A., Blumenfeld, P.C., Paris, A.H.: School engagement: potential of the concept, state of the evidence. Rev. Educ. Res. **74**(1), 59–109 (2004)
34. Lim, T., Louchart, S., Suttie, N., Ritchie, J.M., Aylett, R.S., Stănescu, I.A., Roceanu, I., Martinez-Ortiz, I., Moreno-Ger, P.: Strategies for effective digital games development and implementation. In: Baek, Y., Whitton, N. (eds.) Cases on Digital Game-Based Learning: Methods, Models, and Strategies, pp. 168–198. IGI Global, Hershey (2012). doi: 10.4018/978-1-4666-2848-9.ch010
35. Bellotti, F., Berta, R., De Gloria, A., Primavera, L.: Adaptive experience engine for serious games. IEEE Trans. Comput. Intell. AI Games **1**(4), 264–280 (2009)
36. Brown, M.: Learning Analytics: Moving from Concept to Practice. EDUCAUSE Learning Initiative Briefing (2012)

The Journey: A Service-Based Adaptive Serious Game on Probability

Maira B. Carvalho[1]([✉]), Francesco Bellotti[1], Riccardo Berta[1],
Francesco Curatelli[1], Alessandro De Gloria[1], Giorgia Gazzarata[1], Jun Hu[2],
Michael Kickmeier-Rust[3], and Chiara Martinengo[4]

[1] DITEN, University of Genoa, Via Opera Pia 11A, 16145 Genoa, Italy
`maira.carvalho@elios.unige.it`
[2] Department of Industrial Design, Eindhoven University of Technology,
P.O. Box 513, 5600, MB Eindhoven, Netherlands
[3] Knowledge Technologies Institute, Graz University of Technology,
Inffeldgasse 13/5th Floor, 8010 Graz, Austria
[4] DIMA, University of Genoa, Via Dodecaneso 35, 16146 Genoa, Italy

Abstract. Serious Games (SGs) have a lot of potential in education, possibly making learning more engaging and satisfying. Adaptive Games strive to keep the challenges presented by the game balanced with the player's abilities, as to keep the player in the "flow" state. We have used a Service-Oriented Architecture (SOA) approach to develop a simple adaptive SG for teaching basic elements of probability to high school and entry-level university students, called *The Journey*. The game performs continuously the updating of a user model with the competences of the student and presents the new challenges according to the student's current level. This paper presents details of the educational aspects of the game, as well as of its implementation. It also presents a preliminary validation study and discusses future work.

1 Introduction

Games are being more and more recognized by their importance in education and training settings. Serious Games (SGs) have been shown to have a lot of potential in education [1], making learning more engaging and satisfying than in traditional educational settings [2,3]. More attention is being given to meaningful insertion of games in curricula [4], to supporting authors and educators in the development of SGs [5,6] also in specific situations such as users with motor and cognitive disabilities [7,8], and to appropriately connecting pedagogical practices to the game mechanics [9] in order to create more effective games.

Motivation plays a crucial role in learning, and thus it is important that the learning environment provide the player with an appropriate level of challenge, always balancing on the limits of the learner's competences and skills [3]. Adaptive serious games draw on the research on Intelligent Tutoring Systems and Adaptive Hypermedia to create a personalized learning experience, which has been shown to be beneficial in terms of motivation and learning outcomes [10].

© Springer International Publishing Switzerland 2015
A. De Gloria (Ed.): GALA 2014, LNCS 9221, pp. 97–106, 2015.
DOI: 10.1007/978-3-319-22960-7_10

In this paper, we present *The Journey*, an adaptive serious game for teaching basic elements of probability to high school and entry-level university students, and also report the results of a preliminary evaluation of the game. *The Journey* has been developed following a Service Oriented Architecture (SOA) approach, in which software is built as a set of independent components that are loosely coupled to deliver certain functionalities.

This paper is organized as follows. In Sect. 2, we discuss the basic concepts of adaptive SGs. In Sect. 3, we present the benefits of the SOA approach in SG development and list a few examples. In Sect. 4, we explain the Competence-based Knowledge Space Theory (CbKST) and how it can be used in adaptive SGs. In Sect. 5 we describe the game in detail. Section 6 describes the evaluation of the game. Finally, we present a conclusion and discuss future work on the topic.

2   Adaptive Serious Games

Research in Adaptive Serious Games has roots in the fields of Intelligent Tutoring Systems (ITS) and Adaptive Hypermedia, both with an established tradition in using technology to provide personalized experiences [10]. Inspired by Bloom's findings in the superior performance of tailored tutoring when compared to regular teaching [11], psychologists, educationists, and technicians started to develop technology to take the role of a private teacher and to intelligently provide learners with suitable tutoring. [12]

The concept of "flow" is central to educational game development: the game should provide an adequate level of challenge to the player, neither too hard, causing frustration, nor too easy, causing boredom [3]. A meta-review of more than 300 scientific articles on the educational efficacy of computer games found out that 90 % of the games that reported non-trivial educational results bear some form of educational adaptation or personalization [13]. These results are in line with experimental findings that demonstrated that adaptation results in superior gaming experience and educational gains [14].

The adaptation to be realized in-game can be different from that of traditional virtual environments. Steiner et al. [15] argue that, in this case, subtle ways of adaptation are needed, basing assessment on continuous input and output of information about the learner. Shute and Ke [16] discuss the concept of "stealth assessment", in which learning assessment happens without disrupting the game flow, using observable evidences to infer knowledge, skills or other attributes.

3   Service Oriented Architecture for SG Development

A Service-Oriented Architecture (SOA) is a set of recommendations, policies and practices for software architectural design which implements business processes by using loosely coupled components which are arranged to deliver a certain level of service or set of functionalities [17]. The goal is to manage the complexity of large systems by employing modularization and compositionality [18].

The benefits of using a SOA approach are many, from the reuse of services without the need for code replication to the establishment of formal obligations between service consumer and provider [18]. There are challenges in adopting a SOA approach as well, mostly related to increased complexities in testing and quality assurance processes [17], and the crucial role played by appropriate documentation and definition and description of service interfaces, which, when missing or lacking in quality, can cause difficulties in the development [19].

In game development, a SOA approach can enable easier scalability and usage-dependent payment model. It also releases the games from the dependency on gaming hardware. Providing pervasive gaming experiences becomes easier, as support for different platforms is highly simplified if the core of the gaming experience is service-based [20].

Despite the benefits, current examples of SGs and related technologies that employ SOA are very few. The *Rashi Intelligent Tutoring System*, which teaches human anatomy through a problem-based environment, is built as a web service architecture [21]. The envisioned *Mobile Augmented Reality (MARL)* gaming platform would use a service-based architecture to provide on-demand location-based instruction through a head-mount display [22]. The Serious Games Society has developed the *Serious Games Web Services Catalog* (http://services. seriousgamessociety.org), a repository of web services with documentation and example applications.

4   CbKST Services

The CbKST services' approach to formative, competence-centered assessment is inherited from the Knowledge Space Theory (KST) and the Competence-based Knowledge Space Theory (CbKST) [23]. It assumes a finite set of atomic competences (aptitude, ability, knowledge, or skill) and a prerequisite relation between them, which defines the competence model of the domain. Due to the prerequisite relations, not all subsets of competences are possible competence states. A person's level of knowledge, ability or proficiency is described, theoretically, by exactly one competence state.

The structural model focuses on unobservable competences, making hypotheses about the brain's black box. By utilizing interpretation (p, in Fig. 1) and representation functions (q), the unobservable competences are mapped to observable evidences relevant for a given domain. No one-to-one correspondence is required to link competences to the indicators. CbKST considers indicators on a probability-based level, in order to account for the fact that indicators cannot be perfect evidence for the latent knowledge or ability.

The CbKST services are part of the ProNIFA tools of the ECAAD methodology, in the scope of the NEXT-TELL (http://www.next-tell.eu) and ROLE (http://www.role-project.eu) projects. The Compod services, which were used for this study, are research prototypes and are available online in the NEXT-TELL project website.

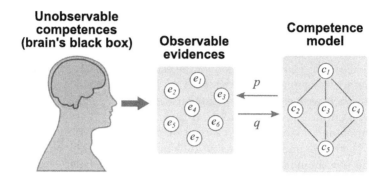

Fig. 1. Interpretation and representation functions in the CbKST model.

5   The Journey

5.1   The Game

The Journey is a simple serious game to teach and train basic concepts of probability theory to high school and entry-level university students. It was developed at the University of Genoa as a prototype implementation of a service-based adaptive SG, employing the CbKST services to provide basic adaptation features. Being a prototype, the game can be further developed in the future.

In the game, the player represents the head of a group of hikers who wants to reach the top of a mountain chain. Players have to understand how to calculate the probabilities of events that are related to the journey, and also use their knowledge to make the best possible decisions along the way.

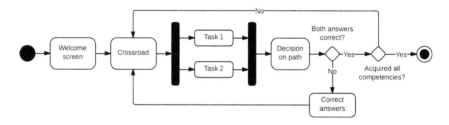

Fig. 2. Game sequence

The game sequence, represented in Fig. 2, is as follows. After the introduction, the player reaches a crossroad (Fig. 3). Two paths are presented, each with different probabilities of success and different lengths. After calculating the probabilities for each path, the player must choose a way. If she calculated the probabilities correctly, the system decides on the success of the choice, following the probability distribution of that path. If successful, the group moves forward to the next crossroad; if not, they have to go back and try the other path. If the

Fig. 3. The crossroads screen of *The Journey*.

player calculates one or both probabilities incorrectly, the game shows the correct answers and takes her back to the crossroad, where a new set of tasks is presented. The process repeats until the end of the game.

We now describe the game using the elements presented by Game Ontology Project [24]. *The Journey* has a **User Interface** based on **Indirect Manipulation**, as decisions are made via a **Menu Interface**. The **Input Device** is the mouse. It shows a **Challenge Segmentation** of gameplay, implemented as **Puzzles**. **Randomness** is also used.

There are two **Goals** in the game: (1) reaching the end of the journey as fast as possible (explicit goal) and (2) acquiring all the competences (not communicated to the player). Similarly, there are two **Goal Metrics**: **Time** and **Score**. The "faster" the player is (in the game's internal time), the higher the score. The score also depends on the performance of the player in the tasks.

5.2 Learning, Assessment and Feedback

The competence model of the game is composed of the following competences and their dependencies:

1. **Probability Space.** The learner understands the relationship of a collection of events and their probability measure within a sample space. The learner is able to estimate the probability of an event from data of observed outcomes. The learner is able to derive that $P(\neg A) = 1 - P(A)$. No dependencies.
2. **Probability of Mutually Exclusive Events.** The learner understands the relationship between two mutually exclusive events in the same probability space, which can be represented by the formulas $P(A \cap B) = 0$ and $P(A \cup B) = P(A) + P(B)$. Depends on competence 1.

3. **Probability of Non Mutually Exclusive Events.** The learner understands that when there are two non-mutually exclusive events in the same probability space ($P(A \cap B) \neq 0$), they can be represented by the formula $P(A \cup B) = P(A) + P(B) - P(A \cap B)$. Depends on competence 1.

4. **Probability of Independent Events.** The learner understands that the probability of two consecutive and independent events is calculated using the formula $P(A \cap B) = P(A) \times P(B)$. Depends on competence 1.

5. **Probability of Dependent Events.** The learner understands that the probability of two consecutive events is calculated differently when the one of the events is dependent on the other. In that case, $P(A \cap B) = P(A) \times P(B|A)$, and consequently, $P(B|A) = P(A \cap B)/P(A)$. Depends on competences 2, 3 and 4.

In the game database, there is a set of tasks for each competence in the model. See below one example question, which refers to the competence Probability space. The values inside the curly brackets are generated by the game.

Up to now, {n} people tried to take this path, but only {x} of them managed to get through. Based on this sample, what is the estimated probability of arriving at your destination through this path?

The concrete implementation of the learning process in "The Journey" is, therefore, via the mechanism of Questions & Answers. The game provides guidance via hints, shown after 3 min of inactivity while working on the tasks.

There are two levels of reasoning that are expected from the player: (1) solving the problems correctly; and (2) deciding which direction to take, considering time and probability of success. Table 1 details how the game supports each of the levels of Bloom's revised taxonomy of learning goals in the cognitive domain [25].

The assessment is based on the answers that the player gives to the challenges, which are sent to the CbKST service. The service updates its model of the player's competences, selects the next tasks that are appropriate to the user's level, and replies to the game suggesting the IDs of the next challenges to be presented to the player. The tasks are chosen from the pool of tasks for that competence. Once all the competences in the model have been acquired, the service informs the game that there are no more tasks, and the group reaches their destination, ending the game.

Feedback is offered to the player only with regard to the answers to the tasks. If the player answers the tasks incorrectly, the game will inform so and offer the correct answers, with the explanation of how to calculate the probabilities correctly. The representation of the competence model itself is not made visible to the player inside the game.

5.3   Implementation Architecture

The Journey has been developed following a Service Oriented Architecture (SOA) approach. It is a Flash Desktop Application using Starling, an ActionScript 3

Table 1. Levels of Bloom's cognitive learning goals covered by "The Journey"

Learning Goal	How the game supports the level
Remembering	Memorizing is not required, as the game shows relevant formulas when needed. Nevertheless, repetition helps remembering.
Understanding	The player needs to understand how the concepts and formulas are relevant to solve the task.
Applying	The player needs to interpret the values of probability distributions and apply that knowledge when making decisions.
Analysing	The player must be able to analyze the information available in the task to be able to apply the correct formulas.
Evaluating	Weakly supported, when the player is asked to choose between paths. To support it more explicitly, in class it could be asked of a student to explicitly justify her choices.
Creating	Not supported

2D framework, for the graphical interface. It is connected to a local SQLite database, which holds the list of tasks for the game and the profile information of each player, and it access the CbKST adaptation service via a REST interface (Fig. 4).

The CbKST service has to be configured in advance with a representation of the competence model. The service does not hold any information about the game tasks, except for the relationship between the tasks IDs and the competences in the model. In addition, the service does not hold information about the players other than their IDs, which is passed to the service in the beginning of a learning session. While the learning session is open, the service holds an instance of the competence state of each player currently using the game, which can be deleted once the learning session is closed. A report on the learning session can be generate when requested.

The source code of the game is available online at http://www.bitbucket.org/elioslab/thejourney.

6   Validation

We performed a preliminary validation of the game in a study with 10 participants (6 males, 4 females) aged between 19 and 21 years old. Participants were asked to play *The Journey* for a maximum of 20 min and to complete identical pre and post-tests, with ten multiple choice questions covering all five competences targeted by the game. In addition, the players were observed during the tests to identify possible usability issues with the game interface.

All participants showed an increase of at least one point in the post-test scores, with an average improvement in the final scores of 1.8 points. Although this study was too small to be considered statistically significant, we were encouraged by the positive preliminary results. The usability issues that were identified

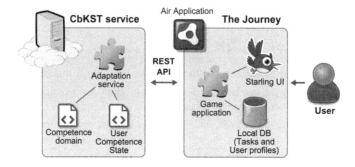

Fig. 4. The architecture of the game.

will be improved for the release of a new version, when a larger user experiment will be carried out to evaluate learning effects.

7   Conclusion and Future Work

In this paper we described the concepts, structure and software implementation of *The Journey*, a serious game to teach probability to high school and entry-level university students, which employs the SOA approach and utilizes a service based on the Competence-based Knowledge Space Theory (CbKST) to realize in-game adaptation. We also reported the results of a preliminary evaluation, which will be used in the development of future versions of the game.

We defend the application of a SOA approach as beneficial for the field of serious games development. SOA can improve the development process through components reuse and enhance product quality by enabling the implementation of features, such as adaptivity, that are still rare in SGs. It also gives the SG developer a significant amount of freedom in the development, while still taking advantage of reusing high quality existing services.

The Journey is a prototype that was used to investigate the benefits and drawbacks of a service-oriented architecture for SG development. Its current implementation can be extended with different functionalities, such as the use of stealth assessment [16] and formative evaluation and feedback [26]. It would be possible, for example, to expose the competence model to teachers and to players via an assessment interface. Another interesting possibility is the creation of a richer learning environment that allows more than one learning technology or game to have access to the same competence model.

We hope that the SOA approach becomes more widespread in the field of SGs and that more developers embrace the possibilities brought by services that are already available.

Acknowledgements. This work has been partially funded by the EC, through the GALA EU Network of Excellence in Serious Games (FP7-ICT-2009-5-258169).

This work was supported in part by the Erasmus Mundus Joint Doctorate in Interactive and Cognitive Environments, which is funded by the EACEA Agency of the European Commission under EMJD ICE FPA n 2010-0012. This work is partially supported by the European Commission (EC) under the Information Society Technology priority of the 7th Framework Programme for Research and Development under contract no 258114 NEXT-TELL.

References

1. van Eck, R.: Digital game-based learning: it's not just the digital natives who are restless. EDUCAUSE Rev. **41**(2), 16–30 (2006)
2. Bellotti, F., Berta, R., De Gloria, A.: Designing effective serious games: opportunities and challenges for research. Int. J. Emerg. Technol. Learn. (iJET) **5**(SI3), 22–35 (2010)
3. Kickmeier-Rust, M.D., Albert, D.: Educationally adaptive: balancing serious games. Int. J. Comput. Sci. sport **11**(1), 1–10 (2012)
4. Hauge, J.B., Bellotti, F., Kickmeier-rust, M., Berta, R., Carvalho, M.B.: Deploying serious games for management in higher education: lessons learned and good practices. In: Escudeiro, P., de Carvalho, C.V. (eds.) Proceedings of the 7th European Conference on Games Based Learning, pp. 225–234 (2013)
5. Bellotti, F., Berta, R., De Gloria, A., Margarone, M.: MADE: developing edutainment applications on mobile computers. Comput. Graph. **27**(4), 617–634 (2003)
6. Bellotti, F., Berta, R., De Gloria, A., Primavera, L.: Supporting authors in the development of task-based learning in serious virtual worlds. Brit. J. Educ. Technol. **41**(1), 86–107 (2010)
7. Curatelli, F., Martinengo, C.: Design criteria for educational tools to overcome mathematics learning difficulties. Procedia Comput. Sci. **15**, 92–102 (2012)
8. Curatelli, F., Bellotti, F., Berta, R., Martinengo, C.: Paths for cognitive rehabilitation: from reality to educational software, to serious games, to reality again. In: De Gloria, A. (ed.) GALA 2013. LNCS, vol. 8605, pp. 172–186. Springer, Heidelberg (2014)
9. Arnab, S., Lim, T., Carvalho, M.B., Bellotti, F., de Freitas, S., Louchart, S., Suttie, N., Berta, R., De Gloria, A.: Mapping learning and game mechanics for serious games analysis. Br. J. Educ. Technol. **46**(2), 391–411 (2015). doi:10.1111/bjet.12113
10. Peirce, N., Conlan, O., Wade, V.: Adaptive educational games: providing non-invasive personalised learning experiences. In: 2008 Second IEEE International Conference on Digital Game and Intelligent Toy Enhanced Learning, pp. 28–35 (2008)
11. Bloom, B.S.: The 2 sigma problem: the search for methods of group instruction as effective as one-to-one tutoring. Educ. Researcher **13**(6), 4–16 (1984)
12. De Bra, P.: Adaptive hypermedia. In: Adelsberger, H., Kinshuk, Pawlowski, J., Sampson, D. (eds.) Handbook on Information Technologies for Education and Training SE - 2. International Handbooks on Information Systems, pp. 29–46. Springer, Heidelberg (2008)
13. Kickmeier-Rust, M., Göbel, S., Albert, D.: 80Days: melding adaptive educational technology and adaptive and interactive Storytelling in digital educational games. In: Klamma, R., Sharda, N., Fernández-Manjón, B., Kosch, H., Spaniol, M. (eds.) Proceedings of the First International Workshop on Story-Telling and Educational Games (STEG'08), CEUR Workshop Proceedings, January 2008

14. Kickmeier-Rust, M.D., Marte, B., Linek, S., Lalonde, T., Albert, D.: The effects of individualized feedback in digital educational games. In: Proceedings of the 2nd European Conference on Games Based Learning, pp. 227–236 (2008)
15. Steiner, C.M., Kickmeier-Rust, M.D., Mattheiss, E., Göbel, S., Albert, D.: Balancing on a high wire: adaptivity key factor of future learning games. In: An Alien's Guide to Multi-Adaptive Educational Computer Games, p. 43 (2012)
16. Shute, V.J., Ke, F.: Games, learning, and assessment. In: Ifenthaler, D., Eseryel, D., Ge, X. (eds.) Assessment in Game-Based Learning, pp. 43–58. Springer, New York (2012)
17. Hurwitz, J., Bloor, R., Baroudi, C., Kaufman, M.: Service Oriented Architecture For Dummies. Wiley, Hoboken (2007)
18. Sprott, D., Wilkes, L.: Understanding service-oriented architecture. Archit. J. 1(1), 10–17 (2004)
19. Papazoglou, M.P., Traverso, P., Dustdar, S., Leymann, F.: Service-oriented computing: state of the art and research challenges. Computer 40(11), 38–45 (2007)
20. Hassan, M.M., Hossain, M.S., Alamri, A., Hossain, M.A., Al-Qurishi, M., Aldukhayyil, Y., Ahmed, D.T.: A cloud-based serious games framework for obesity. Proceedings of the 1st ACM multimedia international workshop on Cloud-based multimedia applications and services for e-health (CMBAS-EH '12), p. 15. ACM Press, New York (2012)
21. Floryan, M., Woolf, B.P.: Optimizing the performance of educational web services. In: 2011 IEEE 11th International Conference on Advanced Learning Technologies, pp. 399–400. IEEE, July 2011
22. Doswell, J., Harmeyer, K.: Extending the 'Serious Game' boundary: virtual instructors in mobile mixed reality learning games. In: Proceedings of the 3rd Digital Games Research Association International Conference - DiGRA 2007, pp. 524–529 (2007)
23. Kickmeier-Rust, M.D., Albert, D.: An Alien's Guide to Multi-Adaptive Educational Computer Games. Informing Science Press, Santa Rosa (2012)
24. Zagal, J.P., Bruckman, A., Computing, C.: The game ontology project : supporting learning while contributing authentically to game studies. In: Proceedings of the 8th International Conference on International Conference for the Learning Sciences (ICLS'08), pp. 499–506 (2007)
25. Anderson, L.W., Krathwohl, D.R., Bloom, B.S.: A Taxonomy for Learning, Teaching, and Assessing: A Revision of Bloom's Taxonomy of Educational Objectives. Longman, New York (2001)
26. Bellotti, F., Kapralos, B., Lee, K., Moreno-Ger, P., Berta, R.: Assessment in and of serious games: an overview. Adv. Hum.-Comput. Interact. 2013, 1–11 (2013)

Improved Multimodal Emotion Recognition for Better Game-Based Learning

Kiavash Bahreini$^{(\boxtimes)}$, Rob Nadolski, and Wim Westera

Welten Institute, Research Centre for Learning, Teaching and Technology,
Faculty of Psychology and Educational Sciences,
Open University of the Netherlands, Valkenburgerweg 177,
6419 Heerlen, AT, The Netherlands
{kiavash.bahreini,rob.nadolski,wim.westera}@ou.nl

Abstract. This paper introduces the integration of the face emotion recognition part and the voice emotion recognition part of our FILTWAM framework that uses webcams and microphones. This framework enables real-time multimodal emotion recognition of learners during game-based learning for triggering feedback towards improved learning. The main goal of this study is to validate the integration of webcam and microphone data for a real-time and adequate interpretation of facial and vocal expressions into emotional states where the software modules are calibrated with end users. This integration aims to improve timely and relevant feedback, which is expected to increase learners' awareness of their own behavior. Twelve test persons received the same computer-based tasks in which they were requested to mimic specific facial and vocal expressions. Each test person mimicked 80 emotions, which led to a dataset of 960 emotions. All sessions were recorded on video. An overall accuracy of Kappa value based on the requested emotions, expert opinions, and the recognized emotions is 0.61, of the face emotion recognition software is 0.76, and of the voice emotion recognition software is 0.58. A multimodal fusion between the software modules can increase the accuracy to 78 %. In contrast with existing software our software modules allow real-time, continuously and unobtrusively monitoring of learners' face expressions and voice intonations and convert these into emotional states. This inclusion of learner's emotional states paves the way for more effective, efficient and enjoyable game-based learning.

Keywords: Game-based learning · Human-computer interaction · Multimodal emotion recognition · Real-time emotion recognition · Affective computing · Webcam · Microphone

1 Introduction

Recent technologies have been adopted by e-learning experts for improving the efficiency, effectiveness and enjoyableness of e-learning [1]. Currently, learners are habitually accustomed to the web-based delivery of e-learning content when communicating, working and learning together with their peers in distributed (a)synchronous settings [2]. It is broadly acknowledged that emotions are important in all learning activities, as they affect information processing, memory usage and performance [3].

© Springer International Publishing Switzerland 2015
A. De Gloria (Ed.): GALA 2014, LNCS 9221, pp. 107–120, 2015.
DOI: 10.1007/978-3-319-22960-7_11

This study is part of our research [4–6] that aims at improving multimodal emotion recognition for better online game-based learning but that can also be applied in e-learning. Game-based learning has several advantages: (1) it is a didactical approach that looks to be in-line with the learners' interests [7], (2) can be very effective for skills training [8], (3) encouraging [9], and (4) it is very fashionable most recently [7]. Learners' vocal and visual input to the technology can be used via a game-approach for enhancing their learning experience. This learning experience therefore becomes more informal, though not pure entertainment. A delicate balance between game play and learning is important [10]. Especially the training of recurrent skills might benefit from a game-based approach, as these require frequent practice where individuals remain to be motivated [11]. Furthermore, as skills training are time-consuming, technology could alleviate the workload of trainers and might also lead to improved face-to-face training as trainers can focus on the training of non-recurrent skills [12]. To accomplish this purpose, the here described and tested software technology from FILTWAM will ultimately be combined with a game-based didactical approach. FILTWAM will be combined with EMERGO for mainly practical reasons. EMERGO is an in-house developed and tested methodology, and open source toolkit for the development and delivery of serious games [13].

FILTWAM uses webcams and microphones to interpret the emotional state of people during their interactions with a game-based learning environment via an affective computing tool. It triggers timely feedback based upon learner's facial expressions and verbalizations. It is designed for distinguishing the following emotions: happiness, sadness, surprise, fear, disgust, anger, and neutral. It mainly offers software with a human-machine interface for the real time interpretation of emotion that can be applied in game-based learning and e-learning. The study is a follow up of our previous studies [4–6]. It aims at extending our game-based learning setting for multimodal emotion recognition. For this, the affective computing tool is composed of face and voice emotion recognition modules. The affective computing tool represents the development of a software system, which is able to recognize and interpret human emotions. The affective computing tool of FILTWAM is built upon existing research [14–17]. Linking two modalities (face expression and voice intonation) into a single system for affective computing analysis is not new and has been studied before [18–21]. A review study by [22] shows that the accuracy of detecting one or more basic emotions is significantly improved when both visual and audio information are used in classification, leading to accuracy levels between 72 % and 85 %.

Although digital learning is widely used true interaction with digital learning artifacts, it is still limited despite the recent developments of input devices. Webcams and microphones not only offer opportunities for more natural interactions with digital learning artifacts (like serious games) but also offer ways of unobtrusively gathering affective user data during learning process.

We performed one of the most widely used linear fusion method in this study that has been reported in [23]. We propose (1) an unobtrusive approach that supports (2) a real-time interpretation of emotion with (3) an objective method that can be verified by researchers, which requires (4) inexpensive and ubiquitous equipment, and offers (5) two interactive software modules.

In this paper, Sect. 2 introduces the FILTWAM framework and its sub-components. The methodological setup of the validation of the software modules is described in Sect. 3. Results and discussion are presented in Sect. 4. Section 5 discusses the findings and limitations of this study and proposes future improvements.

2 The FILTWAM Framework

The FILTWAM framework includes five layers and a number of sub-components within the layers (see Fig. 1). The five layers are introduced as the: (1) Learner, (2) Device, (3) Data, (4) Network, and (5) Application. We used EMERGO in conjunction with FILTWAM in this study; however FILTWAM can also be used with other game-based learning environments.

2.1 Learner Layer

The learner refers to a subject who uses web-based learning materials for personal development or preparing for an exam.

2.2 Device Layer

The device layer is the most important part of FILTWAM. The device reflects the learner's machine, whether part of a personal computer, a laptop, or a smart device. It includes a webcam and microphone for collecting user data. It contains three sub-components named: the web interface, the EMERGO web service client, and the affective computing tool.

2.2.1 Web Interface

The web interface runs a serious game in the device layer and allows the learner to interact with the game components in the application layer. This component indirectly uses the EMERGO web service client. The web interface will receive the feedback/content through Internet and the game-based learning environment in application layer.

2.2.2 EMERGO Web Service Client

The EMERGO web service client uses the affective computing tool; calls the EMERGO web service in the application layer. It reads the affective data and broadcast the live stream including the face emotion recognition data and the voice emotion recognition data through Internet to the EMERGO web service.

2.2.3 Affective Computing Tool

The affective computing tool is the heart of FILTWAM. It processes the facial behavior and vocal intonations data of the learner. It consists of two components for the emotion recognition of both vocal and facial features. The emotion recognition of the vocal

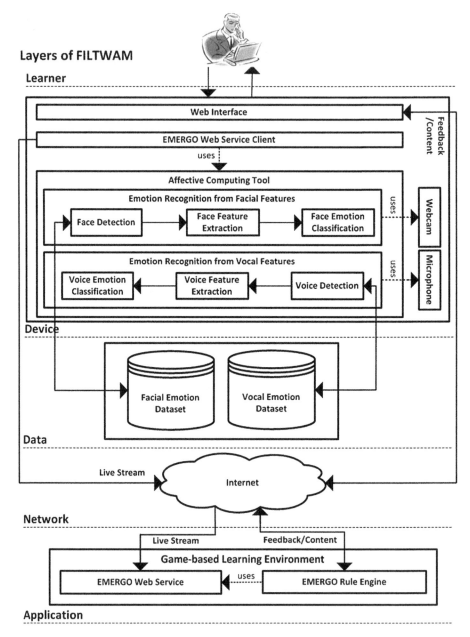

Fig. 1. The FILTWAM framework integrates the face emotion recognition module and the voice emotion recognition module in an online game-based environment. The face emotion recognition sub-component and the voice emotion recognition sub-component have been reported in our previous studies [4–6]).

features uses the microphone voice streams whereas the emotion recognition of the facial features uses the webcam face streams.

Emotion Recognition from Facial Features. This component extracts facial features from the face and classifies emotions. It includes three sub-components that lead to the recognition and categorization of a specific emotion.

Face Detection. The process of emotion recognition from facial features starts at the face detection component. But we do not necessarily want to recognize the particular face; instead we intend to detect a face and to recognize its facial emotions.

Facial Feature Extraction. Once the face is detected, the facial feature extraction component extracts a sufficient set of feature points of the learner. These feature points are considered as the significant features of the learner's face and can be automatically extracted.

Facial Emotion Classification. We adhere to a well-known emotion classification approach that has often been used over the past thirty years which focuses on classifying the six basic emotions [15]. Our facial emotion classification component supports the classification of these six basic emotions plus the neutral emotion, but can in principle also recognize other or more detailed face expressions when required. This component analyses video sequences and can extract an image for each frame for its analysis. This component is independent of race, age, gender, hairstyles, glasses, background, or beard and its development is based on the FaceTracker software [24]. During the analysis, one image that already includes a not-yet determined emotion is compared with all already classified images in the dataset. Then this image will be classified as one of the indicated emotions. It compares the classified emotions with existing emotions in the facial emotion dataset and trains the dataset using a number of learners' faces.

Emotion Recognition from Vocal Features. This component extracts vocal intonations from voices and classifies emotions. It includes three sub-components that lead to the recognition and categorization of a specific emotion.

Voice Detection. The process of emotion recognition from vocal intonations starts at the voice detection component. But we do not necessarily want to recognize the particular voice; instead we intend to detect a voice and to recognize its vocal emotions. This component divides the received voice signal into meaningful parts that will be used in voice feature extraction and voice emotion classification components.

Voice Feature Extraction. Once the voice is detected, the voice feature extraction component extracts a sufficient set of features from the voice of the learner. These features are considered as the significant features of the learner's voice and can be automatically extracted.

Voice Emotion Classification. We have used a similar emotion classification approach than with the facial emotion classification. This component analyses the voice stream and can extract a millisecond feature of each voice stream for its analysis. We used the sequential minimal optimization (SMO)[1] classifier of WEKA[2] software, which is a software tool for data mining.

2.3   Data Layer

The data layer is another separated layer within the FILTWAM. It physically stores the facial and the vocal datasets of the emotions. This layer reflects the intelligent capital of the system and provides a statistical reference for the detection of emotions.

2.4   Network Layer

The network layer uses the Internet to broadcast a live stream of the learner and to receive the feedback from the learner.

2.5   Application Layer

The application layer is the second most important part of FILTWAM. It consists of the game-based learning environment (e.g., EMERGO) and its two sub-components. The game-based learning environment uses the live stream of the facial and the vocal data of the learner to facilitate the learning process. Its sub-components named: the EMERGO rule engine and the EMERGO web service.

2.5.1   EMERGO Rule Engine
The EMERGO rule engine component manages didactical rules and triggers the relevant rules for providing feedback as well as tuned training content to the learner via the device. The game-based learning environment component complies with a specific rule-based didactical approach for the training of the learners.

2.5.2   EMERGO Web Service
The EMERGO web service component receives emotional data from EMERGO web service client component. It provides the training content and feedback to the learner through EMERGO rule engine component. At this stage, the learner can receive a feedback based on his facial and vocal emotions.

3   Method

Our hypothesis is that data gathered via webcam and microphone can be reliably used to unobtrusively infer learners' emotional states. Real-time multimodal emotion recognition of learners can be used for triggering more personalized feedback towards improved online learning. For example, it can be used during online game-based training of communication skills.

---

[1] http://weka.sourceforge.net/doc.dev/weka/classifiers/functions/SMO.html.

[2] http://www.cs.waikato.ac.nz/ml/weka.

3.1   Participants

An e-mail was sent out to employees from Welten Institute at the Open University Netherlands to recruit the participants for this pilot study. The e-mail mentioned the estimated time investment for enrolling in the study. Twelve participants (7 male, 5 female; age M = 42, SD = 10) volunteered to participate. By signing an agreement form, the participants allowed us to capture their facial expressions and voice intonations, and to use their data for the study. No specific background knowledge was requested. They were told that they needed to do some tasks in which their input through a microphone and webcam would be used to help them to become more aware of their emotions.

3.2   Design

Participants were asked to expose seven basic face and voice expressions (happy, sad, surprise, fear, disgust, angry, and neutral) in four consecutive tasks. In this way, in total eighty face expressions and voice expressions of each participant were gathered. During this study, we offered very limited feedback to the participant, just the name of the recognized emotion and its prediction accuracy. In this way, the participant was informed whether or not our affective computing software detected the same 'emotion' as he was asked to 'mimic'.

In the first task participants were asked to mimic the face expressions while looking at the webcam, speak aloud and use the voice emotion that was shown on the face of the person that was on the presented image to them. There were 14 images subsequently presented through PowerPoint slides; the participant paced the slides. Each image illustrated a single emotion. All seven basic face expressions were two times presented with the following order: happy, sad, surprise, fear, disgust, angry, neutral, happy, sad, et cetera. In the second task, participants were requested to mimic the face expressions and to speak aloud the seven basic expressions twice: first, through the slides that each presented the keyword of the requested emotion and second, through the slides that each presented the keyword and the picture of the requested face and voice emotion with the following order: angry, disgust, fear, happy, neutral, sad, surprise. In total, 14 PowerPoint slides were used for the second task. For the first and the second task, participants could improvise and use their own texts. The third task presented 16 slides with the text transcript (both sender and receiver) taken from a good-news conversation. The text transcript also included instructions which face and voice expressions should accompany the current text-slide. Here, participants were requested to read and speak aloud the sender text of the 'slides' from the transcript and were asked to deliver the accompanying face and voice expressions. The forth task with 36 slides was similar to task 3, but in this case the text transcript was taken from a bad-news conversation. The transcripts and instructions for tasks 3 and 4 were taken from an existing OUNL training course [25] and a communication book [26].

3.3   Test Environment

All tasks were performed on a single Mac machine. The Mac screen was separated in three panels, top-left, top-right, and bottom. The participants could watch their facial expressions in the face emotion recognition module of the affective computing software at the top-left panel, they could watch their analyzed voice expressions in the voice emotion recognition module of the affective computing software at the top-right panel, while they were performing the tasks using a PowerPoint file in the bottom panel. An integrated webcam with a microphone and a 1080HD external camera were used to capture and record the emotions of the participants as well as their actions on the computer screen. The affective computing software with the face emotion recognition module and the voice emotion recognition module used the webcam and the microphone to capture and recognize the participants' emotions. The Silverback usability testing software version 2.0 used the external camera to capture and record the complete this experimental session. Figure 2 displays an output of both software modules and the PowerPoint slide for Task 3.

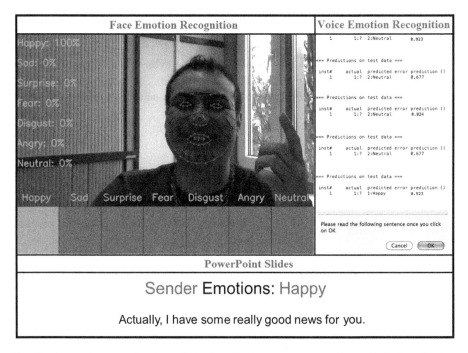

Fig. 2. The main researcher in task 3, the affective computing software including the face emotion recognition module (top-left) and the voice emotion recognition module (top-right), and the PowerPoint slide (bottom).

3.4 Gathering Participants' Opinions

A self-developed questionnaire was used to collect participants' opinions after carrying out the requested tasks. All opinions were online collected via a Google form using 34 items on a 7- point Likert-scale with possible scores: (1) completely disagree, (2) disagree, (3) mildly disagree, (4) neither disagree nor agree, (5) mildly agree, (6) agree, and (7) completely agree. Participants' opinions were gathered for: (1) perceived difficulty to mimic the requested emotions in the given tasks, (2) perceived usefulness of the given feedback to mimic the emotions in the given tasks, (3) perceived instructiveness of the instructions for the given tasks, (4) perceived attractiveness of the given tasks, and (5) perceived concentration on the given tasks. Participants were also asked to report their self-assurance on (1) being able to mimic the requested emotions in the given tasks and (2) their acting skills on a similar 7-point Likert scale.

3.5   Procedure

Each participant signed the agreement form before his/her session of the study started. They individually performed all four tasks in a single session of about 30 min. The session was conducted in a completely silent room with a good lighting condition. The moderator of the session was present in the room, but did not intervene. All twelve sessions were conducted in two consecutive days. The participants were requested not to talk to each other in between sessions so that they could not influence each other. The moderator gave a short instruction at the beginning of each task. For example, participants were asked to show mild and not too intense expressions while mimicking the emotions. All tasks were recorded and captured by both the face emotion recognition module and the voice emotion recognition module of the affective computing software. After the session, each participant filled out the online questionnaire gathering participants' opinions.

4   Results and Discussion

The main purpose of this study focused on the validation of the software with respect to its multimodal detection of emotions. We asked two raters to analyze the recorded streams and carry out validation of the software modules. We do not report the output of our software modules for all tasks in detail in this study; instead we will first present the agreement between two raters, the requested emotions, and the recognized emotions by the two software modules separately.

4.1   Validation Results of the Software

The Kappa value for the validation of the face emotion recognition module based on the requested emotions, recognized emotion, and the raters' rating is reported in Table 1. The Kappa value for the validation of the voice emotion recognition module based on the requested emotions, recognized emotion, and the raters' rating is reported in Table 2.

Table 1. The Kappa value for the validation results of the face emotion recognition module for all the seven emotion for task 1, task 2, task 3, and task 4.

Validation of the Recognized Emotion by the Face Emotion Recognition Software Module							
Happy	Sad	Surprise	Fear	Disgust	Angry	Neutral	Total
0.84	0.66	0.69	0.67	0.66	0.77	0.8	0.76

Analyzing of the Kappa statistic underlines the agreement among the raters, the requested emotions, and the face emotion recognition software module. The result with 95 % confidence reveals that the interrater reliability was calculated to be Kappa = 0.76 (p < 0.001). Therefore a substantial agreement among them is obtained based on Landis and Koch interpretation of Kappa values [27].

Table 2. The Kappa value for the validation results of the voice emotion recognition module for all the seven emotion for task 1, task 2, task 3, and task 4.

Validation of the Recognized Emotion by the Voice Emotion Recognition Software Module							
Happy	Sad	Surprise	Fear	Disgust	Angry	Neutral	Total
0.63	0.50	0.51	0.48	0.41	0.50	0.71	0.58

Analyzing of the Kappa statistic underlines the agreement among the raters, the requested emotions, and the voice emotion recognition software module. The result with 95 % confidence reveals that the interrater reliability was calculated to be Kappa = 0.58 (p < 0.001). Therefore a moderate agreement is obtained among them.

The Kappa value for the validation of the face and the voice emotion recognition module based on the requested emotions, recognized emotion, and the raters' rating is reported in Table 3.

Table 3. The overall Kappa value for the validation results of the face and the voice emotion recognition software modules for all the seven emotion for task 1, task 2, task 3, and task 4.

Validation of the Recognized Emotion by the Face and the Voice Emotion Recognition Software Modules							
Happy	Sad	Surprise	Fear	Disgust	Angry	Neutral	Total
0.68	0.50	0.53	0.50	0.43	0.55	0.73	0.61

Analyzing of the Kappa statistic underlines the agreement among the raters, the requested emotions, the face and the voice emotion recognition software modules. The result with 95 % confidence reveals that the interrater reliability was calculated to be Kappa = 0.61 (p < 0.001). Therefore a substantial agreement is obtained among them.

4.2   Multimodal Fusion of the Two Software Modules

The overall accuracy of our face emotion recognition software module is 75 %, whereas it is 52 % for the voice emotion recognition software module. In order to perform multimodal fusion between the two software modules, we selected linear weighted fusion method, which is a type of rule-based fusion and has been widely used [23]. As we used nominal data types (e.g. Happy and Angry) we do not need to normalize weights of different modalities in our linear fusion to combine the information. We performed a general formula $V_m, 1 \leq m \leq n$ to be a feature vector acquired from mth software module, such as face and voice. We also let $w_m, 1 \leq m \leq n$ be the weight given to the mth software module. Our vectors have the same dimensions and combined by using sum operator through this formula: $V = \frac{1}{n} \sum_{m=1}^{n} w_m \times V_m$. To combine the information of the two software modules we obtained a coefficient using this formula for each emotion category and we applied this coefficient into the validation results. This coefficient leads us to a higher accuracy rate for the combination of the two software modules. In case of differ in recognizing the emotions by the two software modules, the higher accuracy between the two modules prominent in all cases. For example, if the voice emotion recognition module returns disgust and the face emotion recognition module returns surprise, then the feedback 79 %f will be given to the user. This indicates that the accuracy of 79 % is based upon the recognized emotion by the face emotion recognition software module. Table 4 displays the new accuracy using the multimodal fusion and the rules on how the feedbacks are generated.

The uniform distribution of emotions is the average of the diagonal: 78 % (based on Table 4).

Table 4. The overall accuracy using the multimodal fusion between the two software modules.

| | | Face Emotion Recognition | | | | | | |
		Happy	Sad	Surprise	Fear	Disgust	Angry	Neutral
Voice Emotion Recognition	Happy	89.7%	56%f	79%f	58%f	75%f	83%f	90%f
	Sad	80%f	74.4%	79%f	66%v	75%f	83%f	90%f
	Surprise	80%f	56%f	67.8%	58%f	75%f	83%f	90%f
	Fear	80%f	56%f	79%f	50.3%	75%f	83%f	90%f
	Disgust	80%f	56%f	79%f	58%f	63%	83%f	90%f
	Angry	80%f	63%v	79%f	63%v	75%f	100%	90%f
	Neutral	80%f	61%v	79%f	61%v	75%f	83%f	100%

4.3   Participants' Opinions

Here we report the results of the online questionnaire gathering participants' opinions for various aspects (see Table 5). The results indicate that all tasks were regarded moderately difficult and interesting to do. Participants were satisfied with the clarity of the instructions and thought that the feedback was pretty helpful to them. The self-assurance factor was not high among the participants. The results for the concentration factor indicated that participants experienced no distraction during their performance. It can be easily seen that the participants did not regard themselves as actors.

Table 5. The participants' opinions (n = 12).

		Answers by the Participants							
		1	2	3	4	5	6	7	Total
Questions	Difficulty								100%
	It was easy for me to mimic the requested emotions in the given tasks	----	8%	----	33%	33%	26%	----	
	Feedback								
	The feedback did help me to mimic the emotions in the given tasks	----	----	----	17%	17%	50%	16%	
	Self-assurance								
	I am confident that I was able to mimic the requested emotions in the given tasks	3%	3%	48%	10%	16%	20%	----	
	Instructiveness								
	The instructions for the given tasks were clear to me	----	----	8%	----	25%	42%	25%	
	Attractiveness								
	The given tasks were interesting	----	----	----	----	17%	75%	8%	
	Concentration								
	I could easily focus on the given tasks and was not distracted by other factors	----	----	----	----	16%	46%	38%	
	Acting skills								
	I regard myself as a good actor	----	42%	24%	17%	----	17%	----	

1= Completely disagree, 2= Disagree, 3= Mildly disagree, 4= Neither disagree nor agree, 5= Mildly agree, 6= Agree, and 7= Completely agree

5 Conclusion

The FILTWAM framework aims at real-time interpretation of multimodal emotional behavior into emotional states that can be used for better game-based learning. This study examined a multimodal fusion approach for real-time face emotion recognition and voice emotion recognition modules that are part of the FILTWAM framework. We have also examined the two software modules separately. The overall accuracy of our face emotion recognition software based on the requested emotions and the recognized emotions is 75 %. The overall accuracy of our voice emotion recognition software based on the requested emotions and the recognized emotions is 52 %. This is in accordance with [28, 29]. Compare to our previous study [5], the accuracy of our voice emotion recognition dataset improved from 22.2 % to 50 %. The overall accuracy of our multimodal fusion method is 78 % for combination of the two software modules, which falls into the same range as reported in [22].

The results of the questionnaire indicate participants' low self-confidence on being a good actor and the self-assurance factor that was not high among the participants. This issue clearly hints towards an improved feedback mechanism that will be dealt in our upcoming study. We only recruit twelve participants from middle age group volunteered to participate in this study. The possible outcome might be different for younger and older participants. FILTWAM forms part of our research that aims at improving multimodal emotion recognition for better online game-based learning. In this, a future study will use it for researching its suitability towards improved skill acquisition in the context of an online game-based training for communication skills using EMERGO [13].

Acknowledgments.   We thank our colleagues at Welten Institute of the Open University Netherlands who participated in the integration of the face and voice emotion recognition study. We likewise thank the two raters who helped us to rate the recorded streams. We also thank the Netherlands Laboratory for Lifelong Learning (NELLL) of the Open University Netherlands that sponsors this research.

References

1. Anaraki, F.: Developing an effective and efficient eLearning platform. Int. J. Comput. Internet Manage. **12**(2), 57–63 (2004)
2. Hrastinski, S.: Asynchronous and synchronous e-learning. Educause Q. **31**(4), 51–55 (2008)
3. Pekrun, R.: The impact of emotions on learning and achievement: towards a theory of cognitive/motivational mediators. J. Appl. Psychol. **41**, 359–376 (1992)
4. Bahreini, K., Nadolski, R., Qi, W., Westera, W.: FILTWAM - a framework for online game-based communication skills training - using webcams and microphones for enhancing learner support. In: Felicia, P. (ed.) The 6th European Conference on Games Based Learning (ECGBL), pp. 39–48. Ireland, Cork (2012)
5. Bahreini, K., Nadolski, R., Westera, W.: FILTWAM and voice emotion recognition. In: De Gloria, A. (ed.) GALA 2013. LNCS, vol. 8605, pp. 116–129. Springer, Heidelberg (2014)
6. Bahreini, K., Nadolski, R., Westera, W.: FILTWAM - a framework for online affective computing in serious games. In: The 4th International Conference on Games and Virtual Worlds for Serious Applications (VS-GAMES 2012). Procedia Computer Science. Genoa, Italy. vol. 15:45–52 (2012)
7. Kelle, S., Sigurðarson, S., Westera, W., Specht, M.: Game-based life-long learning. In: Magoulas, G.D. (ed.) E-Infrastructures and Technologies for Lifelong Learning: Next Generation Environments, pp. 337–349. IGI Global, Hershey, PA (2011)
8. Reeves, B., Read, J.L.: Total Engagement: Using Games and Virtual Worlds to Change the Way People Work and Business Compete. Harvard Business Press, Boston (2009)
9. Gee, J.P.: What Video Games have to Teach us about Learning and Literacy. Palgrave Macmillan, New York (2003)
10. Connolly, T.M., Boyle, E.A., MacArthur, E., Hainey, T., Boyle, J.M.: A systematic literature review of empirical evidence on computer games and serious games. Comput. Educ. **59**(2), 661–686 (2012)
11. Van Merrienboer, J.J.G., Kirschner, P.A.: Ten Steps to Complex Learning. A systematic approach to four-component instructional design. Routledge, New York (2007)
12. Hager, P.J., Hager, P., Halliday, J.: Recovering Informal Learning: Wisdom. Judgment and Community. Springer, Dordrecht (2006)
13. Nadolski, R.J., Hummel, H.G.K., Van den Brink, H.J., Hoefakker, R., Slootmaker, A., Kurvers, H., Storm, J.: EMERGO: methodology and toolkit for efficient development of serious games in higher education. Simul. Gaming **39**(3), 338–352 (2008)
14. Bashyal, S., Venayagamoorthy, G.K.: Recognition of facial expressions using Gabor wavelets and learning vector quantization. Eng. Appl. Artif. Intell. **21**(7), 1056–1064 (2008)
15. Ekman, P., Friesen, W.V.: Facial Action Coding System: Investigator's Guide. Consulting Psychologists Press, Palo Alto (1978)
16. Kanade, T.: Picture processing system by computer complex and recognition of human faces. Ph.D. thesis. Kyoto University, Japan (1973)
17. Petta, P., Pelachaud, C., Cowie, R.: Emotion-Oriented Systems. The Humaine Handbook. Springer-Verlag, Berlin (2011)

18. Chen, L.S.: Joint Processing of Audio-visual Information for the Recognition of Emotional Expressions in Human-computer Interaction. University of Illinois at Urbana-Champaign. Ph.D. thesis (2000)
19. Sebe, N., Cohen, I.I., Gevers, T., Huang, T.S.: Emotion recognition based on joint visual and audio cues. In: International Conference on Pattern Recognition. Hong Kong, pp. 1136–1139 (2006)
20. Song, M., Bu, J., Chen, C., Li, N.: Audio-visual based emotion recognition: a new approach. In: IEEE Computer Society Conference on Computer Vision and Pattern Recognition vol. 2 (2004)
21. Zeng, Z., Pantic, M., Roisman, G.I., Huang, T.S.: A survey of affect recognition methods: Audio, visual, and spontaneous expressions. IEEE Trans. Pattern Anal. Mach. Intell. **31**(1), 39–58 (2009)
22. Sebe, N.: Multimodal interfaces: challenges and perspectives. J. Am. Intell. Smart Environ. **1**(1), 23–30 (2009)
23. Atrey, P.K., Hossain, M.A., El Saddik, A., Kankanhalli, M.: Multimodal fusion for multimedia analysis: a survey. Multimedia Syst. **16**(6), 345–379 (2010). Springer-Verlag
24. Saragih, J., Lucey, S., Cohn, J.: Deformable model fitting by regularized landmark mean-shifts. Int. J. Comput. Vis. (IJCV), **91**(2), 200–215 (2011)
25. Lang, G., van der Molen, H.T.: Psychologische Gespreksvoering. Open University of the Netherlands, Heerlen (2008)
26. Van der Molen, H.T., Gramsbergen-Hoogland, Y.H.: Communication in Organizations: Basic Skills and Conversation Models. ISBN 978-1-84169-556-3. Psychology Press, New York (2005)
27. Landis, J.R., Koch, G.G.: The measurement of observer agreement for categorical data. Biometrics **33**, 159–174 (1977)
28. Vogt, T., André, E., Bee, N.: EmoVoice – a framework for online recognition of emotions from voice. In: Proceedings of Workshop on Perception and Interactive Technologies for Speech-Based Systems (2008)
29. Dai, K., Harriet, J.F., MacAuslan, J.: Recognizing emotion in speech using neural networks. In: Telehealth and Assistive Technologies, pp. 31–38 (2008)

Serious Games Opportunities for the Primary Education Curriculum in Quebec

Margarida Romero[(⊠)] and Sylvie Barma

Université Laval, 2320 rue des Bibliothèques, Québec G1V 0A6, Canada
{margarida.romero,sylvie.barma}@ulaval.ca

Abstract. Curriculum integration is one of the main factors in the teachers' decision-making process when deciding to use games in formal educational contexts. Based on this observation, we aim to provide primary education teachers with a selection of (serious) games in each of the main areas of the primary education curriculum in Quebec. The taxonomy of the games selected includes Serious Games (SG), designed for educational purposes from the start, but also repurposed games, which, despite not having being intentionally designed for educational purposes, could be diverted for meeting the curriculum objectives of primary education.

1 Introduction

In formal education, the curriculum is the main guideline for the learning activities proposed by the teachers in order to facilitate the learners' achievement of the knowledge and competences defined for each curriculum area and level. The curriculum "lies between the teacher and the learners" [1, p. 96] resulting in a social interaction in an specific formal education context where teachers often use the curriculum as a rationale for the learning activities decision making. Games are often perceived as a diversion from curricular pedagogical goals and even considered by some teachers as "frivolous, unproductive, and apart from the real world" [2, Para. 8]. According to McFarlane, Sparrowhawk and Heald, "obstacles to game use in schools is a mismatch between game content and curriculum content, and the lack of opportunity to gain recognition for skill development" [3, p. 4]. In some cases, educational games are offered to students as a reward but not as a primary learning activity [4]. When games are perceived as a second-order learning activities, the inflexibility of the curriculum and the lack of teaching time is also invoked as a barrier to integrate the adoption of games [5]. Nevertheless, there is an increasing number of Serious Games (SG) addressing the curriculum objectives which could be used for achieving the curricular pedagogical goals in an efficient manner which remains unknown to. We find it relevant to point out that many educators believe that the use of games has many benefits in the educational context [6]. *Serious games* primary purpose is something other than mere entertainment. They "invite the user to interact with a computer application designed to combine elements of teaching, learning, training, communicating and information processing with playful aspects provided by the video game. Such an association is designed to supplement utilitarian content (serious content) with a *videoludic* approach (a game)" [In French, translation by authors][7, p. 11]. This study aims to identify the SG available for

© Springer International Publishing Switzerland 2015
A. De Gloria (Ed.): GALA 2014, LNCS 9221, pp. 121–131, 2015.
DOI: 10.1007/978-3-319-22960-7_12

the primary education curriculum in Quebec but also some limitations teachers are facing if they want to make good use of them in their classes. The paper starts by introducing the pertinence of SG in the context of primary education and the adequacy for the K-12 learners. We then focus on the primary education curriculum of Quebec discussing the universal aspects of this curriculum in relation to other primary education curricula in European countries.

The methodology for identifying the games in relation to the primary education curriculum is introduced in the fourth section, before introducing the results and discussing the opportunities and limits of the present identification of SG for primary education curriculum in Quebec and its potential use in other educational contexts.

2 Learning Through SG in Primary Education

This section aims to explore the interest of Game Based Learning (GBL) and SG in primary education, based on the pedagogical goals of primary education and the opportunities offered by GBL and SG for achieving them.

2.1 Primary Education Goals and Context in Quebec and Europe

Primary or elementary education aims to educate children, addressing "their emotional and intellectual development, the development of their creativity, and their acquisition of social, cultural and physical skills" [8, p. 1], focusing on the main competences and knowledge to be part of society. Primary education has progressed worldwide in the last decades and is close to reach the United Nations goal of achieving the Millennium development goal of Universal Primary Education (UPE). While developing countries focus on actions for facilitating schooling in rural areas and reducing the disparity of gender in education, developed countries discuss the curriculum objectives of primary education for the 21st Century and the learning methodologies to ensure the success of every child. In developed countries, primary education is considered a foundational educational stage for developing literacy, numeracy the key competencies and numeric and language literacies before the secondary education programs. According to the latest data of the OECD family database, the variation in school starting age is very important among OECD countries. In Belgium, France, Italy and Spain almost 100 % of 3–5 year olds are enrolled in formal preschool programs [9]; which aims to prepare children for their primary education. In Quebec, a formal preschool course is optional at five years old and primary school begins at the age of six, which situates Quebec among the schooling systems where the formal curriculum is introduced later. Children backgrounds in relation to their informal and formal pre-schooling education is one of the challenges to be addressed by the primary education teachers during the first years of primary education. The primary education is structured around three main compulsory subjects with apportioned times (French, Mathematics and Physical education and health) and five compulsory subjects with unapportioned times (English Second Language, Arts education, Ethics and religious culture, Geography, history, citizenship education and Sciences and technology) [10]. The schools and the teachers have an important degree of temporal flexibility with unapportioned time subjects, leading to the opportunity of using innovative and interdisciplinary approaches of learning. The interviews to pre-service teachers in Quebec lead to consider a higher opportunity to use (serious) games in primary education than secondary education because of a higher flexibility in the curriculum execution in primary education than secondary education. Despite the greater opportunity to integrate SG in primary education, the effective integration of SG in primary education is still limited to innovative projects [11]. During the last decade, both European and Quebec primary curriculum have changed from an objectives-based to a competency-based pedagogy [12, 13]. In relation to European primary education curriculum, there are important similarities in terms of mathematics, science and technology; Quebec primary education teachers' are used to introduce popular culture and characters in the classroom [14], which could be favorable to help integrating games as popular cultural artifacts in the classroom. In both contexts, European and Quebec elementary schools have been equipped with different types of educational technologies through the last decade, including computer or media labs, laptops and tablet computers and interactive whiteboards in different degrees, creating a big diversity of educational technologies landscapes in each school. While educational technologies are still diverse and not available for all the learners and primary teachers, the integration of computer games faces a technological challenge in their integration to primary education.

3   Methodology for Identifying the (Serious) Games

In order to identify the (serious) games that could be integrated in the primary education curriculum we have developed a two axis criteria. The first axis, considers the curriculum, including the 8 areas of the primary education disciplinary fields: (1) French, (2) Mathematics, (3) Physical education and health, (4) English Second Language, (5) Arts education, (6) Ethics and religious culture, (7) Geography, history and citizenship education; and (8) Science and Technology. The second axis integrates the strategies for adapting (serious) games to the curriculum objectives: (1) using SG or customizing existing games, (2) repurposing existing games and (3) creating new games. We introduce the strategies for adapting (serious) games to the curriculum objectives in the next section before introducing the (serious) games identified for the primary education curriculum.

3.1   Strategies for Adapting (Serious) Games to the Curriculum Objectives

Computer games are techno-pedagogical artefacts which are still quite complex to design by teachers. Despite the growing number of technological solutions which are offered for creating games (e.g. Unity, Ren'py, Scratch…) the techno-pedagogical skills and the time required for developing a game from scratch are important barriers to engage primary education teachers to develop their own computer games. When introducing games in their practice, teachers engage in a decision making process in which they should select an existing game that fits with the curriculum objectives or repurpose an existing entertainment game, which has maybe not being designed initially with an educational objective but which could be used as part of a learning activity [15]. The perfect matching between the pedagogical intentions of the teacher in relation to the curricular objectives and the pedagogical use of (serious) games requires time, adaptations or customization. A study involving pre-service teachers' analysis of different SG, illustrated that SG are in most cases not fully adapted in terms of curriculum objectives, but also in terms of the "design (colors, shapes, pictures etc.), scenarios, characters, levels, points, and feedback", which requires a redesign of the game in order to fit an appropriate curriculum integration in the classroom [16, p. 1351]. In order to face the challenge of adapting the game to the curriculum goal, there are mainly three strategies that we will describe in the next section: (1) customizing existing games, (2) repurposing existing games and (3) creating new games.

3.1.1 Customization of Existing SG

Firstly, there is the possibility the redesign and customization of games to fully match the learners' needs to achieve the curricular goals. Adaptation and customization of the games could be made in terms of difficulty, language, knowledge content, metacognitive supports [17], learner skills and competence assessment SG [18], among other adaptive characteristics of SG. This first strategy requires the SG to be technologically advanced enough in order to support a certain degree of adaptability, but more importantly, this strategy requires technological skills that could became a barrier to the integration of SG in the formal education.

3.1.2 Repurposing Existing Games

Secondly, the teacher could decide to adapt the learning sequence in order to integrate computer entertainment games or SG in a way that could help achieve the curricular objectives and avoid losing the "educational focus" [19]. Popular entertainment games such *Angry Birds* could be repurposed in the context of mathematical learning [20] if the teacher succeeded to integrate the learning objectives and the use of the game within the curricular objectives. Entertainment games can be used as popular content in the classroom, such as the use of newspapers or other type of media, when the teacher organizes the learning sequence as a resource in one of the phases of the teaching or learning process. Playing simulation and virtual words, such *SimCity* could be a possibility to introduce the urban geography curriculum [21], providing an environment of simulation before starting to introduce the concepts of urban geography of the curriculum. Nevertheless, games are often used at the end of the learning sequence as a way to evaluate or transfer the knowledge and competences developed through the learning sequence. Sancar Tokmak and Ozgelen observed pre-service teachers integration of (serious) games for curricular objective, and observed "the computer games selected required students to have pre-knowledge to play. For example, children had to know addition and subtraction process in order to play the computer game on basic operations." [16, p. 1354].

3.1.3 Creating (Serious) Games as a Learning Activity

Finally, we should consider the strategy of creating games as a learning activity helping to achieve the curriculum objectives. Kangas [22] develops creative and collaborative learning competencies through the development of a playful learning environment where the children are invited to co-create and play computer games. The MAGICAL project [23] aims to develop also the creative and teamwork competences through the use of a game-authoring environment where the children create games collaboratively. The game authoring platforms Scratch (http://scratch.mit.edu/) and Ren'py (http://www.renpy.org/) are specially adapted for introducing children to game development, which contributes to their digital literacy skills, their algorithmic, algebraic and geo-metrical mathematical knowledge; but also to the narrative development of the lan-guage curriculum by creating a scenario for the game and their characters [24]. Game creation is a learning activity with multiple opportunities for the primary education curriculum, which could be exploited as an interdisciplinary project in history and geography (game contextualization), arts (game and characters design), first and second language (narrative, character development, scenario and dialogues…), mathematics (algebra, geometry …) and science (game items interactions) (Fig. 1).

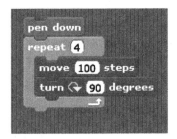

Fig. 1. Programming a square shape with Scratch.

Kafai [25, p. 74] discuss the opportunities of the game creation learning activity for allowing children be placed "in a situation that requires them to design, plan, reflect, evaluate and modify their programs on a constant basis", which could contribute to "development of children's abilities to deal with complex tasks". Game creation and programming has been introduced as learning activities in many schools with initiatives such as the one of *Hour of Code* promoting programming skills among K-12 children in the USA, or the www.code.org tutorial, which "teaches basic coding principles through gameplay" [26, p. 99]. Little by little, these initiatives of informal education are becoming formal; in July 2013, UK has become the first country to integrate programming as an official objective of the primary education curriculum [27]. The creation game strategy requires the teacher to develop her own programming skills or be able to delegate this expertise to other colleagues or the children. In relation to ICTs general uses teachers are sometimes behind part of their pupils; but can develop a classroom management strategy were the more advanced ICT people (often part of the pupils) have the responsibility to help the other members of the Community of Learners

(CoL), including the other pupils and teachers. When teachers joins the learning journey from the same starting point than children in the pedagogical integration of ICTs, teachers models part of the 21st century competencies of learning to learn (lifelong learning), teamwork and collaborative learning, but also solution making strategies to overcome the technological challenges emerging in the classroom.

4 Identification of (Serious) Games for Primary Education

The strategies of games integration described in the previous section constitute the second axis of the matrix for identifying the (serious) games that could help develop the curriculum areas (first axis) of primary education in Quebec. The integration strategies include (1) using SG for children education or customizing existing games, (2) repurposing existing games and (3) creating new games. In order to facilitate the use of the SG identification in other international contexts, we added a column in Table 1, specifying the language availabilities of the games. The game identification has been developed based on a literature review of the serious games in primary education in Quebec using EBSCO and ERIC databases. The games selection was completed with the game identified by 51 pre-service teachers in their third year of their teacher training program in Université Laval in 2014.

Despite the SG available, most educators have remained skeptical about the relevance of using them [6]. It still remains a challenge for most elementary and secondary teachers. So far, very little has been done during the formative years of pre-service elementary teachers to make sure they develop an awareness of resources available to them and understand the potential of SG with their students. Teachers do not feel tech-savvy and are afraid to incorporate new technologies to their practice. However, at the present time, the pervasive use of digital technologies as tools of mediation in cultural practises, both in the West and elsewhere in the world, has to be taken into account. As the Canadian Council on Learning's report on virtual learning stated [30, p. 9]: "Canada's younger generation is primed to exploit the potential of learning technologies. Computers, multimedia programs, chat rooms and other manifestations of the digital age are now common throughout children's developmental years – as almost any parent or educator will attest". Developing pre-service teachers ICT competencies could be a strategy to exploit this potential, and allow future teachers to be more knowledgeable about the ICT technologies that could be integrated in education, in general, and have a better knowledge about the GBL and SG opportunities for achieving their curricular objectives. In this sense, Romero has proposed and introduction to SG integration in the elementary school to the 2014 cohort of the pre-service teachers enrolled in the "ICT integration in primary education" course at Université Laval in 2014. None of the pre-service teachers had ever heard before about the existence of SG and they did not figure out the possibilities to repurpose existing games or create new ones using the game authoring platforms. The introduction to SG integration activity was introduced during 30 min in the classroom and each of the students was required to identify a (serious) game to be integrated in the primary education curriculum. Most of the students (50 over 51) succeeded to integrate a (serious) game in the primary curriculum.

Table 1. Games for primary education according to curriculum areas and the integration strategy.

Curriculum Area (*Axis 1*)	(Serious) Game	Language	Integration Strategy (*Axis 2*)
(1) French	*Les mots du Visuel.* Spelling and ortography.	FR	SG for children education
	Du plaisir à lire. French literacy.	FR	SG for children education
	Magimot. Ortography	FR	SG for children education
	Thélème. Social network for learning French Second Language	FR	SG for children and adults
(2) Mathematics	*La Souris Web.* Geometry, symmetry.	FR	SG for children education
	Timez Attack. Mental calculations [28].	FR	SG for children education
	Bejeweled Blitz. Casual games for learning geometry, shapes and algebra.	EN, FR	Repurposed game
	Angry Birds. Casual games for learning	EN	Repurposed game
	CalculaTice. Mental calculations.	FR	SG for children education
	MathémaTice. Mental calculations.	FR	SG for children education
	Le café des MATHadores. Venn diagrams, algebra, applied mathematics.	FR	SG for children and young
	Math Mountain. Mental calculations.	EN	SG for children education
(3) Physical education and health	*Vinz et Lou mettent les pieds dans le plat.* Nutrition and Health.	FR	SG for children education
(4) English Second Language	*The Sims*, English Second Language	EN	Repurposed game
	Wordspot, English words identification.	EN	SG for children and adults
(5) Arts education	*Crayons Physics*, Arts.	EN	SG for children and adults
(6) Ethics and religious culture	*World of Warcraft*, Using the game to reflect on violence and ethics.	EN	Repurposed game

(*Continued*)

Table 1. (*Continued*)

Curriculum Area (*Axis 1*)	(Serious) Game	Language	Integration Strategy (*Axis 2*)
(7) Geography, history and citizenship education	*Pays du monde*. Geography, list of the countries.	FR	SG for children and adults
	Happy wood. Geography and citizenship.	FR	SG for children and young
	Le code perdu. Citizenship.	FR	SG for children and young
	Civilization. Geography and urban context.	EN	Repurposed game
	SimCity. Geography and urban context.	EN	Repurposed game
(8) Sciences and technology	*Lake Adventures*. Water management and sustainable development.	FR	SG for children education
	Donjons & RaDon. Introduction to physics [29].	FR	SG for children and young
	Énerguy. Energy management and sustainable development.	FR	SG for children and adults
	Crazy Machines. Introduction to physics.	EN	SG for children and adults

5   Discussion

As mentioned previously, this study aimed to identify SG that could be used in the context of the primary education curriculum in Quebec. The (serious) games identification process leads to an observation of a majority of SG in the curricular area of mathematics, followed by science and technology. In mathematics we observe the higher rates of using repurposed games. The strategy of game integration most considered by pre-service teachers was the use of existing SG, designed specifically for the primary education curricular objectives. The rationale behind the use of existing SG is the facility of integration. These results point out the pre-teachers avoidance of customizing, adapting or creating new games due to the technological requirements for developing these strategies. There is a need to allow pre-service teachers to develop the strategies of customization, repurposing and game creations, and stop waiting for the perfect matching between the SG and the curricular objectives. With this objective, we aim to highlight two main ideas to increase the (serious) game integration in the primary classroom. Firstly, teachers' have the possibility to adapt existing games and technology. There is no need to wait for the perfect SG matching perfectly each curriculum objectives. We have observed different strategies that could help introduce existing (serious) games for developing the curriculum objectives through customization, repurposing existing games or by creating games as a learning strategy. Event when the school facilities does not provides computer equipment for all the learners, teachers could organize the classroom activities in order to run games in collaborative challenges, or even invite the children to bring their laptops, smartphones or tablets to the classroom through a "Bring Your Own Device" (BYOD) policy. Introducing games in the classroom should not be limited by the existing (serious) games neither by technology when the teacher is able to customize, repurpose or engage in creating games in technologically diverse contexts. Secondly, teachers do not need to become tech-savvy before integrating computer games in the classroom, they just should change their paradigm from "I'm-the-Teacher-I-know-everything" to a Community of Learners (CoL) paradigm where the teacher is the facilitator of the learning experience but does not control everyone and everything (domain knowledge, technologies, software…) but allows the emergence of collaborative solution solving strategies. In relation to the use of ICTs, teachers are sometimes behind part of their pupils; but can develop a classroom management strategy were the more advanced ICT people (often part of the pupils) have the responsibility to help the other members of the Community of Learners (CoL), including the other pupils and teachers. When teachers joins the learning journey from the same starting point than children in the pedagogical integration of ICTs, teachers models part of the 21st century competencies of learning to learn (lifelong learning), teamwork and collaborative learning, but also solution making strategies to overcome the technological challenges appearing in the classroom. Prensky [31], describe young people as *Digital Natives*, and as the *Game Generation*. Primary education teachers should made be aware of those facts and invited to take part in a Community of Practices (CoP) and other professional events and networks in order to develop a better awareness of the SG integration in the classroom. Developing their personal network to improve their game integration projects successfully and reflect on their practices with other colleagues could reveal an important step in changing their teaching practices for the benefit of the learners.

References

1. Groundwater-Smith, S., White, V.: Improving our Primary Schools: Evaluation and Assessment Through Participation. Harcourt Brace, Sydney (1995)
2. de Winter, J., Griffin, D., McAllister, K.S., Moeller, R.M., Ruggill, J.E.: Computer games across the curriculum: A critical review of an emerging techno-pedagogy. Curr. Electron. Lit. (2010)
3. McFarlane, A., Sparrowhawk, A., Heald, Y.: Report on the educational use of games. Teachers evaluating educational multimedia (2002)
4. Can, G., Cagiltay, K.: Turkish prospective teachers' perceptions regarding the use of computer games with educational features. J. Educ. Technol. Soc. **9**(1), 308–321 (2006)
5. Baek, Y.K.: What hinders teachers in using computer and video games in the classroom? Exploring factors inhibiting the uptake of computer and video games. Cyberpsychol. Behav. **11**(6), 665–671 (2008)

6. Barma, S., Power, M., Daniel, S.: Réalité augmentée et jeu mobile pour une éducation aux sciences et à la technologie. In: Actes du colloque scientifique Ludovia 2010 « Interactivité/ interactions–Enjeux relationnels (2010)
7. Michaud, L., Alvarez, J.: Serious games: Advergaming, edugaming, training. In: Presented at the IDATE, Paris (2008)
8. van der Ree, R.: Arts and Cultural Education at School in Europe. Eurydice, The Netherlands (2008)
9. OECD, PF3.2. Enrolment in childcare and pre-schools. OECD. Social Policy Division (2013)
10. MELS, Basic school regulation for preschool, elementary and secondary education. Education Act (chapter I-13.3, s. 447). Publications du Québec. Éditeur officiel du Québec (2014)
11. Sauvé, L., Kaufman, D., Jeux, et al: Simulations éducatifs: Études de Cas et leçons Apprises. PUQ (2010)
12. Jonnaert, P., Masciotra, D., Barrette, J., Morel, D., Mane, Y.: From competence in the curriculum to competence in action. Prospects **37**(2), 187–203 (2007)
13. Gauthier, C., Saint-Jacques, D.: La réforme des programmes scolaires au Québec. Presses Université Laval, Québec (2002)
14. Saint-Jacques, D., Chené, A., Lessard, C., Riopel, M.-C.: Les représentations que se font les enseignants du primaire de la dimension culturelle du curriculum. Rev. Sci. Léducation **28**(1), 39–62 (2002)
15. Shelton, B.E., Scoresby, J.: Aligning game activity with educational goals: Following a constrained design approach to instructional computer games. Educ. Technol. Res. Dev. **59**(1), 113–138 (2011)
16. Sancar, H.S., Ozgelen, S.: The ECE pre-service teachers' perception on factors affecting the integration of educational computer games in two conditions: selecting versus redesigning*. Educ. Sci. Theor. Pract. **13**(2), 1345–1356 (2013)
17. Bellotti, F., Kapralos, B., Lee, K., Moreno-Ger, P., Berta, R.: Assessment in and of Serious Games: an overview. Adv. Hum.-Comput. Interact. **2013**, 1 (2013)
18. Romero, M., Usart, M., Popescu, M., Boyle, E.: Interdisciplinary and international adaption and personalization of the metavals serious games. In: Ma, M., Oliveira, M.F., Hauge, J.B., Duin, H., Thoben, K.-D. (eds.) SGDA 2012. LNCS, vol. 7528, pp. 59–73. Springer, Heidelberg (2012)
19. Mor, Y., Winters, N., Cerulli, M., Björk, S.: Literature review on the use of games in mathematical learning, Part I: Design. Report of the Learning Patterns for the Design and Deployment of Mathematical Games project (2006)
20. Rodrigues, M., Carvalho, P.S.: Teaching physics with Angry Birds: exploring the kinematics and dynamics of the game. Phys. Educ. **48**(4), 431 (2013)
21. Tüzün, H., Yılmaz-Soylu, M., Karakuş, T., İnal, Y., Kızılkaya, G.: The effects of computer games on primary school students' achievement and motivation in geography learning. Comput. Educ. **52**(1), 68–77 (2009)
22. Kangas, M.: Creative and playful learning: Learning through game co-creation and games in a playful learning environment. Think. Ski. Creat. **5**(1), 1–15 (2010)
23. Kiili, K., Kiili, C., Ott, M., Jönkkäri, T.: Towards creative pedagogy: Empowering students to develop games. In: 6th European Conference on Games Based Learning, p. 250 (2012)
24. Robertson, J., Good, J.: Children's narrative development through computer game authoring. TechTrends **49**(5), 43–59 (2005)
25. Kafai, Y.B.: Learning design by making games. Constr. Pract. Des. Think. Learn. Digit. World, pp. 71–96 (1996)

26. Computer Society Connection, Hour of Code' kicks off to introduce K-12 students to computer programming. IEEE Xplore, **46**(11), 99 (2013)
27. Curtis, S.: Teaching our children to code: a quiet revolution. The Telegraph, London, 11-Apr-2013
28. Fargeot, B., Thibaud, M.: L'utilisation d'un jeu serieux dans l'acquisition de l'automaticite des tables de multiplication en cycle 3. L'exemple de « Timez Attack » . Université Claude Bernard Lyon 1, Institut Universitaire de Formation des Maitres de l'Académie de Lyon, Lyon, France, Mémoire de recherche (2013)
29. Sanchez, E., Ney, M., Labat, J.-M.: Jeux sérieux et pédagogie universitaire : de la conception à l'évaluation des apprentissages. Rev. Int. Technol. En Pédagogie Univ., vol. 8, no. 1–2 Journées scientifiques Pédagogie Universitaire Numérique, pp. 48–57, juillet 2011
30. Canadian Council on Learning, "State of E-learning in Canada," Ottawa, Canada
31. Prensky, M.: Digital natives, digital immigrants part 1. Horiz. **9**(5), 1–6 (2001)

Free Your Brain a Working Memory Training Game

Gonçalo Pereira[1]([✉]), Manuel Ninaus[2], Rui Prada[1], Guilherme Wood[2],
Christa Neuper[2], and Ana Paiva[1]

[1] INESC-ID, Instituto Superior Técnico, Universidade de Lisboa,
Avenida Professor Cavaco Silva, Porto Salvo, Portugal
`goncalo.pereira@gaips.inesc-id.pt`, `rui.prada@tecnico.ulisboa.pt`,
`ana.paiva@inesc-id.pt`
`http://gaips.inesc-id.pt/`
[2] Department of Psychology, Section Neuropsychology, University of Graz,
Universitätsplatz 2/III, 8010 Graz, Austria
`{manuel.ninaus,guilherme.wood,christa.neuper}@uni-graz.at`

Abstract. Working memory training systems are designed to improve
the user's working memory. However, current systems are frequently considered tedious deeply affecting the user's motivation and consequently
the potential for training derived improvements. "Free Your Brain" is a
brain training game combining insights from cognitive neuropsychological theories and flow theories. In this work we describe the game and its
design process specifically establishing the link between the supporting
theoretical background research and the developed solution.

1 Introduction

Technology enhanced learning is currently being used in many different domains
ranging from conflict resolution skills to math teaching [1,2]. Since the discovery
of the possible positive impact that memory training games can have on several
cognitive skills (e.g. knowledge acquisition) some training systems have been
developed [3]. These systems have a potentially great impact for both healthy
people who simply want to improve their cognitive skills and people with specific
neurological disorders (e.g. Attention Deficit Hyperactivity Disorder - ADHD).
However, despite the diversity of training systems and games developed the
effectiveness of such systems is still controversial [4,5].

Cognitive training applications, and specifically working memory training systems are designed to improve the user's working memory. However, conventional
systems are frequently considered tedious or repetitive which deeply affects the
user's motivation to learn and consequently the potential for learning transfer [6].
According to Prins *et al.* [7] working memory training with game elements significantly improves motivation and training performance. To further explore these
benefits in this work we present the brain training game "Free Your Brain" which
addresses this gap in current systems by combining insights into how to keep users
engaged in the learning process by using concepts of Flow theory [8,9] in conjunction with a working memory training task design from neuroscientific studies [4,5].

© Springer International Publishing Switzerland 2015
A. De Gloria (Ed.): GALA 2014, LNCS 9221, pp. 132–141, 2015.
DOI: 10.1007/978-3-319-22960-7_13

The document is structured as follows. In the next section we review existing brain training software. Then, we introduce the main theoretical background research supporting our game, followed by the description of our game and the link between background research and the developed. Finally, we draw some conclusions and present future work.

2   Existing Brain Training Software

Currently there are several commercial brain training software solutions available (e.g. Cogmed[1], Luminosity[2]). However, these solutions cannot support their impressive claims [10] sufficiently either by having controversial studies or by a complete lack of empirical studies (to our knowledge). One of the most scrutinized cases is Cogmed. In [5] Shipstead *et al.* concluded that Cogmed's claims of working memory capacity improvements are unsubstantiated. Regardless of Cogmed's criticism the authors do not exclude the possibility that effective working memory training (in capacity and related abilities) is possible. As a result of the analysis, it is suggested that future approaches should focus on training based on theories for specific working memory aspects and study their transfer effects. In a meta-analysis by Hulme and Melby-Lervåg [10] the previous criticism is reinforced and it is emphasized the need for a more theoretically motivated research that tests those theories. One aspect specifically focused the recommended utilization of multiple measures in the studies performed. Gathercole *et al.* [11] explores the value of the different studies and attempts to address Cogmed's controversy. In this work, the authors call for a balanced evaluation of all the data available relating current problems in assessing the effects of training software to the experimental designs used in several experiments. As such, the authors argue for a more careful experimental design at its different levels: multiple measures, test generalization, random participant allocation, control group.

In summary, even though there are several brain training applications available these do not support trainee motivation or lack empirical evidence [5,10,12]. When such brain training software or cognitive training in general is used for extended periods of time or in an even more crucial context of rehabilitation of neurological patients, motivation quickly decreases and the training outcome could be reduced [13].

3   Theoretical Background

In this section we introduce the fundamental theoretical background research that supported the design process of our brain training game. First we review neurophysiological evidence to the importance of working memory training and determine what tasks are appropriate to perform it. Next we will introduce Flow Theory as a promising contribution towards addressing the boredom typically faced in current brain training games.

---

[1] http://www.cogmed.com/.

[2] http://www.lumosity.com/.

3.1   Neurophysiological

Trying to train working memory is very plausible for patients (e.g. stroke, ADHD, etc.) as well as for healthy adult persons. Working memory is a brain system that allows the human to manipulate and recall a limited amount of retained chunks of information for a brief period of time [14]. Numerous studies demonstrated that working memory is of central importance for acquiring knowledge (e.g. [15]) and is involved in a variety of complex cognitive tasks and abilities (e.g. [3]). Alloway and Alloway [16] showed that working memory is even a better predictor for academic success than intelligence. Thus working memory is also a strong predictor for reading and mathematical skills [17].

Literature on working memory training shows that core training of working memory is especially promising. Core training studies typically involve tasks using sequential processing and frequent memory updating components integrated with a design targeting domain-general working memory mechanisms [4]. One very common and successful approach of core training paradigms is the complex span task. Basic simple span tasks require the participant to remember and recall a number of items which have been presented without interruption. Whereas in complex span tasks participants have to execute, after each presented item, a distractor task. For instance, participants have to remember a sequence of one-digit numbers. These numbers are presented sequentially and after each number the participants have to solve an easy equation (e.g. 6+8=15, true or false?) and maintaining the presented number(s) in their temporary storage. Complex span tasks are a reliable measure of complex cognition [5].

3.2   Flow Theory

Flow or a state of flow, was introduced by Csikszentmihalyi and occurs when a person is completely absorbed by its current activity [8]. Such a state is considered optimal [9] because it is driven by a high intrinsic motivation towards the activity that leads to personal positive experiences such as immersion, enjoyment, fulfillment and skill. However, flow is not easy to achieve since it actually only corresponds to a narrow band of experiences [8]. If a given activity is very challenging but a person has low skill at performing it, instead of flow he/she is lead to a state of anxiety. Conversely, if the person faces a very easy activity and he/she has high skill at performing it, again flow is missed and a state of boredom might be reached.

Even though a flow state can have diverse beneficial psychological impacts on people (such as the mentioned positive experiences) we are especially interested on its impact on learning. Webster *et al.* [18] explored this important link and verified that indeed a flow state has a positive impact in learning. Furthermore, the authors verified this impact in a context of human-computer interaction also expanding the theory's range of applicability from psychology to human-computer interaction.

In [19] Kiili introduced an adapted version of the theory of flow for virtual environments, specifically to game based learning. According to the theory, there are several main "flow antecedents" [20] that should be considered to achieve a state of flow and consequently its learning effects:

- **Clear Goals** - clear goals facilitate the learner's focus on the activity which is related to a higher probability of experiencing flow;
- **Feedback** - helps the learner monitor his/her performance and progress and also avoid distractions, both related to a higher probability of experiencing flow;
- **Playability** - overly complex activities or interaction with the learning system are related with a lower probability of experiencing flow;
- **Sense of Control** - the learner's perception that he/she can develop his/her skills to reduce errors in challenges should be supported. If such a balance between the challenges and skills is offered there is a higher probability of experiencing flow.

Even though "Challenges" and "Skills" were not specifically described they are both fundamental antecedents[3]. These antecedents are actually the key elements of the theory and are better characterized as a comparative dichotomy (e.g. Playability and Sense of Control antecedents). Even though Flow Theory provides several well defined antecedents each individual's experience of flow is unique as it also depends on personal characteristics such as emotions, values and previous experiences [20].

4   Free Your Brain Serious Game

In this section we will detail our approach to design a solution addressing the problems faced by current working memory training software and also how this solution was actually implemented to be tested in a real context.

4.1   Approach

In the development of "Free Your Brain" we specifically intended to address the lack of motivation and the lack of empirical evidence of effectiveness for current working memory training software solutions. Based on our neuropsychological background research by using a complex span task as our core central activity we have a better chance of success in achieving working memory improvements. Therefore, we selected such a task as a basic design choice. To address the lack of motivation we introduced several game elements designed around the central activity expecting to improve motivation and increase the learning outcome. Flow Theory provided us with a set of design guidelines that were used to increase the probability of players achieving a state of flow.

---

[3] Such that they are the frequently used as the basic determinants of Flow Theory prediction.

4.2   Complex Span Task Activity

The game was designed to guide the player through cycles of a complex span task activity. The activity is composed by a sequence of phases that are typically[4] presented in the following order:

1. **Digit Presentation (DP)** the game displays a one-digit number (*key-digit*) that the player must memorize until the unlocking phase;
2. **Decision Task (T)** the game presents a simple arithmetic decision task (e.g. $5 + 6 = 11$) that the player must classify as either true or false;
3. **Unlocking (U)** the player is asked to recall the key-digit initially presented;

This complex span task activity can be parameterized in terms of difficulty by varying the number of $DP{\rightarrow}T$ phase pairs before reaching the U phase. The digits to recall in this phase are all those that were previously presented in each DP phase. The number of digits to remember is therefore directly proportional to the number of $DP{\rightarrow}T$ pair sequences that precede it.

4.3   Game Description

The game is presented to the player as a personal quest of *freeing one's own brain*. Upon entering the game, a player can see a high score table displaying his/her best game sessions in this quest. After this, the player can then start a new session. If it is a first time player then he/she starts at level 0 otherwise at a slightly lower level than in his/her previous session.

Each level is composed by two sequential and equally difficult complex span task activities. If a player is able to successfully complete two equally difficult tasks then he/she advances to the next level. For each level that the player advances the complex span task to solve is increased in difficulty by adding one more $DP{\rightarrow}T$ pair relatively to the previous level. For example, in level 1 the player is presented with the following complex span tasks composed by the following phases: $DP{\rightarrow}T{\rightarrow}U$. However, in level 2 he/she faces tasks with the following phases: $DP{\rightarrow}T{\rightarrow}DP{\rightarrow}T{\rightarrow}U$. Generically, for level n a player faces n phase pairs $DP{\rightarrow}T$ before entering phase U.

As in any game, the player can make mistakes and in the specific case of "Free Your Brain" these occur either at the T phase or at the U phase. An error in any of these phases results in the player restarting the current complex span task from the beginning. However, if the player makes two mistakes, in the same level, it levels down and starts a complex span task with a lower difficulty. This procedure allows the players to train at the optimal level of their capabilities. Furthermore, the adaptive difficulty of the game should ensure maximum performance of the players [21]. The flowchart presented in Fig. 1 represents the possible paths in player progression according to the different phases of levels 1 and 2.

During the game the player receives visual feedback of correct (growing neuron animation) or wrong (shrinking neuron animation) according to the result

---

[4] Assuming an error free progression.

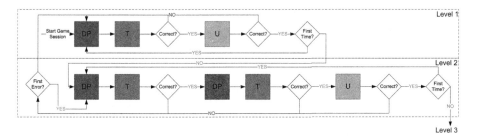

Fig. 1. Components flowchart for levels 1 and 2. DP - Digit Presentation; T - Decision Task; U - Unlocking.

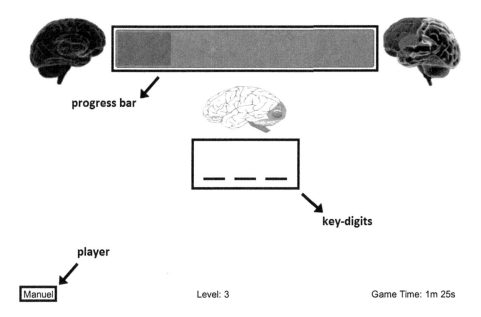

Fig. 2. Game interface

of the T phase. Visual feedback of correct (attempting to or unlocking current level's brain area animation) or wrong (locking current level's brain area animation) is also displayed according to the result of the U phase. When a player either levels up or down this information is emphatically displayed. Finally, the player always has the current score bar visible, see Fig. 2.

4.4   Elements of Flow

In this section we will explore the link between the diverse game elements and Flow Theory.

Clear Goals. A higher probability of experiencing flow exists when a game has clear goals. In line with this "Free Your Brain" has a very simple goal: unlock as many parts of your brain as possible by reaching higher levels in each game session.

Feedback. Several game elements help the player monitor his/her performance and progress which also increases the probability of experiencing flow. Preceding any game session the player can assess his/her overall progress across all game sessions by checking his/her personalized highscore board. After starting a game session the player then has several feedback systems. First, and always present, is the score bar that enables the player to check his/her current session score instantly and compare it with previous ones. Second, there are several visual elements to depict different game events or phases. For the *decision task (T)* phase if a player gives the correct answer then a growing neuron animation is played to convey that information, otherwise a shrinking neuron animation is played to represent a wrong answer.

In the *unlocking (U)* phase the player also receives visual feedback. Initially he/she is presented with a brain image with a specific part of the brain locked. Then according to the digits provided, if correct and it is the first *unlocking (U)* the player faces in that level then a brain struggling to unlock animation is played. If also correct, but it is the second time, then an unlocking animation specific for that level (represented by a specific part of the brain) is played. If the digits provided are incorrect then an animation emphasizing the locking of that part of the brain is played.

Finally, in any level up or down event the player is presented by a visual notification informing his/her about that change in game difficulty.

Playability. Regarding playability several game characteristics contribute to a higher probability of achieving flow. First, the actual tasks included in the activity are very simple: observe a digit, reply correct or wrong, input one or more digits. Additionally, the provided modes of interaction are also very simple by being straightforward to the action the player has to make: click a button displaying correct, a button displaying wrong or simply press key digits in the keyboard.

Another important design decision that contributes to achieving flow is the avoidance of working memory cognitive overload by balancing the amount of visual elements [19]. To this end we excluded from the game all visual elements that did not have a specific function and therefore added value to the learning goals. This game characteristic helps the player avoid distractions and keep focused on the game's central activity.

In the creation of the images and animations for the *unlocking (U)* phase special attention was given to the brain diagrams and their locked or unlocked areas. Each level had a specific region of the brain locked which was unlocked by successfully completing that level. An area unlocked in a given level always appears unlocked in the higher levels to give the player a sense of progression in his/her goal to "unlock the brain".

Sense of Control. The flow antecedent sense of control specifically focus the attainment of the player's specific correct balance between the difficulty of the challenges presented and the player's skills. As recommended by Flow Theory we introduced an adaptation mechanism that adapts the level of difficulty and consequently the challenges presented to the player's proficiency in the activity.

The player's good performance is rewarded by letting the player progress in the game. However, and in order to support the sense of control a player can only level up and face a harder complex span task by completing the same difficulty task twice. If a player makes one mistake it is not immediately leveled down, but given a chance to correct his/her mistake. However, if a second mistake is made, the player levels down so that the complex span task challenge presented is more adequate to the player's current skills and avoids an anxiety state. Furthermore, given our task design the changes in difficulty are progressive and avoid irregular spikes by occurring at a set pace of one $DP{\rightarrow}T$ phase pair per level change.

To ensure that players train/play close the maximum of their capabilities and avoid a boredom state we also introduced a starting level dependent on the previous gaming session's final level. A new session's initial level corresponds to the previous session final level decreased by a pre-determined amount of difficulty (corresponds to one or more levels down).

4.5   Game Implementation

The "Free Your Brain" game was developed as a web application so that the players are able to perform the training online from their own computers. Players log in with personal credentials and the performance of each training session is saved in the webserver.

The technologies used to implement the game were Unity 3D (using C#), MySQL and PHP. We opted for Unity 3D because it is a powerful framework that enables us to build a web-based game efficiently, enables an easy deployment of the game and easy access to the players. MySQL was used to store collected user data persistently for posterior evaluation and to support the level related personalization mechanism. Finally, PHP was used for the creation of an interoperability layer between Unity 3D and MySQL on the webserver hosting the game.

The implementation of the game required the conception of technical solutions to diverse challenges. Given the requisite of high parameterization capability we developed a preferences loading system so that someone deploying the game could easily switch between different versions. A given game version can be easily parameterized or fine tuned by altering different game aspects such as the available decision tasks, the scoring system and game timings.

5   Conclusion and Future Work

In this work we present a working memory training game designed to include insights from both neuroscientific studies and Flow Theory adapted to virtual environments for game based learning. The neuroscientific studies provided the fundamental activity around which the game was designed and the guidelines of Flow Theory were carefully intertwined in the game mechanisms to try to support player motivation. Additionally, given the methodology and choices made in its implementation the game is easily parameterizable to create different versions that can be easily distributed to the player's personal computers.

As future work we intend to empirically study our solution. To this end we are currently undergoing a study to examine if the developed working memory training game leads to an increased training outcome in comparison with a version without game elements. The two versions are exactly the same except for the game elements. In this study we use multiple measures to assess participants' cognitive abilities changes. If transfer effects are found we will conduct a magnetic resonance imaging (MRI) study to examine morphological and functional changes induced by our working memory training game.

Acknowledgment. Work supported by GaLA (Games & Learning Alliance) Network of Excellence funded by the EU in FP7-ICT-2009-5 under grant agreement no: 258169, by FCT(INESC-ID multi annual funding) under project PEst-OE/EEI/LA0021/2013 and FCT scholarship SFRH/BD/66663/2009. The authors are grateful to António Brisson for game development assistance and Vanessa Hinterleitner, René Stefitz for assets creation and Dimitris Skliris for technical assistance.

References

1. Andersen, E., Popovi, Z.: Refraction. In: Grand Prize: Best in Show Award, Disney Learning Challenge, SIGGRAPH 2010, University of Washington
2. Campos, J., Martinho, C., Ingram, G., Vasalou, A., Paiva, A.: My dream theatre: putting conflict on center stage. In: 8th International Conference on the Foundations of Digital Games (2013)
3. Klingberg, T.: Training and plasticity of working memory. Trends Cogn. Sci. **14**(7), 317–324 (2010)
4. Morrison, A.B., Chein, J.M.: Does working memory training work? the promise and challenges of enhancing cognition by training working memory. Psychon. Bull. Rev. **18**(1), 46–60 (2011)
5. Shipstead, Z., Hicks, K.L., Engle, R.W.: Cogmed working memory training: does the evidence support the claims? J. Appl. Res. Mem. Cogn. **1**(3), 185–193 (2012)
6. Green, C.S., Bavelier, D.: Exercising your brain: a review of human brain plasticity and training-induced learning. Psychol. aging **23**(4), 692–701 (2008)
7. Prins, P.J., Dovis, S., Ponsioen, A., ten Brink, E., van der Oord, S.: Does computerized working memory training with game elements enhance motivation and training efficacy in children with ADHD? Cyberpsychology Behav. Soc. Networking **14**(3), 115–122 (2011)
8. Cskszentmihlyi, M.: Beyond Boredom and Anxiety. Jossey-Bass Publishers, San Francisco (1975)
9. Csikszentmihalyi, M.: Flow: The Psychology of Optimal Experience. Harper & Row, New York (1990)

10. Hulme, C., Melby-Lervg, M.: Current evidence does not support the claims made for CogMed working memory training. J. Appl. Res. Mem. Cogn. **1**(3), 197–200 (2012)
11. Gathercole, S.E., Dunning, D.L., Holmes, J.: Cogmed training: let's be realistic about intervention research. J. Appl. Res. Mem. Cogn. **1**(3), 201–203 (2012)
12. Owen, A.M., Hampshire, A., Grahn, J.A., Stenton, R., Dajani, S., Burns, A.S., Howard, R.J., Ballard, C.G.: Putting brain training to the test. Nature **465**(7299), 775–778 (2010). PMID: 20407435 PMCID: PMC2884087
13. Calderita, L., Bustos, P., Suarez Mejias, C., Fernandez, F., Bandera, A.: THERA-PIST: towards an autonomous socially interactive robot for motor and neuroreha-bilitation therapies for children. In: 2013 7th International Conference on Pervasive Computing Technologies for Healthcare (PervasiveHealth), pp. 374–377 (2013)
14. Baddeley, A.: Working memory: looking back and looking forward. Nat. Rev. Neurosci. **4**(10), 829–839 (2003)
15. Pickering, S.J.: Working Memory and Education. Academic Press, Burlington (2006)
16. Alloway, T.P., Alloway, R.G.: Investigating the predictive roles of working memory and IQ in academic attainment. J. Exp. Child Psychol. **106**(1), 20–29 (2010)
17. Gathercole, S.E., Alloway, T.P., Willis, C., Adams, A.M.: Working memory in children with reading disabilities. J. Exp. Child Psychol. **93**(3), 265–281 (2006)
18. Webster, J., Trevino, L.K., Ryan, L.: The dimensionality and correlates of flow in human-computer interactions. Comput. Hum. Behav. **9**(4), 411–426 (1993)
19. Kiili, K.: Digital game-based learning: towards an experiential gaming model. Inter-net High. Educ. **8**(1), 13–24 (2005)
20. Kiili, K., de Freitas, S., Arnab, S., Lainema, T.: The design principles for flow experience in educational games. Procedia Comput. Sci. **15**, 78–91 (2012)
21. Yerkes, R.M., Dodson, J.D.: The relation of strength of stimulus to rapidity of habit-formation. J. Comp. Neurol. Psychol. **18**(5), 459–482 (1908)

Game Design and Development for Learning Physics Using the Flow Framework

Danu Pranantha[1,2]([✉]), Erik van der Spek[2], Francesco Bellotti[1],
Riccardo Berta[1], Alessandro De Gloria[1], and Matthias Rauterberg[2]

[1] DITEN, University of Genoa, Via Opera Pia 11A, Genoa, Italy
{franz,berta,adg}@elios.unige.it, d.pranantha@tue.nl
[2] Faculty of Industrial Design, Eindhoven University of Technology, Den Dolech 2,
Eindhoven, The Netherlands
{e.d.v.d.spek,g.w.m.rauterberg}@tue.nl

Abstract. Instruction, in several knowledge domains, aims at achieving two goals: acquisition of a body of knowledge and of problem solving skills in the field. In physics, this requires students to connect physical phenomena, physics principles, and physics symbols. This can be learned on paper, but interactive tools may increase the learner's ability to contextualize the problem. Computer simulations provide students with graphical models that join phenomena and principles in physics. However, a minimally guided approach may make learning difficult, since it overburdens the working memory. In particular, for developing problem solving skills, students need to be guided and exercise with a variety of physics problems. Intelligent tutoring systems (ITS) can be a useful tool to fill this gap. Thus, we have developed a physics game to support inquiry learning and retrieval practicing using simulation and knowledge based tutorship (QTut), and implemented as a puzzle game that uses driving questions to encourage students to explore the simulation. To address scalability and reusability, the game features different difficulty levels atop of a customizable format. This allows us to explore in-game adaptivity, exploiting task and user models that rely on the flow framework. User tests are being executed to evaluate the usefulness of the game.

1 Introduction

Learning physics aims at achieving two goals: the acquisition of a body of knowledge and the ability to solve quantitative problems in physics. In physics, the body of knowledge is organized into three levels: the macroscopic level corresponds to physical objects, their properties and behaviour; the microscopic level explains the macroscopic level using concepts, theories and principles of physics; and the symbolic level represents the concepts of physics as mathematical formulae [1]. Consequently, physics instructions need to advocate the connection of those levels to the students.

Lack of knowledge and/or misconceptions at the microscopic level lead students to difficulties in solving physics problems [2]. The use of concrete models,

A. De Gloria (Ed.): GALA 2014, LNCS 9221, pp. 142–151, 2015.
DOI: 10.1007/978-3-319-22960-7_14

analogies and graphics may help students to overcome difficulties. In this regard, computer simulations graphically model physical objects and unite the macroscopic, the microscopic, and the symbolic levels. This approach urges students to actively seek questions, explore the simulation, and discover knowledge based on their observations.

However, such a minimally guided approach may harm learning since it does not align with working memory limitations [3]. This, to some extent, necessitates the use of scaffolding, which is essential for inquiry learning [4]. It is also crucial for students to exercise with a variety of physics problems and to perform retrieval practices at microscopic and symbolic levels [5]. In this case, Intelligent tutoring systems (ITS) nurture students in problem solving skills. Thus, combining a physics simulation with a tutoring system in the form of serious games may provide students with a graphical tool for exploration (the macroscopic level) and a training tool for problem solving (the microscopic and the symbolic levels). Serious games have the strengths of appealing and motivating students. A meta analysis also showed that games can be more effective than traditional instructions, but only when considering working memory limitations [6].

To this end, we created an online puzzle game in physics, in particular Newtonian mechanics for the first year university students, that uses simulation to represent physical objects at the macroscopic level and a knowledge tutor (namely QTut) to explain physical phenomenon at the microscopic and the symbolic levels. The game was implemented using HTML5, JavaScript, Box2D-JS, PHP, and Ajax (Asynchronous Javascript and XML) for rich web experiences, JSON (JavaScript Object Notation) for lightweight data storage, and NLTK (natural language tool kit) for natural language processing[1]. We adhered to the flow framework [7] in designing the game to consider experiential learning [8] and followed rapid prototyping to iteratively create prototypes over short period.

2   Game System Design

2.1   Designing Educational Games and the Flow Experiences

The flow framework considers player, game artefact, and task elements for designing optimal experience (flow) in educational games (Fig. 1) [7]. The framework divides the experiential learning in games into three important phases: (a) inducing flow antecedents, i.e. factors that contribute to the flow experience and should be considered in educational game design, (b) achieving flow state, i.e. an experience where players are completely unaware of their surroundings since they are fully concentrated on solving the tasks in games, and (c) getting the outcomes of being in the flow experience in gaming (flow consequences) which include learning and exploratory behavior.

Flow antecedents include clear goals, good cognitive/immediate feedback, and autonomy for performing cognitive task and using game artefacts [9], with the addition of playability for the artefacts. The premise is, therefore, games that

---

[1] http://www.nltk.org/.

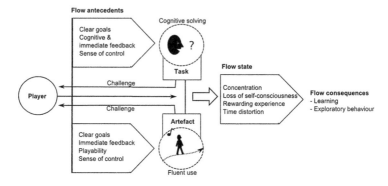

Fig. 1. The flow framework.

are well equipped with the antecedents in form of proper challenges (stimuli) are more likely to promote users reaching the flow state and, subsequently, learning. This emphasizes the importance of integrating the antecedents into game mechanics and gameplay.

2.2 Game Mechanics, Gameplay, and the Flow Antecedents

To develop the game mechanics and the gameplay, we considered two educational artefacts in the physics game: a simulation and a tutoring tool (QTut). Tasks in the game include understanding physics concepts (conceptual knowledge) and solving physics problems (procedural knowledge). To be easily grasped, we selected puzzle guessing as the primary mechanic of the game with the tutor as scaffolding. Table 1 shows the game mechanics in relation with flow antecedents.

Using the game mechanics we constructed the gameplay. All game levels are initially locked except at the base level (level 1). For simplicity, all tasks in a level have equal weights for scoring. However, each level has three most difficult tasks, with each indicated by a star. If a student answers a starred task, he will receive one star.

A level has a topic related to its preceding and succeeding levels. For instance, force and torque can be two successive levels. If a level is unrelated to its preceding, the tutor presents an introduction to denote a topic transition. A student may progress to a level (i.e., unlock a level) if he has passed its preceding level. A student completes a level if he earns at least two stars and scores above a certain threshold. During the game, a student may query the tutor about concepts, formulas, and terminologies. Moreover, relevant tools, e.g. ruler and calculator, can be used to help solving the puzzles. There is no timeout in the game but we use the timer for logging purpose.

3 Game Development

To develop the game artefacts, we started from identifying challenges in the development of the game, devising the solutions, implementing each solution as

Table 1. Game mechanics and flow antecedents of artefacts and tasks in game for learning physics.

No	Game mechanics	Flow antecedents	Elements
1	A task is defined as a puzzle where the system poses the puzzle and the player solves the puzzle in turn	Clear goal	Task
2	Game level consists of a sequence of puzzles		
3	Game level are either unlocked or locked		
4	Required metrics for unlocking a level are game score and collectibles (e.g. star) in its preceding level		
5	Both the selected and the correct answers are immediately highlighted after a user answering the puzzle	Cognitive feedback	
6	The tutor immediately provides customized text-auditory feedback		
7	Puzzles are given with increasing difficulties in each level	Sense of control	
8	Topics are interrelated for successive game levels		
9	Checkpoints are available in each game level		
10	The tutor may provide hints	Clear goal	Artefact
11	Proper symbols for representing game levels (e.g. grid lock to represent locked levels)		
12	Scaffolding using visual feedback from the simulation	Immediate feedback	
13	Scaffolding using text-auditory responses from the tutor		
14	Grouping functions of game elements into the same grid to ease navigation	Sense of control	
15	Freedom to explore the simulation (to select, to move, to rotate, to collide objects)		
16	Functionality to reset the simulation		
17	Freedom to query the tutor		
18	Providing relevant tools to solve the puzzles if necessary		
19	The use of simulation to mimic real object behavior	Playbility	
20	The use of tutor to mimic teacher		
21	Cartoonish visual graphics for the simulation		
22	Selectable cartoonish avatars for the tutor		
23	Musical background during play		

a module, and ended with integrating the modules into a complete system. We considered three challenges in developing the game system: extensibility refers to the ease to produce a variety of games for different topics, scalability means the ease to attach new modules to the system, and reusability corresponds to the use of some modules for other purposes. Therefore, to address the challenges, we created game format and knowledge based tutor, and implemented the system in a modular fashion.

3.1 Game Level and Game Format

We used game levels and created game format to allow extensibility [10]. The game level clusters learning topics into levels based on their complexity. The game format sets each game level as series of tasks -a puzzle set- drawn from the database (a JSON file). A task - or a task item- is either a closed ended question about a simulated event or an action request in the simulation area. Figure 2 described a puzzle set that consists of several task items. Each task item has two types of data: the scaffolding data and the simulation data.

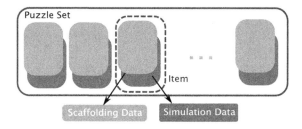

Fig. 2. A puzzle set and a task item.

Using the game format, a game consists of a sequence of inter-related tasks that can be easily created to learn problem solving skills. Some tasks can be recalled several times to promote a retrieval practice, which is essential for learning [5].

3.2 Knowledge Based Tutor

Beside the scaffolding data in the task item, we created QTut, a knowledge based tutor. QTut allows students to query some information in relation to the task at hand.

To support the extensibility of QTut, we created *knowledge triplet* (Qs, R, DA), where Qs refers to a list of query samples; R represents a response to a list of query samples Qs; and DA denotes dialog act (Program 1). The knowledge triplet (subsequently called triplet) represents QTUt knowledge on learning topics. Consequently, the number of triplets is contingent on the coverage of the learning topics in the game.

Table 2. An example of N-gram TF-IDF table with 2 triplets.

N-gram words	TF-IDF of triplet 1	TF-IDF of triplet 2
Net force	0.40	0
Normal force	0	0.4
Force	0.10	0.10

```
Program 1 (A knowledge triplet):
{  "Qs": ["Define normal force","What is normal  force"],
   "R": "Normal force  (N) is the component (perpendicular to the surface
        of contact) of the contact force exerted on an object by,
        for instance, the surface of a floor or wall, preventing the
        object from penetrating the surface",
   "DA": { "key": ["what", "define"],
           "intention": "ASK_EXPLAIN" }
}
```

Using NLTK, we use the triplets to construct a N-gram term frequency - inverse document frequency (TF-IDF) table (Table 2) that measures how concentrated the occurrence of a given word in a collection of triplets. Words with high TF-IDF numbers imply a strong relationship with the triplet they appear in, suggesting that if that word were to appear in a query, the triplet could be of interest to the student.

To match a user query to a triplet, we also transformed the user query into a set of N-gram words. We developed a Naive Bayes classifier to determine the similarity between the set of query words and the triplets using TF-IDF information. QTut subsequently ranks the similarity values in descending order and removes triplets that have similarity values below a certain threshold. QTut performs intention matching on the DA of the remaining triplets with the following rules: if it finds a match, then returns the corresponding triplet; otherwise, returns the triplet with the highest similarity value.

QTut has two response modes: "text" and "text-auditory". For text-auditory mode, we use a free text-to-speech (TTS) web service[2] to convert texts into speeches. The procedure is that QTut sends the texts to the TTS web API using HTTP GET and the TTS web API subsequently synthesizes the speeches and sends them to QTut. This supports both extensibility and scalability.

3.3 Modular System

To facilitate scalability and reusability, the game system is divided into functionality modules (Fig. 3): (a) the tutoring module delivers questions, provides hints and feedbacks, and responds to queries; (b) the physics simulation module

---

[2] VoiceRSS Text To Speech (http://voicerss.org/).

handles all graphical events based on laws in physics; (c) the delivery module draws a task item from the puzzle set either in random, sequential, or difficulty based order; and (d) the data module accesses, organizes, and manipulates game database (i.e., game contents, game configuration, and user log).

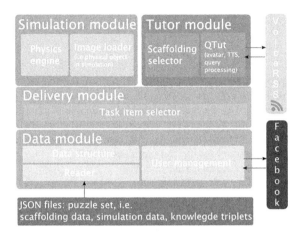

Fig. 3. A stack of modules as a complete system architecture.

To minimize the needs of user management and to support the game distribution, the system is connected to a social networking platform (Facebook) using *Facebook Javascript API*[3]. The system extracts user information on Facebook to be stored into the database.

3.4 Graphical User Interface (GUI)

Good GUI is essential to improve goal clarity and sense of control of artefacts. To this end, the layout of the game GUI was designed using grid systems to group all elements according to their functionalities. This allows the game users to easily comprehend and navigate the interface [11]. Figure 4 shows the wireframe of the game GUI: tutor area on the top right consists of a tutor avatar and an input text to enter query for the tutor, information area on the middle presents feedback and task from the tutor, and the simulation area on the bottom plays physics events. The final GUI of the Physics game prototype is shown in Fig. 4(b).

The GUI elements (e.g., buttons and playable objects) use the feedforward and feedback concept to allow intuitive interaction. Feedforward is the information that occurs during or after user action, e.g., on-screen messages indicating what to do. Feedback is 'the return of information about the result of a process or activity' [12], e.g., clicking on a button opens a new window. Figure 5(a) shows the use of feedforward and feedback in a Logout button and Fig. 5(b) shows the

---

[3] Facebook Developer API (https://developers.facebook.com/).

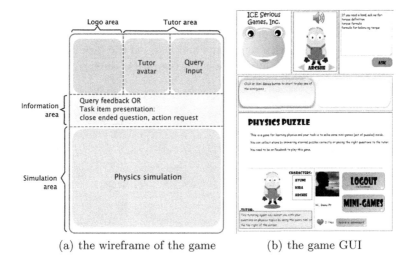

(a) the wireframe of the game   (b) the game GUI

Fig. 4. Wireframe of the game vs. the game GUI

(a) Feedforward and feedback (b) Feedforward of a ruler
in a Logout button   in simulation

Fig. 5. Examples of feedforward and feedback.

feedforward for using a ruler in simulation. Feedforward conveys an implicit message that the logout button is click-able by changing its color upon mouse-over event; and the feedback responds to user action (a click) by changing the logout button into a login button. Feedforward is also used to help students in problem solving. For instance, a calculator button appears if a task item asks student to calculate force. The physics simulation shows a ruler if student needs to measure length or distance.

3.5   The Game Prototype

The game prototype has two levels: force and torque. The first level consists of nine close ended questions. The questions are either conceptual or procedural problems. The second level has six action requests that demands student to interact with objects in the simulation area. Figure 6(a) shows a list of game levels where all levels are locked except level 1 (force). Figure 6(b) shows a task item in the first level that asks about stationary state. Figure 6(c) shows a task item in the second level that demands student to balance the mobile toy. Each correct answer is awarded with ten points and a star-if the task item is a starred task item. A student passes a level if he earns two stars (three stars are available in each level) and scores above 50 %.

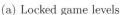
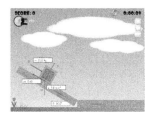
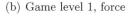
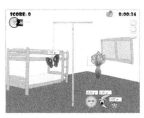

(a) Locked game levels   (b) Game level 1, force   (c) Game level 2, torque

Fig. 6. Game levels

4   Conclusions and Future Works

In this paper, we have presented our work on designing a physics game to support inquiry learning and retrieval practicing using simulation and knowledge based tutor (QTut). The game was implemented as an online puzzle game that used driving questions to encourage students to explore the simulation. We addressed three challenges in designing the system: extensibility, scalability, and reusability. Consequently, we defined game levels and game format to cope with extensibility. Also, knowledge triplets were designed to represent QTut knowledge. The system was divided into modules to allow scalability and reusability. The game GUI was designed using feedforward and feedback concepts on a grid system.

This work provided a baseline for creating educational games using the flow framework. We set the tasks with the increasing difficulties but we have not implemented difficulty adaptation into the system. It will be beneficial to explore the mechanism for difficulty adaptation. Task and user models proposed by [13] may fit to our case since our game prototype has leveled gameplay. In the future, we will test the game for its usefulness by assessing user performance and user perception of the games which is essential for serious games [14].

Acknowledgment. This work was supported in part by the Erasmus Mundus Joint Doctorate in Interactive and Cognitive Environments, which is funded by the EACEA Agency of the European Commission under EMJD ICE FPA n 2010-0012. This work also is co-funded by the EU under the FP7, in the Games and Learning Alliance (GaLA) Network of Excellence, Grant Agreement nr. 258169.

References

1. Johnstone, A.H.: Why is science difficult to learn? things are seldom what they seem. Comput. Assist. Learn. **7**(2), 75–83 (1991)
2. Heyworth, R.: Procedural and conceptual knowledge of expert and novice students for the solving of a basic problem in chemistry. Int. J. Sci. Educ. **21**(2), 195–211 (1999)
3. Kirschner, P., Clark, R.: Work: an analysis of the failure of constructivist, discovery, problem-based, experiential, and inquiry-based teaching. Educ. Psychol. **41**(2), 75–86 (2006)
4. Jong, T.D.: Technological advances in inquiry learning. Science **312**(5773), 532–533 (2006). (New York, N.Y.)
5. Karpicke, J.D., Blunt, J.R.: Retrieval practice produces more learning than elaborative studying with concept mapping. Science **331**(6018), 772–775 (2011). (New York, N.Y.)
6. Wouters, P., van Nimwegen, C., van Oostendorp, H., van der Spek, E.D.: A meta-analysis of the cognitive and motivational effects of serious games. J. Educ. Psychol. **105**(2), 249–265 (2013)
7. Kiili, K., de Freitas, S., Arnab, S., Lainema, T.: The design principles for flow experience in educational games. Procedia Comput. Sci. **15**, 78–91 (2012). 4th International Conference on Games and Virtual Worlds for Serious Applications(VS-GAMES 2012)
8. Kolb, D.A., et al.: Experiential Learning: Experience as the Source of Learning and Development, vol. 1. Prentice-Hall Englewood Cliffs, Upper Saddle River (1984)
9. Csikszentmihalyi, I.S.: Optimal Experience: Psychological Studies of Flow in Consciousness. Cambridge University Press, Cambridge (1992)
10. Pranantha, D., Bellotti, F., Berta, R., DeGloria, A.: A format of serious games for higher technology education topics: a case study in a digital electronic system course. In: International Conference on Advanced Learning Technologies, pp. 13–17, Rome. IEEE (2012)
11. Elam, K.: Grid Systems: Principles of Organizing Type (Design Briefs). Princeton Architectural Press, New York (2004)
12. Wensveen, S.A.G., Djajadiningrat, J.P., Overbeeke, C.J.: Interaction frogger: a design framework to couple action and function through feedback and feedforward. In: Designing Interactive Systems: Processes, Practices, Methods, and Techniques, pp. 177–184, New York, NY. ACM (2004)
13. Bellotti, F., Berta, R., De Gloria, A., Primavera, L.: Adaptive experience engine for serious games. IEEE Trans. Comput. Intell. AI Games **1**(4), 264–280 (2009)
14. Bellotti, F., Kapralos, B., Lee, K., Moreno-Ger, P., Berta, R.: Assessment in and of serious games: an overview. Adv. Hum. Comput. Interact. **2013**, 1 (2013)

Mind Book – A Social Network Trainer for Children with Depression

Andreas Schrammel[1]([✉]), Helmut Hlavacs[1], Manuel Sprung[1],
Isabelle Müller[2], M. Mersits[2], C. Eicher[2], and N. Schmitz[2]

[1] Entertainment Computing, University of Vienna,
Währinger StraßE 29, 1090 Vienna, Austria
andreas_schrammel@chello.at,
{helmut.hlavacs,manuel.sprung}@univie.ac.at
[2] Clinical Child and Adolescent Psychology,
University of Vienna, Liebiggasse 5, 1010 Vienna, Austria
isabelle.mueller@univie.ac.at

Abstract. In this paper we present the therapeutical social network MindBook. MindBook is a web page designed to strengthen the self-esteem of children with depression, and show them that a positive self-expression causes positive feedback from friends in the social network. Depression therapy follows the Modular Approach to Therapy for Children with Anxiety, Depression, Trauma or Conduct Problems (MATCH-ADTC), including videos, audio and images to be consumed by the children. MindBook also includes additional features like games and a week planner to help the children to include real life activities into their daily lives. We present the results of two studies including children from different age groups, for evaluating the effect of MindBook on children and the system usability.

Keywords: Children · Depression · Social network · Self-presentation

1 Introduction

One in ten children and adolescents aged 5–16 years suffers from mental or behavioural disorders that significantly impairs functioning, and 40 % suffer from more than one class of disorders [2]. Despite the availability of effective psychological treatments only one third of children and adolescents with mental disorders receive services for their illness. The consequences of untreated mental health problems are profound. Shortage of mental health professionals trained in effective psychological treatments, the complexity and comorbidity of youth mental and behavioural problems, and the restricted flexibility of many evidence-based treatment protocols may be reasons for limited access to effective treatment. Changes in the financing of effective interventions and redesign of effective treatment protocols in a more flexible modular approach are important to solve this problem. However, these changes by themselves are unlikely to eradicate unmet

© Springer International Publishing Switzerland 2015
A. De Gloria (Ed.): GALA 2014, LNCS 9221, pp. 152–162, 2015.
DOI: 10.1007/978-3-319-22960-7_15

need for treatment. Surveys show that the majority of those who received no treatment actually felt that they did not have an emotional or behavioural problem requiring treatment. This highlights the need for awareness interventions to improve the perception of need among those suffering from mental disorders, and the need to deliver preventive interventions in formats that will be more accessible to children and adolescents.

In this paper we introduce MindBook, a computer-game based cognitive behavioural training for children with depression. The game concept is based on common cognitive behavioral therapy (CBT) strategies for depression [6], and uses a simulated social network similar to Facebook. Skills and tools to cope with depression are taught by psychoeducational elements and should be applied by children within the virtual environment of MindBook.

2   Related Work

Learning in a playful way has been proven to be very effective and motivating, thus provoking the development of games that aim primarily to a learning effect instead of fun [1]. Nowadays these games are often used for training, education, advertising, or simulation. The virtual reality allows testing situations that are too dangerous, expensive or impossible to train in reality [5]. For this "genre" the term "serious games" has been coined.

Several serious games have shown a positive effect on people suffering from depression, including SuperBetter[1], Personal Zen[2], and PTSDCoach.[3]

The great popularity the games on Facebook, and the fact that serious games become more and more popular leads to the idea to combine serious games with social networks. Most serious games are designed as single player games and searching for the right solution can be very frustrating and time consuming. Therefore the advantages of social networks can be used to succeed in the game. Konert et al. [3] propose to apply the concepts of *Peer Tutoring* [7] and *Peer Assessment* [4] on serious games in conjunction with social networks. Konert and his colleagues developed a framework which offers two main functionalities. The first supports the *exchange of user-generated content*. This enables users to store content related to the game in a database and other users can access this information if they need hints to proceed. On the one hand this meets the concept of *Peer Tutoring* because information can be shared and accessed by every player. On the other hand the concept of *Peer Assessment* is met because shared solutions can be also rated by the community. The second functionality concerns *influencing the game*. This means that the players include their social networks into their gaming experiences. This can increase the players awareness for the game and also invite other people from the social network to participate in the game. The second point provides more incentives, if additionally to text, the posts also invite to take part in the game.

---

[1] https://www.superbetter.com/.
[2] http://www.personalzen.com/.
[3] http://www.ptsd.va.gov/public/materials/apps/PTSDCoach.asp.

3   Mind Book – A Social Network Trainer for Children with Depression

The common use of social networks includes children as well as adults. Many children and young adolescents are very active on Facebook. This frequent usage can be enriching for the children's social lives, but there are also hidden risks. Social networks offer a broad platform for ostracism and mobbing. Furthermore children with low self-esteem could be discouraged by social exclusion and negative tendencies could be increased.

To counteract these tendencies the idea of a *Therapeutical Social Network* named *MindBook* was born. Children should have the feeling that they are part of a social network and therefore it was important that the application's look is similar to Facebook (see Fig. 1).

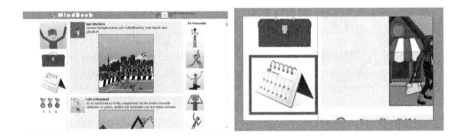

Fig. 1. MindBook mainpage

Fig. 2. Introduction video

Though the functionality is different to conventional social networks. Mind-Book follows the goal of strengthening the children's self-esteem and to show that feedback is more positive, when the self-expression is positive. Children should learn to present themselves in a positive way. Based on the self-portrayal of the children we want to provide feedback to the children. To avoid that children are discouraged by negative feedback of their friends we included a clutch of games and a week planner to help children structure their activities. In addition we planned a reward system for positive self-expression and completion of planned activities.

To achieve this goal already offline existing psychological practices were implemented in this therapeutical social network. This practices are taken from a well working psychological protocol called *Modular Approach to Therapy for Children with Anxiety, Depression, Trauma or Conduct Problems* (MATCH-ADTC) [6]. This protocol is a collection of different procedures on the individual disease patterns. The approach of MindBook is to transfer (some of) the modules for the depression-therapy into a therapeutical social network.

Most of the core modules for depression identified in Weisz and Chorpita [6] are implemented in MindBook. Loosely speaking there are two major types of implementation of the modules. One is representing the content in form of video clips, images or audio files the child consumes. The second type are games the user has to play through. Following the core modules implemented in MindBook are listed in alphabetic order and in what MindBook modules they are realized (Table 1):

Table 1. MindBook modules.

Activity selection	Hobby selection: Choose hobbies from a predefined list (e.g., singing, etc.) Weekplanner: Plan one activity per day they like to do in the following week
Cognitive Coping – BLUE	Game – Memory: Replace negative thoughts by positive ones.
Cognitive Coping – TLC	Image – Change the channel: Try to not to think about negative things Image – Talk to a friend: Talking to friends can distract from bad vibes. Image – Search for the rainbow: Every cloud has a silver lining. Game – Video decision: Figure out the positive solutions for a problem.
Getting Acquainted	Userprofile: Presenting basic information like name, age and hobbies. Feelingsweather: Show how you feel via a weather scale.
Learning About Depression – Child	Various psychoeducational videos: Helpful tools for depression.
Learning to Relax	Audio – Muscle relaxation: 3 different audio clips that help to relax. Video – Slow your breathing: Conscious breathing helps to relax. Video – Chilloutzone: "Flee" to your personal chilloutzone.
Presenting a Positive Self	Feelingsweather: Show how you feel via a weather scale. Posting to friends: Positive presentation leads to positive feedback. Profileheaderimage: Shades of gray depending on the feelingsweather.
Problem solving	STEPS: Five steps to solve problems.

Educative videos and games are introduced step by step over the first five sessions of MindBook. After this five sessions all the tools are available in the toolbox, where the children can use them when needed.

To find out the children's mood the *feelingsweather* (a weather scale from thundery to bright sunshine) is recorded at the beginning of each session from the last session until the day of the actual session. Depending on this data a feelings baseline b is computed, that influences the friends added and shown in the application and the news they post on the child's pin board. The formula for the baseline computation is

$$b = (0.75 \times actualWeather) + (0.25 \times averageWeather),$$

where the *actualWeather* is the weather for the actual date and the *averageWeather* is the average of the weather value from the beginning of the MindBook usage until the day before the actual date. The graying of the profile header image is influenced by the average weather value for the whole usage.

To fulfill the requirement as a therapeutical social network the therapeutically significant parts have to be highlighted. We discussed how it can be guaranteed, that the children follow the therapeutic contents without distraction by the rest of MindBook. Due to the fact that overlays are a very common tool in modern web applications, we have decided to use this technique for the therapeutic relevant parts inside the application.

To increase the effect of focusing the children to the overlays' content the rest of the page in the background is grayed out and inactive. To close an overlay the expected action has to be fulfilled. This actions can be saving the inserted data or changes or the end of a game or video. The parts realized in overlays are:

- Login checkup
- Videos
- Games
- Hobby selection
- Logout

Further parts implemented in overlays are the tools from the toolbox, but those (except of the games) can be closed by the user by clicking the overlay.

After the selection of the current mood in the *first session*, the layout and functions are described by a screenshot video and the children can explore Mind-Book on their own. As in all social networks they have their own profile page with basic information about themselves. Here the children can also select their hobbies. Further more it is possible to plan different activities to be done during the following week, a task that should help children to structure their daily lives.

The application also contains a *toolbox*, where the children find the tools already introduced in the past sessions. These can be used by the users to copy with difficult daily situations. In the sessions two to five, children are asked in the login overlay not only to specify their feelingsweathers but also if they have filled in the task sheets at the end of the last sessions, and how many of the planned activities of the last week have been actually been carried out. Furthermore from the second session on children can change the mood of their profile images. After the confirmation of the overlay the children have five minutes to explore the news or already unlocked tools in the toolbox. Then the educative video for the current session starts and introduces the content. From session six on children can use MindBook as they like, without new therapeutic content. However they always can access the introduced tools via the toolbox.

The converted MATCH modules for depression therapy are introduced over the first five sessions as follows: In the first session the whole application and its areas are introduced. In this introduction the posts of friends, links to different subsites and the header are explained. The first session focuses on the introduction and the module *activity selection*. The week planner is explained in the introductory video (see Fig. 2) and when the children open their profiles, an educative video explaining the importance of hobbies in daily life is started. Subsequently users are asked to select hobbies. At the end of this session the task sheet *How to express my feelings* is shown.

The second session teaches how to *relax*. This is achieved by presenting relaxing audio files and videos showing how to copy with daily stress. The importance of relaxation is again stressed by an introductory video. This session ends with the possibility to download the task sheets *My chilloutzone "and" Relaxation at home.*

Session three concentrates on *problem solving* and the *TLC part of cognitive coping.* First the five steps of problem solving are introduced, followed by asking children to solve problems shown in a sequence of videos by selecting one out of three possible solutions (see Fig. 3a). The task sheet in this session also deals with the five steps of problem solving.

(a) Video decision   (b) Memory

Fig. 3. The games in MindBook

In session four users learn how to replace negative with positive thoughts. This covers the module *cognitive coping - BLUE* of the MATCH protocol. First the topic is introduced again by a video, and the following game is explained. The game is inspired by the well-known children's game memory. In this game the negative thoughts should be replaced by their positive counterpart (see Fig. 3b). The positive thoughts are sunny whereas the negative ones are a thunderstorm.

The content of each card are audio files that are played by hovering/clicking the card. At the end of this session the task sheets *Changing B-L-U-E Thoughts* and *Double Bubbles on My Own* are provided.

Session five is the last guided session and summarizes the first four sessions. Users fill in a questionnaire about their experiences with MindBook and can select the tools that worked best for them.

After these five sessions the children can use the application on their own and rely on the tools whenever they need them.

4   Experimental Evaluation

To retrieve the data for an experimental evaluation two studies were executed. The first was conducted with some school classes and the second one with a couple of voluntary children.

4.1   Effect on Children

The target of the first study was to investigate the psychological effects on the children. This examination was made with some classes in two schools. One investigation was made in an elementary school, the other in a high school. Children worked through the first five MindBook sessions, where the third and fourth session were linked together due to time reasons. We chose these two sessions because the topics are most similar in these two units. Unfortunately in the high school it came to problems with the Internet in the fifth session so it could not be completed. Therefore data is evaluated for the first four sessions. The evaluation showed that the children in the mean are using the system longer at the last session than in the first.

Figure 4 shows that the onlinetime the children spent in MindBook increased from session to session.

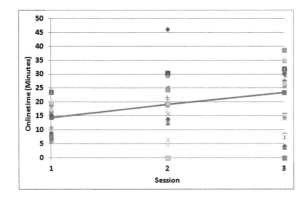

Fig. 4. Onlinetime per session (session 3 and 4 are linked together as one session)

The feelingsweather is an indication for the children's emotional state. Unfortunately the children not always recorded the feelingsweather of the days between the appointments but this is fixed in the actual version of MindBook, so that the children can not progress without recording it. In the mean the feelingsweather is in the positive half but there are also outliers in the negative half. But many children record a better feelingsweather at the end of MindBook usage than at the beginning (see Fig. 5).

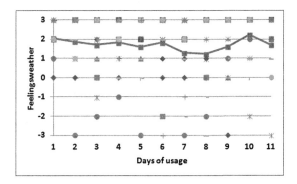

Fig. 5. Feelingsweather per day of usage

4.2 Usability Evaluation

The second evaluation investigated how easy and intuitive the system is to be used. For this evaluation we visited a high school and a judo club where we asked children for their participation. For the evaluation we divided the participants into three age groups: 6–10 years (20 % of the participants), 11–14 years (50 %) and older than 14 years (30 %).

The children are all experienced with computers and except of the age group from 6–10 all of them are familiar with Facebook on computers as well as on mobile devices. This knowledge suggests a basic understanding for the handling of different applications and the concept of touch surfaces.

To retrieve the data the children were confronted with tasks that all could be met before or in the first MindBook session. This is due to the reason that the participants do not have existing accounts. The tasks are:

1. Create a user account
2. Login and fill in the login overlay
3. Plan a week
4. Set your hobbies
5. Return to the main page

To evaluate the usability of MindBook application we investigated the questions about *handling* MindBook (Is the given order of data input fields followed by the child? Is it obvious that always four profile images belong together? Does the child autonomously click buttons for progress like saving data, login? Is the meaning of the feelings weather in the login overlay obvious to the child? Is the concept of "Drag and Drop" intuitive and if not is it necessary to show it or suffices an explanation? How many hobbies are selected and if there are more than ten selected is it obvious that ten is the upper limit?), *Videos* (How long do the videos need to load? Do children watch the videos attentively? Do children try to skip videos?), and *Time* (How long does it last until the child finds the correct link? How long does the child need to fulfill all tasks (without watching videos)? How many time is spent watching videos (including waiting to load them)?).

Observations of the related activities made during our experiments led to the following conclusions.

- **Input Order:** First we observed if the children follow the given sequence of fields to input data. This observation was made in the registration process and during the login. At the account registration 80 % of the children followed the given order, whereas at the login 100 % adhered the order of "Username" and "Passwort".
- **Profile Images:** The second issue observed during the registration process was if the children recognize that the four profile images in a row belong together and can be selected via the radio button on the left side. 60 % of the participants were aware of that fact, whereas the other 40 % needed a hint to select their profile image.
- **Autonomous Saving:** The next point observed answers the question if it is obvious to the children that all of the tasks mentioned above except of the last one ("Return to the main page") have to be finished with saving the inserted data. Three out of five necessary confirmations were made autonomously by 100 % of the participants.
- **Drag and Drop:** Another very important question was, if the concept of "Drag and Drop" is intuitive to the children. Due to the fact that this concept is more common on mobile devices than on the computer, 50 % of the children needed help in the loginoverlay. In the weekplanner, where drag and drop is used to plan the week the concept was clear to 90 % of the children.
- **Hobbies:** In the fourth task we were interested if the children find the part of MindBook where they can select their hobbies, how many hobbies they will select and if it is obvious that ten hobbies is the upper limit for this selection. 90 % of the participants identified the profile page as correct place to set their hobbies. The other 10 % needed a hint to find the page. The majority of the children selected less than ten hobbies. For the 20 % that selected ten hobbies it was obvious that this is the upper limit.
- **Feelings Weather:** Further we were interested if the meaning of the feelingsweather is obvious to the children. It turned out that the presentation is self-explanatory and their were no questions what this pictures mean and what to do with them.

As mentioned above the videos give the children information about the upcoming tasks. So it is necessary to watch the videos attentively, because the more attentively a video is watched the easier the task is to be fulfilled afterwards. The results of this inspection are split into the age ranges mentioned above. The evaluation shows that particularly the video before the hobby selection is watched less attentive than the other ones. Further it turned out that the children in the age from 6 to 10 are the most inattentive in sum. A reason for the great inattention at the last video could the duration of the video be.

Also interesting for the evaluation is the question how long the children need to fulfill tasks. Figure 6 gives an overview over the consumed mean time grouped by age and picture the time searching and clicking links, working without the time consumed watching videos, the total time watching videos, the total time to fulfill all tasks (total time working) and the whole time including the announcement of the tasks.

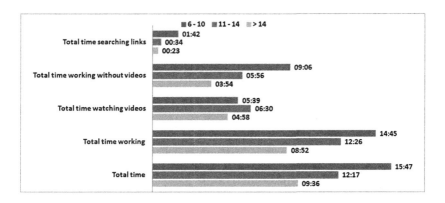

Fig. 6. Mean time per age

- **Find and Click the Correct Link:** Finding the correct link is important to progress with the tasks. With exception of the participants that not followed the introductory video (video 2) attentive, none of the children had problems finding the correct link. The slightly longer time of the age group 6–10 is due problems handling the mouse.
- **Time to Fulfill All Tasks:** This point shows the time the children needed to fulfill all tasks without the time needed from the tester to announce the tasks. This is also dependent from the video loading time, therefore the graph is also pictured for the time working without watching videos. This clearly shows that the experience with computers is advantageous for the use of MindBook but not indispensable.
- **Time Watching Videos:** This graph shows the time the children spent on watching the videos respectively waiting for them to be loaded.
- **Difference Between Slowest and Fastest:** The greatest difference between the slowest and the fastest time working without watching videos is found in

the age group 11–14 This could be on the one hand due to the experience with computers and on the other hand due to the difference in attention span. In this age group the children gain a lot of new experiences and learn to focus on one task.

5   Conclusion

In this paper we present the therapeutic social network MindBook. MindBook is simulation of a social network, but also contains instructive content like audio and video presentations, as well as simple games. The purpose of MindBook is to help children with depression at various levels, including giving them a toolbox for help in difficult situations, structure their daily lives by planning activities, and presenting themselves in a positive way in real social networks.

We evaluated MindBook in two series of experiments. We observed that children do like using MindBook, that the general mood is improved, and we also analysed age dependent differences in using MindBook.

References

1. Abt, C.C.: Serious Games. University Press of America, Boston (1987)
2. Green, H., McGinnity, A., Meltzer, H., Ford, T., Goodman, R.: Mental health of children and young people in great britain, 2004. Technical report, Office for National Statistics, UK (2005). ISBN 1-4039-8637-1
3. Konert, J., Göbel, S., Steinmetz, R.: Towards social serious games. In: Proceedings of the 6th European Conference on Games Based Learning (ECGBL), vol. 1, pp. 258–261. Academic Bookshop, October 2012
4. Stepanyan, K., Mather, R., Jones, H., Lusuardi, C.: Student engagement with peer assessment: a review of pedagogical design and technologies. In: Spaniol, M., Li, Q., Klamma, R., Lau, R.W.H. (eds.) ICWL 2009. LNCS, vol. 5686, pp. 367–375. Springer, Heidelberg (2009)
5. Susi, T., Johannesson, M., Backlund, P.: Serious games - an overview. School of Humanities and Informatics, University of Skövde, Sweden, Technical report, May 2007
6. Weisz, J. R., Chorpita, B.F.: "Mod squad" for youth psychotherapy, restructuring evidence-based treatment for clinical practice. In: Kendall, P.C. (ed.) Child and Adolescent therapy: Cognitive-Behavioral Procedures, 4th edn. chap. 12, pp. 379–397 (2011)
7. Westera, W., Wagemans, L.: Help me! Online Learner Support through the Self-Organised Allocation of Peer Tutors. 1. LMedia: Publications and Preprints (2007)

Using Avatars for Course Management and Immersion

Martin Sillaots[(⊠)]

Tallinn University, Tallinn, Estonia
martins@tlu.ee

Abstract. Gamification is the use of game elements in non-game environment. One element among others is avatar. The use of avatar in the context of learning can make students to feel themselves more safe and relaxed. It can lead to the more active participation and to immersion. To find out what is the effect of using avatars in education, several courses were designed like games, and feedback information was collected It was found that implementation of avatars was useful for creating anonymous scoreboards, however it did not had any strong effect on immersion. For better results avatar should be combined with other game elements e.g. story.

Keywords: Avatar · Character · Gamification · Game elements · Course design

1 Introduction

Avatar in Sanskrit means bodily incarnation of a God. In computer games and in virtual environments avatar represents the user in the virtual world. In general avatars are used for presenting the user identity and activities to others and to the user itself [1]. Using avatars and other game elements in non-game environment is often called gamification [2]. This approach is frequently used in marketing and business conditions [3]. Education is one field where game elements have started to use lately [2]. The most frequently used game elements are badges, experience points and scoreboard but gamification is not only implementing competition in educational condition. Avatars can be used for course management as a usernames for students in the virtual learning environment (VLE). Some researchers report that using avatars can increase the social presence and built stronger connections between group members [4]. How avatars can be used in course management? Does the avatar increase the immersion to the course? To answer to those questions one Game Design and three courses of Research Methods were designed like games. Later a survey was conducted among students to find out how they perceived different game elements (goals, avatar, scoreboard, luck, competition, collaboration and feedback) and does the gamification lead to the deeper immersion? The model of Flow [5] was used for measuring the immersion among students. This article focuses on the single game elements – avatar.

© Springer International Publishing Switzerland 2015
A. De Gloria (Ed.): GALA 2014, LNCS 9221, pp. 163–173, 2015.
DOI: 10.1007/978-3-319-22960-7_16

2 Avatar Design

Gamification is the use of game elements and game-like thinking in non-gaming environment [2]. Examples of gamification vary from the single game-like learning activity [2] to the entire course designed like a game [6]. Game elements that can be used for gamification are: challenging goals, interactive activities, rich and instant feedback, collaboration, competition, rules, experience points, scoreboards, levels, luck, risk, game world, characters, game aesthetics, story etc. Different elements should be balanced on each other to keep the user in the zone of flow [7]. When goals are clear and activities are organised in engaging way the participants loose the sense of time and they stop worrying about themselves. This phenomenon is called immersion [8].

Characters are avatars and non-player characters (NPC) [9]. When implementation of NPC's requires environment similar to the computer game [10], the avatar design can be integrated with creating the student's profile for the course [6]. This character can be used as an avatar during the entire course. Students can pretend that they are somebody else (e.g. talented game designer or researchers). It can increase the immersion to the course [11]. Research has shown that using avatars can increase the social presence and establish stronger connections in the group. Users who had a chance to design their avatar reported greater satisfaction and felt closer to their classmates than users who did not had a chance to design their avatar. Without giving players a unique identity, the students become less engaged with the content of the game [12].

Avatars are used for providing starting point for the game story, for enabling emotional engagement and visual looks. For commercial videogames it is also strong selling point [9]. Three different approaches how avatars are used in the video games:

- Game is not avatar based – player interacts with the game directly (first person).
- Semi-specific avatar – avatar is controlled by the player as a puppet.
- Specific avatar – avatar is a centre point for the story, they have sophisticated personality and players control avatars to certain limit [9].

Depending on course design course can be seen as a first person game – students interact directly with the course environment or they have direct control over semi-specific avatar in the VLE.

Character design can be driven by the art or by the story. In the first case the graphical appearance (physical type, visual look and other elements) is created. In the second case the character background story is written (role, attitudes, values, personality, behaviour, etc.) [9]. In the end both approaches complement each other. In the educational conditions students can be asked to come out with the avatars related with the course content. E.g. in the course of Research Methods students are encouraged to come up with avatars like Dr. Evil or Mad Professor. This assignment can also involve the design of the icon and story for the avatar. Describing the avatar personality can be related with the combination of archetypes [13] and with the story [14].

3   Using Avatars in Education

Avatars are used decades in virtual worlds and in game environments. Several studies have investigated what motivates the users to design their personal characters and what affects their choices during the design [15–17]. Researchers have found that users like to play with their identity. It enables them to change the world (at least on virtual level). It provides possibility to be somebody else. Similar approach is commonly among the users of dating portals – users physical and virtual selves tend to be different [18]. Participation in online environments is like identity workshop [16]. Avatar design is also part of so called creative play where users are allowed to design elements of virtual world [9].

The use of avatars in learning conditions is mostly related with VLE [4] and with design of serious games [12]. Researchers suggest that using avatars will increase the sense of presence and increase the course satisfaction and motivation [19]. The use of avatars in on-site education is not new [6] but how it effects on student engagement and immersion, is not investigated. Immersion describes the level of user engagement during the gameplay [8]. It is also described by the players ability to induce the feeling of being part of the game world [20].

From the pedagogical point of view, it is of interest whether the use of avatars increases the sense of being present in the course? The current article introduces several cases where avatars were used in the classroom conditions as gamification elements. This approach is based on the theory of possible selves [21], according to which to users try to create their avatars so that they fit best to the environment. The ensuing research question is, when this freedom is provided in the educational conditions does it lead to the deeper immersion?

4   Case Courses

To increase the students' engagement in learning activities four courses were designed like games:

- Game - Course of Game Design for Cross-Media bachelor curriculum, 35 students (23 finished)
- Seminar 1 - Research Seminar One for ICT bachelor level, 60 students (48 finished)
- Seminar 2 - Research Seminar Two for ICT bachelor level, 25 students (19 finished)
- Research - Research Methods for Educational Technology and IT management master curriculums, 31 students (29 finished)

Most of the students who did not finish the course reassigned officially already during the first two weeks of the course. All courses took place during the autumn semester 2013. The content of the courses depended on subject but the learning activities were designed in similar way. In the beginning of the semester it was announced that the course is organized as a game. The goals and the rules of the game were introduced. First assignment was the design of personal avatar. Creating the imaginary personality was mostly needed for representing the student on scoreboards. This solved the issue related with the law of personal data protection. By the law, it is forbidden to compare and publish students' learning results publicly. Same avatar was used as a user name for the course online environment. For course management the Elgg online portfolio was used. It was applied for delivering the learning materials and for uploading students' assignments. For registering to the VLE, students created their avatars. Also during the classroom activities students were approached by avatar names. Students acted under their avatar names in the virtual and physical learning environment.

The avatar design activity involved several subtasks. Students were asked to find a name for their character, design graphical icon for representing them and write a short story to describe their background. In this way both the art and story driven character design was implemented. In the end of the avatar design activity some students were randomly selected for introducing their character to the rest of the class and answering to the avatar related questions.

Students were encouraged to use avatar names that are somehow related with the content of the course. E.g. students from the course of Research Methods picked names like Doc, Dr. House, Dr Dre etc. Surprisingly small amount of students used the possibility to act under a fake name during the course. For most of them it was fine to use their first name. It was recommended to bind the avatar story with the personal learning goals for this course but also purely fantasy-based stories were accepted (Table 1).

In the Game course students formed teams and designed new games from idea to working prototype. Every activity consisted three elements: creating the artefact (e.g.

Table 1. Examples of avatars created by the students

Avatar name: Unicow	Avatar name: Whistler
Avatar story: Having only one horn since birth, she was made fun of by the other cows. Driven by the urge to find a place where she would belong to, she stumbled upon the legend of unicorns. Now, believing she's one unicorn, she has set out to find the mystical creatures. Will she find the unicorns? Will she ever acquire magical powers? Find out in the next episode.	Avatar story: My mission is to understand the relationships between team members and to find ways how to increase the collaboration between conflict members. I believe that conflicts create conditions for better results.

game idea, team description, gameplay, core mechanics, etc.), presenting the artefact in front of the class and asking questions from other teams. In the course of Research Methods and Research Seminars students formed groups and investigated different aspects of research methods. They read scientific articles at home, analysed them in the beginning of each class in groups and introduced the summary of the article in the front of the class. One group introduced the article from the positive perspective, another team from the negative angle. In both cases students were encouraged to start discussion around the aspects of game design or research methods. The order of presentation was generated with the help of random number generator. In this way the game element of luck was implemented.

Some of the activities were related with the competition between individuals. E.g. in the Game course all students were asked to introduce the idea for the new game in teams. The best idea was selected for further development. In the same way students of Research Methods introduced personal research plans for their group. The best plans were selected per group. Best ideas and plans were presented in the front of the class. Winners earned extra points.

Some research methods (dada collection, data analyse, paper formatting and presenting research results) were introduced in the format of quiz. Traditional presentations were mixed with questions. Before explaining the theory the question was asked and students were asked to answer in groups. Theoretical explanations were provided after the answers. Points were distributed based on quiz results.

Courses ended with the final exam (Big Boss Fight). Teams from the Game course introduced their game specifications and demonstrated digital prototypes in the front of visitors from game industry. Course of Research Methods ended with online assignment of writing essay about student's personal research plan. Seminar 1 ended with written test and Seminar 2 with presenting students' personal research plans in the front of fellow students and faculty staff members.

Most of the activities involved cooperation inside of the groups, competition between groups and provided immediate feedback. Every activity generated certain amount of experience points (XP). Based on XP's students were listed in the scoreboard. Levels (grades) were based on score. After the exam students were asked to conduct self-evaluation. They had a chance to adjust the amount of points that were collected during the teamwork. Courses included also several bonus activities and possibilities to earn extra XP's like: testing and evaluating game prototypes from different project, participating on online surveys and providing links to additional learning materials.

5 Methodology

In the end of every course the students were asked to fill in an online survey, in order to find out how students adopt game elements in none-game environment. Different game elements and flow aspects were measured. Two questions were related with the use of avatar. 90 students out of 131 (69%) who ended the course answered to the questionnaire.

The questions were expressed in the form a Likert scale, and with a free text field for additional comments. The interval scale with values: Yes = 4, Rather yes = 3, Rather no = 2, No = 1 was used for the answers. The neutral answer was left out intentionally to force students to take clearer standpoints. Arithmetical averages and standard deviation were calculated per every question and for the group of questions.

Table 2. Scales for the questions and results

Options	Value	Min	Max
Yes	4	3.26	4.00
Rather yes	3	2.51	3.25
Rather no	2	1.76	2.50
No	1	1.00	1.75

During the data analysis, average results were tied with text-based explanations. The consequent interpretation key was the following. The range from 1 to 4 was divided in to 4 equal intervals. When the average score belonged to the range from 4 to 3.26 it would indicate that avatars were successfully implemented to the course and accepted by the students (Yes). If the aggregated result felled in the range from 3.25 to 2.51, then the use of avatars was partly successful (Rather yes). If the result fell between 2.5 and 1.76, then the concept of avatars was not successfully integrated (Rather no). 1.75 to 1 means failure (No). All quantitative estimations are illustrated with qualitative feedback to find out are the numbers valid and reliable (Tables 2 and 3).

6   Results

In general, the implementation of the game element – Avatar was not successful. The average rating for using the avatars in the course design was 2,27. It means that using avatars was not justified form the students' point of view.

Table 3. Students' estimations to the use of avatars (means, standard deviations and numbers of data points).

Questions	Game			Seminar 1			Seminar 2			Research			Total	
	M	SD	N	M	SD	N	M	SD	N	M	SD	N	M	SD
Design of a personal avatar was good for the immersion	3.07	0.96	15	2.88	0.86	42	2.75	1.16	8	2.29	1.12	24	2.74	1.01
Avatar influenced my behaviour during the course	1.53	0.92	15	1.88	0.76	43	1.88	0.83	8	1.79	1.02	24	1.80	0.86
Total	**2.30**			**2.38**			**2.31**			**2,04**			**2,27**	

The lowest score (2,04) was given by the students from the course of Research Methods and the highest (2,38) by the students of the Research Seminar 1. Most likely, this is caused by the age differences between those two groups. Younger bachelor students may find themselves more engaged with the game like environment compared to mature master students. It is surprising that avatars were so badly received by the students from the Course of Game Design (2,30).

According to the results it seams that creating an avatar helps students to immerse with the course in some level (total result for the question 2,74 - rather yes) (Figs. 1 and 2).

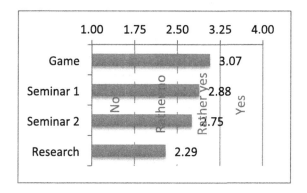

Fig. 1. Average results per courses to the question - Design of a personal avatar was useful for immersion.

28 % of students accepted and 30 % rather accepted that design of the avatar was good for the immersion. 29 % of students rather not and 12 % did not agreed with this statement. Most of the Game Design and Seminar 1 participants agreed that avatar influenced the immersion. Students from Seminar 2 provided equal amount of positive and negative answers. Most of the students from the course of Research Methods did not find avatar useful for immersion.

In positive comments students said about designing avatar, for example:

- It was interesting experience to create different personality.
- It reduced the stress level during the course.
- Avatar design helped me to clarify my goals for this course.
- In general I recommend making new personality for the course because students can act more boldly in the anonymous conditions.
- It was fun thing to do and good chance to show your creativity.
- Avatar can tell a lot about your personality.

Respectively, in negative comments students said, for example:

- I really don't understand why the avatar was needed. I think this gamification should work also without avatar.
- In this case avatar was more like pseudonym, but everybody knew who is who.
- To me it was just another meaningless task that I had to do.

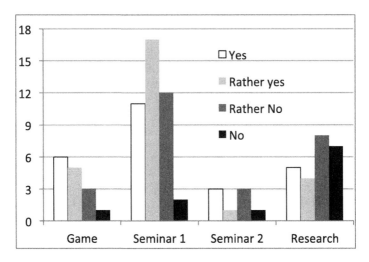

Fig. 2. Distribution of answers to the question - Design of a personal avatar was useful for immersion

- People lost their interest towards avatars soon when they created it. Most of the students did not put much effort on their avatar design. It would be better to ask students to draw their personal avatar. Also some elements in the avatar story should be compulsory. E.g. background, current situation, future plans, etc. It would be interesting to reflect the game through entire course by asking students to write the blog entries from their character point of view.
- Avatar was only needed for protecting the identity and abiding the law of protection of personal data.

Most of the students did not find that the avatar was influencing their behaviour during the course (average result for the question 1,80 - rather no) (Figs. 3 and 4).

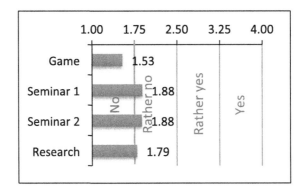

Fig. 3. Average results per courses to the question - Avatar influenced my behaviour during the course.

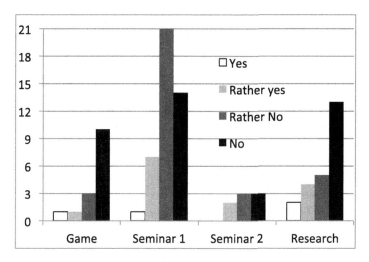

Fig. 4. Distribution of answers to the question - Avatar influenced my behaviour during the course

4 % agreed and 16 % of students rather agreed that avatar influenced their behaviour during the course. 36 % rather not and 44 % of students did not find any influence. It is not so clear why the avatar design had the smallest impact on the course of Computer Games. It was expected that the content of the course and the game like format would have fit nicely together. Most likely this result was influenced by the low rate of general immersion during the course caused by other factors like course environment and management of learning activities – not described in this article.

In the positive comments students mention, among other:

- Thanks to my avatar I had more positive attitude during the course.
- In general I'm brave soul but avatar created some extra courage.
- I felt that thanks to the avatar I was thinking differently.
- I liked the fact that nobody knows who is the person behind my avatar name. I don't have to worry about my position in the scoreboard nor about the nature of my comments in VLE. But I think avatars have much stronger effect in online courses.

In negative comments they say:

- I was just myself (this comment was mentioned 4 times)
- I did not felt any effect on my behaviour (3 times).
- It was little embarrassing to see my avatar name presented during the course.
- Making the avatar felt a little bit silly.

7 Discussion

The goal of this article was to find out how the game element avatar can be used in course design and how the students accept this element, and how large is the influence of the avatar to the immersion? Although for some of the students creating the new personality was an interesting activity that increased the engagement during the course, the majority of the students did not experience any deeper immersion caused by the avatar. Some of them even doubted the meaningfulness of the gamification in this aspect.

The main reason why avatar was not increasing the immersion among students could be due to the fact that the main goal for the avatar design was to generate safe names for the course scoreboard. This goal of the course design was met but the rest of the potential of the use of the avatars was not covered. It may be that for creating deeper immersion, avatars should be integrated with a larger number of game elements. One possibility is to bind avatars with the story. When story-based learning activities, such as developing dialogue skills [22] and solving conflicts [23] are more known, then the design of the entire course as a story is not so common [24]. One possible way to connect avatars and the course with a story is to design the course as a character's journey [14]. In the beginning of the course students are asked to design their personal avatars. The character and the story of the avatar should be related with the content of the course. In this way the course could create a personal meaning to the students. During such a course the character evolves by collecting and storing the pieces of information that are needed to achieve their goals and the evidences that demonstrate their achievements. In the end of the course, the students are asked to conduct a self-evaluation by comparing their initial objectives with achievements. In this way every student is telling a personal story during the course.

Although designing characters for the course can be an interesting case of gamification, this seams to be unnecessary for most of the students. Maybe it's reasonable to focus on elements that support gamified leaning activities and leave the avatar design for more virtual environments like games and online social networks.

Acknowledgments.   This research was supported by SEGAN (LLP-EC 519332) network and Tallinn University Institute of Informatics.

References

1. Benford, S., Greenhalgh, C., Rodden, T., Pycock, J.: Collaborative virtual environments. Commun. ACM **44**, 79–85 (2001)
2. Kapp, K.M.: The Gamification of Learning and Instruction: Game-based Methods and Strategies for Training and Education, p. 336. Pfeiffer, San Francisco (2012)
3. Huotari, K., Hamari, J.: "Gamification" from the perspective of service marketing. In: CHI 2011. Vancouver (2011)
4. Annetta, L.A., Holmes, S.: Creating presence and community in a synchronous virtual learning environment using avatars. Int. J. Instr. Technol. Distance Learn., 27–44 (2006)
5. Sweetser, P., Wyeth, P.: GameFlow: a model for evaluating player enjoyment in games. Comput. Entertain **3**(3), 24 (2005)
6. Sheldon, L.: The Multiplayer Classroom: Designing Coursework as a Game. Cengage Learning PTR (2011)
7. Csikszentmihalyi, M.: Flow: The Psychology of Optimal Experience. Harper & Row, New York (1990)

8. Baños, R.M., Botella, C., Alcañiz, M., Liaño, V., Guerrero, B., Rey, B.: Immersion and emotion: their impact on the sense of presence. Cyberpsychol Behav. **7**, 734–741 (2004)
9. Adams, E.: Fundamentals of Game Design, 2nd edn, p. 700. New Riders, Berkeley (2009)
10. Duch, A., Petit, J., Rodríguez-Carbonell, E., Roura, S.: Fun in CS2. In: Foley, O., Restivo, M.T., Uhomoibhi, J.O., Helfert, M. (eds.) Proceedings of the 5th International Conference on Computer Supported Education, pp. 437–442. SciTePress, Aachen (2013)
11. Sweeney, P.: Sharing a facebook avatar constructively in the classroom. Soc. Inf. Technol. Teach. Educ. Int. Conf. **2012**, 3785–3790 (2012)
12. Annetta, L.A.: The "I's" have it: a framework for serious educational game design. Rev. Gen. Psychol. **14**, 105–112 (2010)
13. Campbell, J.: The Hero with a Thousand Faces, 3rd edn, p. 432. New World Library, Navaro (2008)
14. Campbell, J.: The Hero's Journey. New World Library, Novato (2007)
15. Ducheneaut, N., Wen, M.H., Yee, N., Wadley, G.: Body and mind. In: Proceedings of the 27th International Conference on Human Factors in Computing Systems - CHI 09, pp. 1151–1160. ACM Press, New York (2009)
16. Kafai, Y.B., Fields, D.A., Cook, M.: Your second selves: avatar designs and identity play in a teen virtual world. In: Proceedings of DiGRA 2007 Conference of the Situated Play (2007)
17. Castronova, E.: Theory of the Avatar. Working Papers, 44 (2003)
18. Hancock, J.T., Toma, C., Ellison, N.:The truth about lying in online dating profiles. In: Proceedings of CHI 2007, pp. 449–452. ACM, New York (2007)
19. Mazlan, M.N.A., Burd, L.: Does an avatar motivate? In: 2011 Frontiers in Education Conference (FIE), pp. T4 J–1–T4 J–6. IEEE (2011)
20. Wirth, W., Hartmann, T., Böcking, S.: A process model of the formation of spatial presence experiences. Media Psychol. **9**, 493–525 (2007)
21. Markus, H., Nurius, P.: Possible selves. Am. Psychol. **41**, 954–969 (1986)
22. Ferguson, W., Bareiss, R., Birnbaum, L., Osgood, R.: ASK Systems: an approach to the realization of story-based teachers. J. Learn. Sci. **2**, 95–134 (1992)
23. Paulus, T.M., Horvit, Z.B., Shi, M.: "Isn"t It just like our situation?' engagement and learning in an online story-based environment. Educ. Technol. Res. Dev. **54**(4), 355–385 (2006). doi:10.1007/s11423-006-9604-2
24. McQuiggan, S.W., Rowe, J.P., Lee, S.Y., Lester, J.C.: Story-based learning: the impact of narrative on learning experiences and outcomes. In: Woolf, B.P., Aïmeur, E., Nkambou, R., Lajoie, S. (eds.) ITS 2008. LNCS, vol. 5091, pp. 530–539. Springer, Heidelberg (2008)

Serious Game Mechanics, Workshop on the Ludo-Pedagogical Mechanism

T. Lim[1(✉)], S. Louchart[1], N. Suttie[1], J. Baalsrud Hauge[2], J. Earp[3],
M. Ott[3], S. Arnab[4], D. Brown[5], I.A. Stanescu[6], F. Bellotti[7],
and M. Carvalho[7]

[1] Heriot-Watt University, Riccarton, Edinburgh EH14 4AS, Scotland, UK
{t.lim,s.louchart,n.suttie}@hw.ac.uk
[2] Bremer Institut für Produktion und Logistik (BIBA), Bremen, Germany
baa@biba.uni-bremen.de
[3] Consiglio Nazionale delle Ricerche (CNR), 16149 Genoa, Italy
{jeff,ott}@itd.cnr.it
[4] Serious Games Institute, Coventry University, Coventry CV1 2TL, UK
s.arnab@coventry.ac.uk
[5] Serious Games Interactive, 2100 Copenhagen, Denmark
djb@seriousgames.net
[6] National Defence University "Carol I", 50662 Bucharest, Romania
ioana.stanescu@adlnet.ro
[7] University of Genoa, 16145 Genoa, Italy
{franz,Maira.Carvalho}@elios.unige.it

Abstract. Research in Serious Games (SG), as a whole, faces two main challenges in understanding the transition between the instructional design and actual game design implementation and documenting an evidence-based mapping of game design patterns onto relevant pedagogical patterns. From a practical perspective, this transition lacks methodology and requires a leap of faith from a prospective customer in the ability of a SG developer to deliver a game that will achieve the desired learning outcomes. A series of workshops were thus conducted to present and apply a preliminary exposition though a purpose-processing methodology to probe various SG design aspects, in particular how serious game design patterns map with pedagogical practices. The objective was to encourage dialogue and debate on core assumptions and emerging challenges to help develop robust methods and strategies to better SG design and its interconnectedness with pedagogy.

Keywords: Game mechanics · Learning mechanics · Ludo-pedagogy mapping · Pedagogically-driven game design · Patterns

1 Introduction

Serious Games (SGs) design is fundamentally different to Entertainment Games (EGs) design [1] and the impact of game-play design needs to be understood with regards to the pedagogical nature of SGs and their ability to facilitate learning. SGs and EGs arguably share the same medium of expression, in that they are developed using

© Springer International Publishing Switzerland 2015
A. De Gloria (Ed.): GALA 2014, LNCS 9221, pp. 174–183, 2015.
DOI: 10.1007/978-3-319-22960-7_17

common or similar technologies (Unity SDKs, Android Game APIs, etc.) and use common engagement processes and concepts in their designs (e.g. game mechanics, flow). As a result, it is often difficult to identify the role, place and space in which the key aspect of learning can or does take place besides the obvious specific learning content of SGs. Yet, learning has to be supported if it is to be implemented efficiently as common, well-known pedagogical practices and methodologies suggest [2]. In the case of SGs this could be achieved through the use of game mechanics (GMs), in the same way player engagement is structured in EGs.

The notion of Serious Games Mechanics (SGM) stems from findings on SG literature [3], workshops [4–6] and SG analysis. One important aspect of the work on SGMs, thus far, relates to the distinction between SGMs and GMs. One could rationally argue that there is no real difference between a GM used in a EG, and a similar or identical GM used in a SG, and negate the need for a distinction to be drawn. Conventionally agreed and recognised GM for EGs do not in most cases map onto education practices and do not offer a generally suitable fit for quick and efficient SG design solutions. GMs represent the tools through which educational content is implemented in SGs but their understanding in this context is limited and overdue. The SGM concept considers GMs within the specific context of learning and the acceptance that context determines whether or not a GM can be regarded as a SGM or not. The duality of GM/SGM is an important factor in determining the use of GMs in education as it recognises that the distinction is in essence contextual rather than the form. In this article, we identify SGMs as GMs expressed within the remit of educational purpose, learning process and educational content structure.

2 Bridging the Ludo-Pedagogical Design Knowledge Gap

Identifying SGMs is complex in the sense that it needs to overcome the two main challenges that stem from the transition between the instructional design and actual game design implementation and the insolvency in evidence mapping of Game Design Patterns onto relevant pedagogical patterns. These represent the main gaps in knowledge in Serious Game design from both academic and industrial perspectives (Fig. 1). From the discussions with a number of Serious Game designers it was clear that this transition lacks methodology and requires a leap of faith from a prospective customer in the ability of a SG developer to deliver a game that will achieve the desired learning outcomes.

Game mechanics are core components of any game design as it governs the dynamism of play and, in turn, influences the engagement of the learner-player. The general construction of game mechanics involves rules that control processes not only for interactivity but which also link other gaming mechanics into a system of systems. This poses a granularity problem as it can be all too easy to over generalise or get over analytical with regards to game genres, agenda or contexts. In order to avoid the risk of getting endlessly entangled in the attempt to characterise, structure and represent the whole GM spectrum in its entirety, it is evident that an alternative is required so as to provide deeper insights into serious game design patterns and instructional/pedagogy-driven design elements.

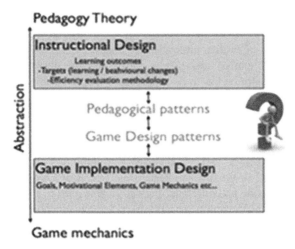

Fig. 1. Knowledge gap in serious game design.

2.1 Pedagogical Patterns

In a desire to bridge the gap identified above, workshop attendees proposed to investigate potential links between Pedagogical patterns and game design patterns so as to develop a "toolbox" for serious game designers in order to inform the process of game design from a pedagogical perspective without having to deal with the high-level theoretical background. Details of pedagogical patterns can be found at the following links [7–10].

Since these patterns are directly relevant to the practitioner one could presume that they are therefore organised in a way that should also be relevant to Serious Game developers. Pedagogical patterns (see Table 1) focus on a wide variety of pedagogical approaches such as active learning, feedback, experiential learning, perspective taking etc. From a Serious Game production perspective, it is crucial to understand how pedagogical patterns could be used to inform design decisions for Serious Game design.

2.2 Game Design Patterns

Past works [11–13] on Game Design Patterns could also be relevant to SGMs if it could be mapped out onto relevant pedagogical patterns. From a process perspective, the workshop attendants concluded that a potential approach towards identifying the missing link between instructional design (learning outcomes) and actual game implementation design could follow the process illustrated in Fig. 2.

These findings suggest that applying a process-oriented method to align educational and game design perspectives would provide a more definitive explanation of SGM. The solution presented in Table 1 imply that delving deeper into the nuances of educational game design patterns in conjunction with a learning mechanic and game mechanic (LM-GM) mapping framework [6] would be necessary.

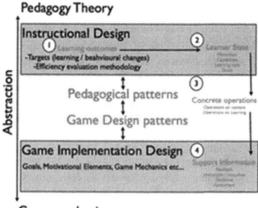

Fig. 2. Identifying the missing link between instructional design and game implementation design.

Table 1. Pedagogical pattern example

Source:	http://csis.pace.edu/ ~ bergin/PedPat1.2.html#earlybird
Name:	Early Bird
Thumbnail	The course is organized so that the most important topics are taught first. Teach the most important material, the "big ideas," first (and often). When this seems impossible, teach the most important material as early as possible.
Audience/context	This has very wide applicability to almost every domain. If design is more important than programming, then find a way to do design as early as you can. If functions are more important than if-statements in programming then do them first. If objects are more important than functions, then do them first.
Forces	Students need to see where they are headed. They need to see that detail presented early in the course will relate to important ideas. Students often remember best what they learn first. This can be both positive and negative, of course. Important (big) ideas can be introduced early, even if they can't get complete treatment immediately.
Solution	A course is mined for its most important ideas. These ideas become the fundamental organizational principle of the course. The ideas and especially their relationships are introduced at the beginning of the course and are returned to repeatedly throughout the course. Order class topics in order of importance and find ways to teach the most important ideas early.
Discussions/ consequences implementation	The most important things in a course or curriculum receive more focus from the instructor and the students. Students can be made more aware of what is paramount.

(Continued)

Table 1. (*Continued*)

Source:	http://csis.pace.edu/ ∼ bergin/PedPat1.2.html#earlybird
	Implementation is difficult. Often only simple aspects of an important idea can be introduced early. Sometimes it is enough to give important terms and general ideas. Some "big" ideas are thought of as advanced. It is difficult to introduce some of these early. Hard thought and preparation are needed in curricular design. Sometimes a really big, but difficult, concept can be introduced incompletely. Then as other material that relates to it is covered, the relationship to the big idea is carefully explored. Professors need to be able to analyse deeply what are the consequences of developing material in a particular order. It is often helpful here to have a forum in which ideas can be discussed and refined. It is also often necessary to develop your own materials, which requires time and effort.
Special resources	Time and deep thought are clearly required. Discussion groups with other educators who share similar ideas about the most important concepts in a domain are very helpful.

3 The SGM Approach

Serious Games, like games in general represent a complex system of intertwined experiences influencing on one another so as to motivate a player not only to play and engage with a proposed experience, but also to express and reflect on a gaming activity during and after experiencing it. These activities correspond to various levels of GMs including motivational elements, competition, challenge which are all inter-related elements through which a gaming experience can be defined. Purposeful learning is in itself an aspect specific to Serious Games. The methodological approach towards identifying SGMs is to focus on the nature of Game Mechanics associated with the specific aspect of purposeful learning. All of these elements can be described in terms of Purpose, Process and Structure, in the sense that SGMs elements are designed for a reason and have a purpose with regards to a gaming and learning experience.

The element of competition for instance could be defined at an abstract level as a process into which a player is provided with a task (score goals, collect things), presented with a challenge (score more goal than an opponent, collect things in a defined period of time) and ultimately made to review his/her performance (leader board, final score results). From a structural perspective, there are many elements determining the actual nature of the challenge and specific GMs can be identified as clear patterns for defining competition. For instance, a player Vs player competition will require specific elements that are not necessarily present in other types of competitions related games. For instance a player vs player approach could be looking at mechanics related to a duel or a direct competition. A massively on-line multiplayer game will, however, implement different elements such as a leader board for instance. A leader board would serve no purpose in the player Vs player approach but would act as an essential mechanic in a multiplayer game. Finally each game or SG element has to have a purpose bounding the actual gaming system framework and set of activities to the player experience. In the case of a player Vs player approach, the purpose would be to provide a safe competitive environment for friends to interact or a framework to support social connection (i.e. the concept of party games etc.).

SGMs are thus viewed as the relationship between pedagogical patterns and game design patterns. The process of investigating the links between the two lies between the instructional design requirements and the actual game/game-play design. This is not obvious and direct links between the low-level game implementation aspects and high-level instructional design aspects of SGs remain obscure.

A three-step approach termed purpose-processing methodology (PPSM) was devised to explore SG elements and specifically identify SGMs. The PPSM could then be used as a design tool or an evaluation tool for SG design.

4 The SGM Workshops

The SGM workshops constitute the main activity of the research on Serious Game Mechanics (SGMs) for the fourth and final year of the GALA EC project. A series of workshops were conducted at different venues to disseminate, collect and validate currently developing knowledge in the area of SGMs. The first workshop ran in the UK followed by first international workshop at GameDays 2014 (Darmstadt, April 1–4) then at GaLA Conference'14 (Bucharest, July 1–4). The next workshop was conducted at the Summer School for serious games (Pori, July 22–24) followed by the ACM meeting on Serious Games (November 3–7, 2014). The workshop was designed as follows:

1. *Introduction to Serious Games Mechanics and Pedagogy (SGMs)*

SGMs are seen as the relationship between pedagogical patterns and game design patterns (Suttie et al., 2012). The process of investigating the links between the two lies between the instructional design requirements and the actual game/game-play design. This is not obvious and direct links between the low-level game implementation aspects and high-level instructional design aspects of SGs remain obscure. This session will provide a definition of SGM and suggest a purpose-processing methodology (PPSM) to identify the link. This talk will also introduce the use of the PPSM towards identifying the role of narrative as a motivational and reflection tool in SG design. The PPSM could then be used as a design tool or an evaluation tool for SG design.

2. *Game Play Session*

During this session the participants will try out the presented methodological approach and framework. Participants will be divided in groups working with two different aims: (1) to analyse (and provide suggestions to improve) existing games; (2) to design new gameplays. All workshops will use with Playing History – The Plague, a serious games developed by Serious Games Interactive (SGI).

3. *SGM Card Game*

This activity is based on the board game "cards against humanity". The intention is to encourage participants to be creative and analytic at the same time. This session is used

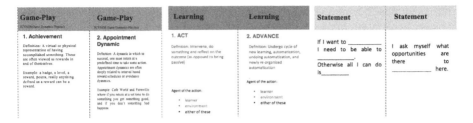

Fig. 3. Example SGM cards

as a basis to identify and formulate new SGMs and their required elements given a theme. Sample cards are shown in Fig. 3.

4. *Reflection and Conclusion (Games and Pedagogy)*

Based upon the result of the game play session, an expert panel will analyse, discuss and show how different aspects of the proposed methodological approach and framework can effectively support the design process, increasing the quality of the outcome and decreasing the time to market. The panel will also discuss typical challenges in the design process as well as challenges in finding the right SGMs for specific purposes. Participants were also asked to complete a Systems Usability Report, which is a self-report using a Likert-type scale of 0 (fully disagree) to 4 (fully agree) to rate the PPSM.

5   Outcomes, Challenges and Opportunities

The SGMs workshops were targeted to gain insights about the effects of game mechanics via the identification of SG specific mechanics for a pedagogical purpose. The activities were designed to reverse engineer SG development from the game design to the learning benefit provided through instructional design and to pro-actively identify and generate SGMs from the learning outcome from a game design perspective. Given the ambitious aims set for the workshops, a number of objectives were required to be met. Two of the key objectives are presented:

1. Positioning SGMs with regards to other SG design/analytical frameworks

One important aspect of the workshop is validating the PPSM against related State-Of-The-Art methodologies in this area. SGMs are a very specific aspect of SGs and therefore only a very limited range of applications and approaches are related to this work. Current work to establish pedagogical transmission factors vary in its diversity and mainly comprises:

a. Specific adaptable learning approaches such as the case method in which one specific approach is modelled within a gaming environment for game design in a number of different topics (GenCSG - Generic Case Study Game [14])
b. Classifications of games by design approach or game mechanics. Djaouti's [15] gamebrick classification is particularly useful in the context of SGMs as it relates to

the ludic elements present in SGs. It does not cover the purpose of the game mechanics despite describing it. However it is very relevant to the PPSM approach as it provided a bottom-up description of linking elements between learning and playing.

c. Platform facilitating the design of simple SGs based on a limited set of design elements.

d. SGM design workshops in the vein of triadic game design. The aim was for participants to design SGMs as part of their SG design. The SGM card game was highly promising as a generative approach, although the SGMs generated may potentially be few due to them being limited to the design of one particular game.

2. Evaluating the efficiency of the Purpose, Process, Structure methodology (PPSM)

From the research perspective of SG design, it is difficult to relate to any other comparative practical contexts to gauge the usefulness and applicability of SGMs (both the pedagogy and the structure of game design). A number of SGMs have already been identified via a case study exercise during the workshop on the topic of narrative SGMs. This served as a benchmark for the understanding of SGMs and later validated at a generic level through the activities of workshop participants. SGMs are meant to be generic, thus these should be applicable in a number of different topics and fields. A direct comparison of SGMs oriented tool or exercise is still possible even though there is a no single tool that compounds the characteristics of SGMs. The workshop provided the opportunity for designers, developers, researchers and academics to express their expertise and domain knowledge on SGM-type analytics to identify a quantitative/qualitative comparison evaluation methodology.

6 Conclusion

The SGM workshop clearly indicated a need for a more common vocabulary on the relationships and associations of ludo-pedagogical mechanisms, in the anticipation of resolving some of the many dichotomies between game designers and educational/ instructional designers. These are critical components that for the defragmentation process that can be currently observed in the SG field. Even more important, the current dichotomy between game design and pedagogical practices should be regarded as a serious obstacle in the uptake of SGs.

Developers and end-users revealed that having a pragmatic means to enable the formalisation and transition of SG methodologies to deliver aligned learning outcomes is clearly needed. While there are many methods/frameworks for SG design and implementation, there are very few that encapsulates the SG design process. SG researchers and professionals are yet to put forward a design methodology in which pedagogical purposes and the epistemic values of game structures to a learning procedure or process are both encompassed in a single homogeneous structure. The question of how to design and implement the internal game mechanisms to ensure learning is not simply a tangential outcome of an incentivised programme through gameplay and it is yet to be fully and comprehensively answered.

Independent assessments of the PPSM suggests it to be a pragmatic tool which can be used to untangle the overall dichotomy between pedagogy and game design in terms of practice-based patterns and specific Serious Games frameworks. PPSM could potentially identify which game mechanics can be used to encourage particular ways of learning to achieve specific kinds of pedagogical goals, also including assessment of curricular content knowledge or skill acquisition. Early work indicate that key narrative elements (narrative SGMs) that give consistency and meaning to SGs could be structured to be reusable and made interoperable. As a forefront for an SG design toolbox, the PPSM has shown to be a generic, yet systematic, means to establish game-pedagogy implications and potential benefits of associated pedagogic practices.

Acknowledgments. This project is partially funded under the European Community Seventh Framework Programme (FP7/2007 2013), Grant Agreement nr. 258169 and EPSRC/IMRC grants 113946 and 112430.

References

1. Suttie, N., Louchart, S., Lim, T., Macvean, A., Westera, W., Brown, D., Djaouti, D.: Introducing the "serious games mechanics" a theoretical framework to analyse relationships between "game" and "pedagogical aspects" of serious games. Procedia Comput. Sci. **15**, 314–315 (2012)
2. Arnab, S., Berta, R., Earp, J., De Freitas, S., Popescu, M., Romero, M., Usart, M.: Framing the adoption of serious games in formal education. Electron. J. e-Learn. **10**(2), 159–171 (2012)
3. Lim, T., Louchart, S., Suttie, N., Hauge, J.B., Stanescu, I.A., Ortiz, I.M., Moreno-Ger, P., Bellotti, F., Carvalho, M.B., Earp, J., Ott, M., Arnab, S., Berta, R.: Narrative serious game mechanics (NSGM) – insights into the narrative-pedagogical mechanism. In: Göbel, S., Wiemeyer, J. (eds.) GameDays 2014. LNCS, vol. 8395, pp. 23–34. Springer, Heidelberg (2014)
4. Lim, T., Louchart, S., Suttie, N., Hauge, J.B., Stanescu, I.A., Bellotti, F., Carvalho, M.B., Earp, J., Ott, M., Arnab, S., Brown, D.: Serious game mechanics, workshop on the ludo-pedagogical mechanism. In: Göbel, S., Wiemeyer, J. (eds.) GameDays 2014. LNCS, vol. 8395, pp. 186–189. Springer, Heidelberg (2014)
5. Games and Learning Alliance conference (GALA) (2014). http://www.galaconf.org/2014/
6. Baalsrud-Hauge, J., Lim, T., Louchart, S., Stanescu, I.A., Ma, M., Marsh, T.: Game mechanics supporting pervasive learning and experience in games, serious games, and interactive & social media. In: The 14th International Conference on Entertainment Computing (ICEC) (2015). http://icec2015.idi.ntnu.no/?page_id=19
7. http://patternlanguagenetwork.wordpress.com/about/
8. http://www.pedagogicalpatterns.org/
9. Rogers, Y., Muller, H.: A framework for designing sensor-based interactions to promote exploration and reflection in play. Int. J. Hum Comput Stud. **64**(1), 1–14 (2006). doi:10.1016/j.ijhcs.2005.05.004
10. Good, J., Robertson, J.: CARSS: a framework for learner-centred design with children. Int. J. Artif. Intell. Educ. **16**(4), 381–413 (2006)
11. Bjork, S., Holopainen, J.: Games and design patterns. In: Salen, K., Zimmerman, E. (eds.) The Game Design Reader, pp. 410–437. MIT Press, Cambridge (2006)

12. Kelle, S., Klemke, R., Specht, M.: Design patterns for learning games. IJTEL **3**(6), 555–569 (2011)
13. Karagiorgi, Y., Symeou, L.: Translating constructivism into instructional design: potential and limitations. Educ. Tech. Soc. **8**(1), 17–27 (2005)
14. Marfisi-Schottman, I., Labat, J.M., Carron, T.: Building on the case teaching method to generate learning games relevant to numerous educational fields. In: 2013 IEEE 13th International Conference on Advanced Learning Technologies (ICALT), pp. 156–160, July 2013
15. Djaouti, D., Alvarez, J., Jessel, J.P., Methel, G., Molinier, P.: A gameplay definition through videogame classification. Int. J. Comput. Games Technol. **2008**, 4 (2008). doi:10.1155/2008/470350

Author Index

Printed in the United States
By Bookmasters